D0593199

STATISTICS FOR
THE BIOLOGICAL SCIENCES

WILLIAM C. SCHEFLER

State University College at Buffalo

ADDISON-WESLEY PUBLISHING COMPANY
Reading, Massachusetts
Menlo Park, California · London · Amsterdam · Don Mills, Ontario · Sydney

This book is in the
Addison-Wesley Series in the Life Sciences

Consulting Editor:
Johns W. Hopkins III

ISBN 0-201-06725-0
HIJKLMNOP-HA-7987

PREFACE

This book is an outgrowth of a beginning course in biometrics taught by the author to junior-level biology majors at the State University College at Buffalo. The content of the book reflects a conviction that it is both possible and desirable to teach useful principles of experimental statistics without resorting to the kind of rigorous mathematical treatment that seems to terrify the average biology student into a state of virtual helplessness.

Two things relative to the reader's background are assumed. First, it is necessary to be able to handle mathematical concepts and formulas found in a beginning algebra course. Second, a reasonably good background in biology will be helpful in following the kinds of examples used.

Notation is kept as simple as possible. Modern summation notation, so useful to the mathematician but so confusing to the biologist, is avoided almost entirely. Shortcuts through methods involving coding and group data are shown, and machine formulas are developed and used.

For the most part, problems listed at the end of each chapter are kept as simple as possible, so as to avoid long hours of busywork on time-consuming problems; practice and understanding can be gained equally well from problems with fewer data. Even-numbered problems are worked out in a step-by-step fashion, and the solutions are presented in Appendix B.

Some of the more basic principles of experimental design are presented in conjunction with statistical procedures. An attempt is made throughout the book to emphasize the uncertainty attached to scientific findings and conclusions.

Many of the basic statistical procedures useful to the biologist are considered, but certain sections, such as the chapters on analysis of variance and covariance, may be left out without doing violence to the organization of the rest of the book.

The philosophy underlying this book holds that statistics is not just another course in mathematics. It is a way of thinking, and should be part of the background of every modern biologist. It has its own special body of principles, and the understanding of these principles need not be dependent on an aptitude for higher mathematics.

This book does not pretend to be a scholarly work in biostatistics, and it does not attempt to make statisticians out of biologists. It does propose to furnish biology students, biology teachers, and research biologists with a substantial amount of basic statistical theory, logically rather than mathematically derived, which will hopefully prepare them for their most critical task—to talk intelligently about statistics to a statistician!

I am grateful to the various authors and publishers who gave me permission to reprint the tables which appear in Appendix C of this book. The source for each table is given in the footnote below the table.

I am indebted to the Literary Executor of the late Sir Ronald A. Fisher, F.R.S., to Dr. Frank Yates, F.R.S., and to Oliver and Boyd, Ltd., Edinburgh, for permission to reprint the tables of the t-distribution and the r to Z transformation from their book, *Statistical Tables for Biological, Agricultural and Medical Research*.

Buffalo, N.Y.   W.C.S.
January 1969

CONTENTS

1
DESCRIPTIVE STATISTICS

1.1 INTRODUCTION

It is increasingly difficult to participate in experimental biology without a practical working knowledge of statistics. It is even difficult to read a professional journal without the background necessary to critically interpret statistical treatments associated with so many experimental designs. One might argue that a knowledge of biostatistics, or *biometrics*, is as important to the modern biologist as the ability to use and interpret a pH meter, or to understand a complex chemical formula.

On the other hand, it would be unreasonable to expect the biologist to design and build pH meters, amino acid analyzers, and other complex pieces of equipment in order to use them intelligently. It is equally unnecessary to be a mathematician in order to acquire a practical knowledge of statistics and its applications to experimental situations. The mathematical statisticians have obligingly "designed and built" the tools of statistics, and the less mathematically inclined biologist can easily learn to use these tools in practical situations.

The concepts and principles of statistics constitute a special body of knowledge. It should not be regarded as "another course in mathematics." Actually, it involves a method of reasoning; and more methods of so-called "critical thinking" may be contained in a statistics course than in a score of average science courses.

This book assumes no mathematical background beyond an ability to perform rather basic algebraic manipulations. On the other hand, consistent with the idea that statistics involves a specialized body of knowledge, it may be read with equal profit by the more mathematically inclined biologist.

1.2 ORIGIN AND USE OF STATISTICS

Originally, statistics apparently dealt with facts and figures gathered for various purposes by government agencies. The periodic census carried on by various governments is a modern example of this activity. The term "statistics" thus appears to have been derived from the state, or government.

This type of statistics is essentially *descriptive* in nature. The number of people making up the population of a city, the number of persons killed in auto accidents last year, or the number of deer counted in a specific area are examples of descriptive statistics. In cases like these we are simply describing the situation in terms of available facts and figures.

As biologists, we are interested in descriptive statistics, but for experimental purposes we use them mainly as a basis for *inferential statistics.* Inferential statistics, or inference, is the major statistical tool of the experimental biologist, and will be considered in detail beginning with Chapter 4.

The specialized application of statistical principles known as biometrics had many of its beginnings in agricultural experimentation. Even today, some biometrics references speak of experimental subjects as "plots," even when the subjects are rats, human beings, etc. Experimental factors are often divided into "levels"; this practice originated in connection with levels of fertilizer concentration, etc.

The use of statistics in biology cannot be separated from principles of experimental design. In fact, the biologist planning an experiment involving statistical analysis of the data *must include an appropriate statistical treatment as an integral part of the design.* A common error, often made by otherwise competent biologists, involves the gathering of data with the blithe assumption that a statistical test useful and appropriate to the situation will be automatically available. This can result in a mass of data which is useless without an appropriate statistical technique. Along this same line, there is a tendency for some experimenters to manipulate data in order to discover "trends" or "differences." Actually, with enough manipulation almost any data will show apparent trends; but to what extent does such manipulation violate the integrity of the original design?

In brief, statistical procedures must be established before—not after—the experiment is performed and the data collected. One of the major objectives of this book is to acquaint the biologist with some common statistical procedures and the kinds of designs and data with which they are used.

1.3 MISUSE OF STATISTICS

Statistics is sometimes unfortunately associated with the old adage that "figures don't lie but liars do figure." In fact, the British Prime Minister Disraeli was so disenchanted with our favorite subject that he stated three classes of falsehoods—"lies, damned lies, and statistics!"

It must be admitted that statistics, like most useful and effective tools, can be and is misused on occasion. There may be deliberate misuse by those who are thoroughly competent in the use of statistics and who use this skill to cleverly misinterpret and misrepresent data in order to serve special interests. Exaggerated or downright fraudulent advertising claims are all too familiar examples of statistical quackery. The campaign oratory of the politician is often laced with deliberately one-sided "statistical evidence" designed to further his own political fortunes. The examples of deliberate misuse are numerous, and the reader is referred to Huff, *How to Lie with Statistics*, for an entertaining exposé of the seamier side of our subject.

Sheer incompetence may also play a part in the misuse of statistical procedures. It is possible for well-meaning and otherwise skillful experimenters to get into difficulty because perfectly good statistical tools are misused as a result of ignorance. This is why a knowledge of experimental procedures is incomplete without an awareness of the appropriate statistical techniques.

Also, it is essential to realize that *a statistical test is only as good as the data it is supposed to test*! An experiment that is poorly designed and carelessly executed *will* yield data, and a statistical analysis *will* yield results based on these data, but these results will obviously be unreliable! Thus it is important to recognize that a statistical test does not automatically reject invalid data, and that the responsibility for validity of the data rests with the experimenter.

It is, therefore, the primary obligation of the experimenter to (1) formulate an appropriate experimental design, (2) include suitable statistical procedures as part of the design, and (3) carry out the mechanics of the experiment with the care, precision, and objectivity for which science is noted in the Sunday supplements.

It is obviously unfair to condemn statistics because it is sometimes misused, either by sharp operators or by bumbling, if well-meaning experimenters. No one would consider rejecting the scalpel as a useful life-saving tool because on fortunately rare occasions it may be wielded by an unscrupulous or incompetent surgeon. Like the scalpel, the statistical test does not have a mind of its own and its usefulness depends on its user.

Having put off the actual study of statistics about as long as we decently can, we will now stop talking about it and start doing something about it. We will begin, therefore, with the very basic concepts involved in describing a distribution.

1.4 DESCRIBING A DISTRIBUTION

A series of measurements or counts is called a *distribution*. Table 1.1 shows such a distribution, purposely kept very simple so the principles involved can be shown without getting all tangled up in arithmetic at this stage of the game.

Table 1.1

X	x	x^2	
10	+5	25	
8	+3	9	$N = 8$
6	+1	1	$\sum X = 40$
5	0	0	$\bar{X} = 5$
5	0	0	$\sum x = 0$
3	−2	4	$\sum x^2 = 64$
2	−3	9	$S^2 = 8$
1	−4	16	$S = 2.82$

First, note that there are 8 numbers, or members, in the distribution shown in Table 1.1. This is the N number of the distribution, therefore $N = 8$.

Also note that upper-case X is used to denote the members of the distribution. In general, throughout this book we will use upper-case letters to designate original, or raw data.

If we sum all the X's in the distribution, we obtain $\sum X = 40$. The Greek letter sigma ($\sum$) is used to denote "the sum of," and is one of the most frequently used symbols in statistics. It should be noted that in some statistics books a more formal summation notation is used. More formally, we would say,

$$\sum_{i=1}^{n} X_i = 40.$$

This tells us to sum all the X_i's in the distribution, from the first X through the nth X; thus it is simply a way to symbolize that *all* X's in the distribution are summed. The expression

$$\sum_{i=2}^{5} X_i$$

tells us to sum those members of the distribution beginning with the second X and including the fifth X. In other words,

$$\sum_{i=2}^{5} X_i = X_2 + X_3 + X_4 + X_5.$$

For the most part we will avoid more formal summation notation by assuming that in every case $\sum X$ implies $X_1 + X_2 + X_3 + \cdots + X_n$. Later, when different subscripts become necessary for proper identification of symbols, they will be kept as simple and descriptive as possible.

Now let's turn back to our distribution in Table 1.1. It may be seen that dividing $\sum X$ by N yields 5 as the result. This quantity is called the *mean* and is symbolized by $\bar{X}$. The mean, an already familiar concept, may be defined as *the sum of all the members of a distribution, divided by the number of members in that distribution.* Symbolically, the mean is represented by

$$\bar{X} = \frac{\sum X}{N},$$

which is a simple formula obtained directly from the definition. Although the mean is commonly called the "average" it is really only one kind of average, since it is only one measure of *central tendency* of a distribution. The *median* is another measure of central tendency, and may be defined as *that measurement which has 50% of the members of the distribution above it and 50% below it.* In our distribution in Table 1.1 it may be seen that the median is 5. The median may also be called the 50th percentile, since 50% of the members of the distribution are below it.

There is an important difference between the median and the mean which becomes immediately obvious if the first member of our distribution is changed from 10 to 100. By definition, the median would remain 5, but the mean would become 16.25. From this it may be seen that the mean is affected by extreme measurements, but the median remains unaffected by extremes.

A third measure of central tendency is the mode. In French, *la mode* means "fashion," and that which is most fashionable is that which is seen more often! In the case of Table 1.1, the number appearing most often is 5.

Note that in our distribution, the mean, median, and mode coincide. This is not necessarily the case in all distributions; in fact, to have the mean, median, and mode coincide exactly in a "real life" set of data would be unusual.

It may be seen that three different measures of central tendency may be designated as the "average" of a distribution. In our work we will concentrate on the mean, since it plays the most useful role in the kind of statistics most applicable to biological experimentation. Later, we will see why this is so.

So far, we have described the distribution in Table 1.1 in terms of central tendency. This does not complete the description, however, for another very important value remains to be calculated. Suppose two large groups take the same test (in statistics, naturally) and upon evaluating the results we find that both group means are 50. Does this imply that both groups are the same, relative to this test, or at least very similar? We might be tempted to think so unless we look further at the two distributions of scores. Suppose that in the first group the scores fall very close to 50, and in the second group the scores range all the way from 0 to 100, with a sprinkling of 10's, 20's, 80's, 90's, etc. Now we see that despite the identical means, one of these groups is homogeneous with respect to the statistics test, while the other group is definitely heterogeneous. Therefore, even though the means are the same, the nature and make up of the two groups are actually quite different.

The second important descriptive feature of a distribution is therefore the *degree of dispersion of the measurements around the mean*. This measure is called the *variance* and Table 1.1 contains the data necessary to calculate it.

If we take the mean, $\overline{X} = 5$, and determine the deviation of each member of the distribution from it, we will obtain a column of deviations from the mean. Note that lower-case x is used to designate a deviation from the mean. Also note that each x is signed according to whether the individual measurement is larger $(+)$ or smaller $(-)$ than the mean.

Adding these deviations (x's), and keeping the signs in mind, we obtain zero as their sum. It is a very important fact that *the sum of signed deviations from the mean of any distribution of measurement data will always equal zero*. It is also true that the sum of the deviations from any number other than $\overline{X}$ will *not* equal zero.

Our next step in calculating the variance is to square each deviation, resulting in the x^2 column. Note that the squaring procedure gets rid of the minus signs. Adding these squared deviations yields 64, which is the sum of squared deviations from the mean. This may be symbolized by $\sum x^2$, or

$\sum (X - \bar{X})^2$, or simply by S.S. or ssq. Also, when you see the term, "sum of squares," remember that it refers to the *sum of squared deviations from the mean.*

Finally, we divide $\sum x^2$ by N, or 64 by 8, obtaining 8 as the variance. Using S^2 as our symbol for variance the definition formula becomes

$$S^2 = \frac{\sum x^2}{N} \quad \text{or} \quad S^2 = \frac{\sum (X - \bar{X})^2}{N},$$

since x and $(X - \bar{X})$ mean the same thing, i.e., a deviation from the mean.

The variance, then, is a measure of dispersion around the mean of a distribution, and is calculated by dividing the sum of squared deviations from the mean by N. For this reason, the variance is sometimes referred to as the *mean square.*

Having calculated the variance, we can now extract the square root of the variance to obtain still another very important value attached to our distribution. Since the variance, S^2, obtained above is 8,

$$S = \sqrt{S^2} = \sqrt{8} = 2.82.$$

This value, 2.82, is called the *standard deviation* and is an extremely important and basic statistical tool. In the next chapter we shall see how the standard deviation bears an important relationship to the normal distribution, or normal curve.

A value called the *coefficient of variation* is sometimes useful when comparing a distribution having a large mean and a large standard deviation with a distribution having a small mean and small standard deviation. This is calculated simply by dividing the standard deviation by the mean, or

$$\text{coefficient of variation} = \frac{S}{\bar{X}}.$$

While the validity of the coefficient of variation has been questioned by some biostatisticians, it is occasionally useful for comparing variability between, say, horses and mice.

1.5 MACHINE COMPUTATION

The method for computing variance described in the preceding section is simple enough, but if you review the number of steps involved you can see that calculating the variance of a large mass of data by this method would be tedious and time consuming. For this reason, various shortcuts have been developed. With a good desk calculator, for example, the work involved in computing variance can be cut to a fraction of what would otherwise be involved. In using a calculator, we need a different version of our formula for variance. This "machine formula" is

$$S^2 = \frac{\sum X^2 - (\sum X)^2/N}{N}$$

or its algebraic equivalent,

$$S^2 = \frac{N \sum X^2 - (\sum X)^2}{N^2},$$

which is preferred by some because it involves only one division process. One "run" through the data with a calculator will yield $\sum X^2$ and $\sum X$. These quantities, along with N, can be substituted in one of the above formulas, and S^2 can be calculated very quickly.

There is nothing mysterious about these computing formulas; they result from the expansion of the term $\sum (X - \bar{X})^2$ in the basic definition formula, followed by algebraic manipulation to produce $\sum X^2 - (\sum X)^2/N$, which is an algebraic identity to $\sum (X - \bar{X})^2$.

1.6 CODING

If a desk calculator is not available, our work can be simplified by the procedure of coding.

Suppose that we have a distribution such as that in Table 1.2. It can be simplified by subtracting a constant from each number. In this case, we subtract 47 from each member and this yields a new distribution, labeled X_c. We find the mean of this new distribution by $\sum X_c/N$, obtaining $\bar{X}_c = -2$. If we now add back the constant (47), we obtain 45, which is the mean of the original distribution. In performing this operation we have made use of the fact that *subtracting a constant from each member of a distribution will yield a new distribution, the mean of which plus the constant will yield the mean of the original distribution.*

We can also calculate the variance, and therefore the standard deviation, by applying the procedure of Section 1.4 directly to the coded distribution, X_c. Thus subtracting the mean (-2) of the coded distribution from each member yields the deviations from the mean labeled x_c. Squaring these, we get the associated x_c^2 values, and summing this column yields $\sum x_c^2$. We now divide $\sum x_c^2$ by $N = 7$ and obtain 22.27 as the variance. It is important to note that we do *not* add back the constant since the *variance of a coded distribution will always be the same as the variance of the original distribution*

Table 1.2

X	X_c	x_c	x_c^2	
50	+3	+5	25	
49	+2	+4	16	$N = 7$
47	0	+2	4	$\sum X_c = -14$
47	0	+2	4	$\sum x_c = 0$
46	−1	+1	1	$\sum x_c^2 = 156$
40	−7	−5	25	$S^2 = 22.27$
36	−11	−9	81	$S = 4.72$

1. Code by subtracting 47.

2. $\bar{X} = \dfrac{\sum X_c}{N} + \text{subtracted constant}$

$$= -2 + 47 = 45$$

3. $S^2 = \dfrac{\sum x_c^2}{N} = \dfrac{156}{7} = 22.27$

$$S = \sqrt{S^2} = \sqrt{22.27} = 4.72$$

from which it was derived. Remember, when the mean of a distribution is calculated by coding, the subtracted constant is restored, but when the variance is calculated, the constant is not restored.

The chief advantage of coding is that it permits us to work with small numbers. While not as convenient as a calculator, it is still a useful work-saving device.

1.7 GROUP DATA METHOD

Another way to handle large quantities of data involves grouping the data according to *class intervals*. Table 1.3 shows a distribution that has been

Table 1.3

	X	f	x_c	fx_c	x_c^2	fx_c^2
40–44	42	3	+2	6	4	12
35–39	37	5	+1	5	1	5
30–34	32	7	0	0	0	0
25–29	27	6	−1	−6	1	6
20–24	22	3	−2	−6	4	12
15–19	17	2	−3	−6	9	18
		$N = 26$		$\sum fx_c = -7$		$\sum fx_c^2 = 53$

grouped in this manner. Let us assume that the particular distribution in Table 1.3 consists of the following measurements:

26	18	36	22	28	31
29	15	36	37	26	
38	32	25	30	30	
43	39	21	27	32	
42	41	21	33	33	

Our first step is to set up a convenient number of class intervals, which include the extremes of the range found in the data. In this case, we have six intervals with an interval size (i) of 5. Since we are talking about a smooth continuous distribution, we assume that each interval has *real* upper and lower limits, i.e., the real lower limits of the bottom interval are 14.50 and the real upper limits are 19.50. The second interval has real limits of 19.50 and 24.50, and so on.

We assume that all measurements or cases found in a particular interval are at the midpoint of that interval. Since, in reality, they are *not* all at exactly the midpoint, some error is introduced by this method. From this, it follows that a small class interval will introduce less error than a larger one. In general, the error involved will be small enough for practical purposes.

The column labeled (X) contains the assumed midpoint values of measurements found within the interval. The (f) column consists of the frequencies of measurements found within associated class intervals. Adding the (f) column yields the N number, 26.

Now we apply a form of coding to our grouped data. Note that we start with zero at the interval which looks as though it could contain the mean of the distribution. It is not necessary to start there; it is simply more convenient, since it will enable us to work with smaller numbers. The midpoint of the interval chosen (32 in this case) is called the *arbitrary origin*. Now go up in increments of $+1$, $+2$, $+3$, etc., and down in decrements of -1, -2, etc. This column, x_c, represents our coded values, and if you refer to the original X column of midpoints, you will see that we are really working in increments of 5. Now, we multiply each coded value (x_c) by the associated frequency, f, and obtain fx_c. Adding the (fx_c) column yields $\sum fx_c$, which is merely part of a shortcut method for computing the mean.

Squaring the x_c values yields x_c^2 and multiplying each x_c^2 by the associated f value yields fx_c^2. Summing the (fx_c^2) column gives us $\sum fx_c^2$. The data are now complete, and we have what we need to calculate the mean, variance, and standard deviation of the distribution.

To calculate the mean, we use the group-data formula as given by

$$\bar{X} = A + i\left(\frac{\sum fx_c}{N}\right),$$

where A is the arbitrary origin and i is the size of the class interval. Thus, in the case of our distribution,

$$\bar{X} = 32 + 5\left(\frac{-7}{26}\right) = 32 + 5(-0.27) = 32 + (-1.35) = 30.65.$$

Note the similarity to the coding.procedure of Section 1.6, where we added the subtracted constant back at the end of the calculations.

The group-data formula for variance is

$$S^2 = i^2\left[\frac{\sum fx_c^2}{N} - \left(\frac{\sum fx_c}{N}\right)^2\right].$$

A little study will show that this somewhat formidable looking formula is similar to the formula for variance developed in Section 1.5. Applying the values from our data in Table 1.3,

$$S^2 = 25\left[\frac{53}{26} - \left(\frac{-7}{26}\right)^2\right] = 25(2.04 - 0.072) = 25(1.97) = 49.25.$$

Taking the square root of 49.25 yields 7.02 as the value for the standard deviation.

If a calculator were available, $\bar{X}$ and S^2 would be computed directly from the raw data. Using the definition formula for the mean, $\bar{X} = \sum X/N$, we would divide 791 by 26, obtaining 30.42. Using the machine formula for variance,

$$S^2 = \frac{\sum X^2 - (\sum X)^2/N}{N} = 25,453 - \frac{(791)^2}{26} = 53.40.$$

The square root of 53.40 yields a standard deviation value of 7.31. A comparison of the values obtained by the group data method and by direct computation reveals a discrepancy. Again, this is explained by the fact that not all members of the distribution were actually located at the interval midpoints. Decreasing the size of the class interval would significantly decrease the error in this case.

We have seen that describing a distribution involves the calculation of two basic values. First, the mean is computed as the measure of central tendency. Second, to avoid the pitfall met by the statistician who drowned in a river having a mean depth of two feet, we determine the degree to which the measurements vary around the mean; this degree of dispersion is measured by the variance.

In the next chapter we shall apply these concepts to one of the most significant products of human thought—the normal curve.

PROBLEMS

1.1 In the following distribution, identify the mean, the median, and the mode (see Section 1.4):

3, 14, 20, 2, 18, 3, 13, 12, 15.

1.2 In the following distribution, compute the mean, the variance, and the standard deviation (see Section 1.4):

6, 12, 11, 7, 8, 10, 6, 12, 9.

1.3 In the following distribution, compute the mean and the standard deviation (see Section 1.4):

1, 8, 10, 9, 14, 13, 14, 12, 8, 11.

1.4 In the following distribution, compute the mean, the variance, and the standard deviation, using the method of coding (see Section 1.6):

63, 68, 62, 66, 68, 67, 63, 70, 69, 73, 68, 67.

1.5 Determine the mean, the variance, and the standard deviation of the following distribution, using the coding procedure (see Section 1.6):

95, 78, 105, 99, 101, 92, 108, 83, 112.

1.6 Compute the mean, variance, and standard deviation of the following distribution, using the group data method (see Section 1.7):

	f
70–79	4
60–69	7
50–59	12
40–49	9
30–39	5
20–29	3

1.7 Arrange the following distribution according to the appropriate class intervals and compute the mean, variance, and standard deviation, using the group data method:

26, 43, 38, 36, 16, 29, 34, 37, 30, 12, 23, 25, 33, 16, 21, 10, 17, 26, 28, 10, 25, 28, 27, 28, 25.

1.8 Find the mean, the variance, and the standard deviation of the following distribution (a) by the group data method, and (b) by the machine method:

81, 75, 79, 57, 64, 69, 70, 69, 77, 79, 61, 83, 67, 63, 64, 72, 73, 80, 75, 64, 76, 74, 72, 73, 65, 74, 70, 71, 69, 69, 60, 60, 73, 59, 70, 69, 67, 66, 66, 62, 65, 70, 69, 68, 68, 68, 67, 76, 74, 70.

2
THE NORMAL DISTRIBUTION

2.1 MEASUREMENT DATA

There are numerous characteristics found in the biotic and physical environments which can be measured in some fashion. Variables such as height, weight, length, temperature, and hemoglobin content are some familiar sources of measurement, or *continuous* data.

These data are continuous because they may assume any value at all on a given continuum existing between two limits. To illustrate, suppose that a large population of birds has bills ranging in length from 9 to 15 mm. It would then be theoretically possible to find birds in this population with bill lengths matching every conceivable measurement between the two extremes. It is as though the bill of one bird suddenly started to grow, like Pinocchio's nose, from 9 mm to 15 mm without missing any possible measurement along the way!

In practice, measurements are limited by the precision of the measuring instruments and by human error. Even the most sophisticated analytical balance cannot supply the *exact* weight of an object, and even the most precise instruments are subject to error in use and interpretation. We therefore take measurements to the nearest centimeter, millimeter, milligram, microgram, or whatever is dictated by the nature and precision of the instrument, admitting that the reported measurement will almost certainly deviate from the true value. Actually, when a measurement is reported as being 50 mm, this implies that the true value lies somewhere between 49.50 mm and 50.50 mm.

In practice, continuous data is therefore to some extent *discrete*, or discontinuous. Also, variables such as pulse rate or the number of fin rays on a fish are discrete in nature, but under certain conditions may be treated as measurement data.

2.2 NORMALLY DISTRIBUTED DATA

Figure 2.1 shows a *histogram* based on measurements obtained from 120 lima beans drawn one at a time from a half-bushel container. Each bean was measured to the nearest millimeter along its longest axis. The histogram is constructed by plotting length as the abscissa and frequency as the ordinate.

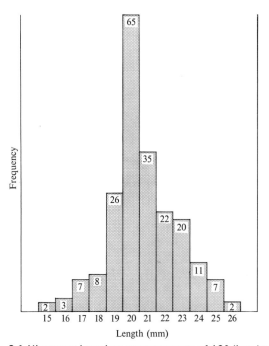

Fig. 2.1 Histogram based on measurements of 120 lima beans.

The area of each bar therefore represents the frequency of cases found between the real upper and lower limits of the associated measurement. Thus since 65 cases are associated with a length of 20 mm, this means that 65 cases have measurement values between 19.50 mm and 20.50 mm.

It is important to note that even with this relatively small sample, the majority of cases tend to cluster around the central portion of the histogram.

Also, as we move toward the left on the abscissa, toward shorter lengths, the frequency decreases, and there is a corresponding decrease in frequency as we move to the right toward larger measurements.

Now, suppose that we have available a very large population of field mice. Suppose further that we have built a better mousetrap and we are able to catch every mouse in the population and measure its tail to the nearest millimeter. A histogram plotted from our data would probably look very much like the one shown in Fig. 2.2. Keep in mind that this is a theoretical histogram based on a very large population of mice and a very good mousetrap!

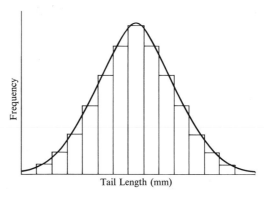

Fig. 2.2 Theoretical histogram based on mouse-tail measurements.

Again, we can see a clustering of cases around the center with a gradual tapering off as we move toward more extreme measurements in both directions.

It is a notable and highly useful fact that many traits found in nature are distributed in this fashion. Carried to its ultimate, we obtain the curve superimposed on the "mouse tail" histogram in Fig. 2.2.

2.3 THE NORMAL CURVE

The curve shown in Fig. 2.3 is called the *normal curve*, and is without doubt one of the most useful theoretical tools ever discovered. The standard normal curve is bell shaped, with the tails dipping down to the base line. In theory, they are asymptotic to the base line and do not touch it, proceeding to infinity. In practice, we usually ignore this and work with practical limits.

The perpendicular erected at the center of the curve in Fig. 2.3 represents the mean of the distribution. Since it obviously splits the distribution repre-

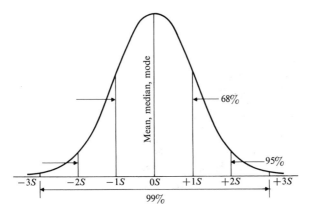

Fig. 2.3 Normal curve relationship between standard deviation and area.

sented by the curve into two equal parts, it must also represent the median. Finally, we note that the frequency density is highest at this point, so the mode is also found at this same perpendicular. Thus, in the standard normal curve, the mean, median, and mode coincide.

2.4 NORMAL CURVE AREAS

In Chapter 1 it was mentioned that the standard deviation bears an important relationship to the normal curve. Looking again at Fig. 2.3, it may be seen that the curve is divided into areas according to standard deviations.

Note that standard deviations to the right of the mean are $(+)$, since they represent points *above* the mean; standard deviations to the left, or below the mean are therefore $(-)$. Figure 2.3 shows that approximately 68% of the total area of the curve is found between $+1S$ and $-1S$, 95% of the area is located between $+2S$ and $-2S$, and 99% of the curve is between $+3S$ and $-3S$.

It will be noted that the standard deviation is located on the curve at the point where the curve changes from concave to convex, or vice versa. Looking at it mathematically, it is the point at which the slope of the curve changes sign.

The question may arise as to why 68% of the curve area is contained between $+1$ and -1 standard deviations, and why 95% lies between $+2$ and -2 standard deviations, etc. This question may perhaps be best answered by pointing out that this is the mathematical nature of the curve, and may be compared to the Pythagorean theorem describing the relationship of the sides of a right triangle to its hypotenuse. We cannot "explain why" $c^2 = a^2 + b^2$, but it is nevertheless true and presents us with a useful tool. The same may be said about the relationship of the standard deviation to the normal curve.

You will recall that any given area of the curve also represents a certain frequency of cases. Therefore, the entire curve area includes *all* cases in the distribution. That half of the curve to the right includes the upper 50% of the cases, 68% of the cases are included between $+1S$ and $-1S$, and so on.

To illustrate, suppose that we have a distribution with $N = 500$, $\bar{X} = 50$, and $S = 5$. What percent of the distribution would be below 55?

If $S = 5$, 55 would be one S, or one standard deviation above the mean. We have just calculated a standard score, or z-score, and we used the following simple relationship:

$$Z = \frac{X - \bar{X}}{S} = \frac{55 - 50}{5} = 1.$$

A standard score, or z-score, is the number of standard deviations above or below the mean of a distribution.

It may be seen from Fig. 2.4 that since 55 is one standard deviation above the mean, approximately 34% of the area lies between 55 and the mean itself. Since 50% of the total area lies to the left of the mean, it follows that 50% + 34%, or 84% of the distribution lies below 55.

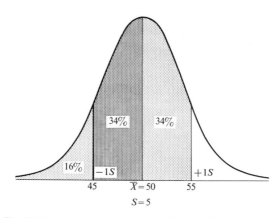

Fig. 2.4 Relationship of values of 55 and 45 to curve areas.

By similar reasoning, a measurement of 45 would be equivalent to a standard score of -1, or one standard deviation *below* the mean. Since 34% of the area lies between $-1S$ and the mean, 16% of the total distribution would lie below 45. Also, since $N = 500$, 16% of 500, or 80 members of the distribution would lie below 45.

So far, so good. Now to get just a little more complicated, what percent of the curve area would lie below 57.50? Applying our formula for the standard score, we find that

$$Z = \frac{X - \bar{X}}{S} = \frac{57.50 - 50.00}{5} = 1.50.$$

Since this is positive, 57.50 is situated 1.50 standard deviations above the mean. Now we must resist the temptation to interpolate between one and two standard deviations and their associated areas. Note that from the high point at the mean the curve dips sharply down toward the tails on either side. Thus as we go in either direction from the mean along the base line, the amount of area contained between two perpendiculars will sharply decrease. Table IV in the appendix gives the area equivalent to various standard scores. Turning to Table IV, we find that a standard score of 1.50 is equivalent to an area of 0.4332, or 43.32%. Remember, the areas given in Table IV are always considered as located between the *mean* and a *perpendicular erected at the specific standard score involved.*

Thus if 57.50 is 1.5 standard deviations above the mean, and this implies that 43.32% of the curve area lies between 57.50 and the mean, it follows that 50% + 43.32%, or 93.32% of the distribution lies below 57.50.

Looking at another kind of problem, what percent of the curve area lies between the standard scores +1.50 and +2.00? Again, we must resist the temptation to subtract 1.50 from 2.00 and look up the area equivalent to the resulting 0.50! Remember, the table areas are always between the perpendicular erected at the *mean* and the perpendicular erected at the

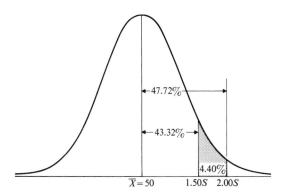

Fig. 2.5 Computing the area between 1.50 and 2.00 standard deviations.

standard score! Just to make certain you are convinced, let's look up 0.50. This turns out to be equivalent to 19.15% of the curve area, which is considerably greater than the actual area between +1.50 and +2.00 standard deviations, since between the two perpendiculars erected at these standard scores the curve dips sharply and the area between them is drastically reduced.

To find the correct area between +1.50 and +2.00 standard deviations, we first find the area between the mean and each of these standard scores. Thus, directly from Table IV, we find that

$$2.00 = 47.72\%, \quad \text{and} \quad 1.50 = 43.32\%.$$

Subtracting 43.32% from 47.72% yields 4.40%, which is the correct area between +1.50 and +2.00 standard deviations. Figure 2.5 may help to make the foregoing example clearer.

2.5 DEPARTURES FROM NORMALITY

Table IV in the appendix, and thus our use of it, depends on a distribution having a shape similar to the standard normal curve. Unfortunately, not all distributions follow the standard curve to perfection, and in some cases, the departure from normality is enough to prevent our using the procedures described in this chapter.

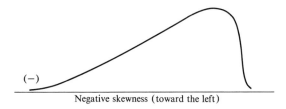

Negative skewness (toward the left)

Fig. 2.6 An illustration of skewness.

Figure 2.6 illustrates a case of *skewness*; in this case, the curve is skewed to the left, or negatively skewed. Such a curve might be obtained from plotting age at death against frequency, since in the normal population there are many more deaths among older individuals than among younger ones. A curve skewed in the other direction would be skewed to the right, or positively skewed, having a preponderance of cases on the lower end of the scale.

Skewness represents a lack of symmetry. A curve may be symmetrical, however, and yet not be normal due to its curvature, or kurtosis. Figure 2.7 illustrates two extremes of kurtosis. Curve (a) is flattopped and is referred to as platykurtic. This may arise from combining two populations having the same variance, but significantly different means. Curve (b) is peaked and has long tails; it is commonly called leptokurtic. This type of kurtosis may result from a mixture of two populations having the same mean, but significantly different variances.

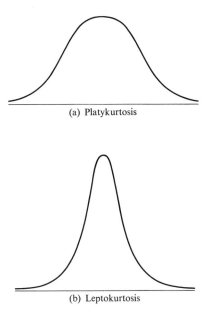

(a) Platykurtosis

(b) Leptokurtosis

Fig. 2.7 Curves illustrating kurtosis.

Actually, it is rather amazing how far a distribution may depart from normality and still not affect statistical results to an appreciable degree. Badly skewed distributions can present problems; however, they can sometimes be "straightened out," or normalized, by special treatments of data called transformations.

The principles involved with the normal curve are basic to experimental statistics; applications of these principles will be considered in subsequent chapters. In the next chapter we shall consider probability and the application of normal curve concepts to the calculation of probability.

PROBLEMS

2.1 From a large field of corn, 714 ears were collected in a random fashion. Each ear was measured to the nearest centimeter. Construct a histogram based on the data shown below (see Section 2.2):

Class interval	f	Class interval	f
24–25	11	16–17	220
22–23	45	14–15	100
20–21	80	12–13	60
18–19	190	10–11	8

2.2 Construct a histogram based on the following group data (see Section 2.2):

Class interval	f	Class interval	f
81–83	2	66–68	10
78–80	3	63–65	6
75–77	5	60–62	4
72–74	7	57–59	2
69–71	12		

2.3 Compute Z, or the standard score of X, in each of the following (see Section 2.4):

a) $X = 40$, $\bar{X} = 30$, $S = 5$ b) $X = 51.50$, $\bar{X} = 45$, $S = 8$
c) $X = 8.92$, $\bar{X} = 10$, $S = 3$ d) $X = 142$, $\bar{X} = 159$, $S = 12$

2.4 Compute the percentage of the normal curve area that would be found *above* each of the following standard scores (see Section 2.4):

a) 1.50   b) −1.50   c) 2.25   d) 1.96

2.5 Compute the percentage of the normal curve area that would be found *below* each of the following standard scores (see Section 2.4):

a) −0.40   b) 1.25   c) −2.00   d) 0.50

2.6 Compute the percentage of the area of the normal curve that would be found *between* each of the following standard scores (see Section 2.4):

a) −0.50 and 0.50   b) 1.25 and 1.50
c) −1.10 and −0.65   d) 1.40 and 1.65

2.7 Given the following standard scores, in each case compute the total area left in the tails of the normal curve (see Section 2.4):

a) −1.64 and +1.64   b) −1.96 and +1.96
c) −2.58 and +2.58   d) −0.95 and +1.25

3
PROBABILITY

3.1 KINDS OF PROBABILITY

The term "probability" is one commonly used in ordinary conversation. In describing an event as probable, we imply that it is likely, or it is to be expected, or it is "in the cards." There is a difference, however, between stating, "It will probably rain tomorrow," and the statement, "The probability of rain tomorrow is 0.50."

In statistics, we attempt to express probability in precise quantitative terms. The basis for this quantitative expression may be built into the situation, as with a coin. In that event it is called *a priori* probability, i.e., established "before the fact." Or, we may formulate a quantitative statement based entirely on past experience; in this case we are dealing with *empirical* probability.

To illustrate, we assume, on the basis of meiotic division, that one-half the sperm produced by the human male carries the *X*-chromosome and one-half carries the *Y*-chromosome. If this is true, then the *a priori* probability that any random birth will produce a boy is $\frac{1}{2}$. On the basis of experience, however, we know that, over a period of time, more boys than girls are born, and the *empirical* probability that a boy will result from a random birth is actually about 0.51 in the white population of the United States.

A probability statement may predict all the way from certainty that an event *will* occur to certainty that it *will not* occur. If it is certain that a specific event will occur, the probability of its occurrence is 1. If there is no chance at all it will occur, the probability is 0. Probability statements may therefore run from 0 to 1, and are usually expressed as fractions or decimals. It should be emphasized that while we may refer to "certainty" when tossing coins or throwing dice, in practical biological problems the concept of certainty is foreign to the careful experimenter. We are almost never certain of anything except the proverbial death and taxes!

3.2 INDEPENDENT EVENTS

Consider an honest coin, having heads on one side and tails on the other. If we assume that landing and balancing on edge is an impossibility, it follows that when such a coin is tossed it *must* land with either heads or tails facing up. Since there is no reason why one side should be favored over the other, the probability of obtaining a head is $\frac{1}{2}$ and the probability of a tail is also $\frac{1}{2}$. Since one *or* the other *must* occur, it follows logically that the probability of either a head *or* a tail coming up in any single toss of an honest coin is 1, or certainty.

Suppose that we toss a coin and it turns up heads. The probability of this happening is $\frac{1}{2}$. Now, if we toss the same coin again, what is the probability of a head on the second toss? A little reflection shows that, provided the coin is tossed in a random manner, the second toss will not be at all influenced by the results of the first toss. In other words, the second event is *independent* of the first event, and the two tosses are classified as independent events. It follows that if we toss an honest coin 10 times and obtain 10 heads in a row, although we might be inclined to bet our life's savings that a tail is "due" on the next toss, the probability of a tail on the eleventh toss is still $\frac{1}{2}$!

Suppose that we now toss a penny and a nickel together. What is the probability they will both turn up heads at the same time? Since the probability in each case is $\frac{1}{2}$, we have the following situation:

Penny	Nickel
$H(\frac{1}{2})$	$H(\frac{1}{2})$

Look at this situation from an intuitive point of view. While you might bet a considerable amount that a single coin would turn up heads, how much would you be willing to bet that a thousand coins tossed into the air would all turn up heads? You know instinctively that this is not a good bet, and extending the example to a million coins makes the point even more obvious. As the number of coins increases, the probability they will all turn up heads decreases. Since probability is expressed in fractions, we will obviously multiply the separate probabilities of two or more independent events in order to obtain the *lesser* probability that they will occur simultaneously.

In our example involving the nickel and penny we therefore *multiply* $\frac{1}{2}$ by $\frac{1}{2}$ to obtain $\frac{1}{4}$ as the probability that two heads will occur. This illustrates the *product rule* for calculating the probability that two or more independent events will occur simultaneously, or in a row.

What is the probability of obtaining a head and a tail when two coins are tossed? Consider the following:

Penny	Nickel
1. $H(\frac{1}{2})$	$T(\frac{1}{2})$
2. $T(\frac{1}{2})$	$H(\frac{1}{2})$

Note that in this case the desired event can be obtained in two ways, or by two different combinations. The penny can turn up heads and the nickel tails, or vice versa. Either combination satisfies the condition specifying one head and one tail. Calculating the separate probabilities of combinations (1) and (2), we have

$$1.\ \tfrac{1}{2} \times \tfrac{1}{2} = \tfrac{1}{4}, \qquad \text{and} \qquad 2.\ \tfrac{1}{2} \times \tfrac{1}{2} = \tfrac{1}{4}.$$

Since the event stipulated can happen as *either* (1) *or* (2), we *add* the probabilities of the ways by which a head-tail combination can be produced. Thus $\frac{1}{4} + \frac{1}{4} = \frac{1}{2}$, the probability of obtaining a head and a tail from a single toss of two coins or from tossing one coin twice in a row.

This is called the *addition rule*, and is applied to situations where a specific event can occur in more than one way.

It follows that the probability of two tails is the same as that for two heads, or $\frac{1}{4}$. Thus the probability of obtaining two heads, *or* one head and one tail, *or* two tails is $\frac{1}{4} + \frac{1}{2} + \frac{1}{4}$, or 1. In other words, if we toss two coins we are *certain* to obtain one of these three results.

Note how the product and addition rules are illustrated in the following example, involving three coins, where the possibilities are three heads, two heads and one tail, two tails and one head, or three tails:

$$H(\tfrac{1}{2}) \times H(\tfrac{1}{2}) \times H(\tfrac{1}{2}) = \tfrac{1}{8}$$
$$\left.\begin{array}{l} H(\tfrac{1}{2}) \times T(\tfrac{1}{2}) \times T(\tfrac{1}{2}) = \tfrac{1}{8} \\ T(\tfrac{1}{2}) \times H(\tfrac{1}{2}) \times T(\tfrac{1}{2}) = \tfrac{1}{8} \\ T(\tfrac{1}{2}) \times T(\tfrac{1}{2}) \times H(\tfrac{1}{2}) = \tfrac{1}{8} \end{array}\right\} \tfrac{3}{8}$$
$$\left.\begin{array}{l} H(\tfrac{1}{2}) \times H(\tfrac{1}{2}) \times T(\tfrac{1}{2}) = \tfrac{1}{8} \\ H(\tfrac{1}{2}) \times T(\tfrac{1}{2}) \times H(\tfrac{1}{2}) = \tfrac{1}{8} \\ T(\tfrac{1}{2}) \times H(\tfrac{1}{2}) \times H(\tfrac{1}{2}) = \tfrac{1}{8} \end{array}\right\} \tfrac{3}{8}$$
$$T(\tfrac{1}{2}) \times T(\tfrac{1}{2}) \times T(\tfrac{1}{2}) = \tfrac{1}{8}$$
$$\text{Total} = 1$$

We will leave coins for now and turn to the ancient, if not always honorable, art of rolling dice. A die (sing.) is a cube having six sides; therefore, the probability that any one side will come up in a single roll is $\frac{1}{6}$. This of course assumes that the die is not "loaded." (But we do not speak of such things in polite company!)

To win on the first roll with a pair of dice, we must roll *either* a 7 *or* an 11. What is the probability of winning on the first roll?

First, we must consider 2 dice, and each is in reality rolled independently of the other, constituting separate, independent events. A 7 could therefore be rolled in any one of the following ways:

Die I	Die II
$4(\frac{1}{6}) \times 3(\frac{1}{6}) = \frac{1}{36}$	
$3(\frac{1}{6}) \times 4(\frac{1}{6}) = \frac{1}{36}$	
$6(\frac{1}{6}) \times 1(\frac{1}{6}) = \frac{1}{36}$	
$1(\frac{1}{6}) \times 6(\frac{1}{6}) = \frac{1}{36}$	
$5(\frac{1}{6}) \times 2(\frac{1}{6}) = \frac{1}{36}$	
$2(\frac{1}{6}) \times 5(\frac{1}{6}) = \frac{1}{36}$	
Total $= \frac{6}{36}$, or $\frac{1}{6}$	

The probability of rolling a 7 is therefore the sum of the probabilities of the various ways by which a 7 could be made; the total probability of rolling a 7 is therefore $\frac{1}{6}$.

On the other hand, only two possible combinations can produce an 11:

Die I	Die II
$6(\frac{1}{6}) \times 5(\frac{1}{6}) = \frac{1}{36}$	
$5(\frac{1}{6}) \times 6(\frac{1}{6}) = \frac{1}{36}$	
Total $= \frac{2}{36}$, or $\frac{1}{18}$	

Since we can win on the first roll with *either* a 7 *or* an 11, the total probability of winning is calculated by the addition rule. Thus $\frac{1}{6} + \frac{1}{18} = \frac{2}{9}$, which is the probability of winning with the first roll of the dice. If we now wanted to know the probability of winning twice in a row, we know intuitively that the probability of this happening would be *smaller*; therefore, applying the product rule, we have $\frac{2}{9} \times \frac{2}{9} = \frac{4}{81}$.

3.3 DEPENDENT EVENTS

In the situations seen thus far, a particular event has had no effect on the probabilities of subsequent events. Now, suppose that you choose a card from a well-shuffled deck and it happens to be an ace. The probability of drawing an ace was $\frac{4}{52}$, since there are four aces in a standard deck of 52 cards. Suppose further that you throw the ace out the window and choose another card from the deck. Since the deck has been depleted by one card and one ace, the probability that the second card drawn is an ace is $\frac{3}{51}$. It may be seen that, in this case, the probability of the second event was indeed affected by the results of the first.

What is the probability of drawing three aces in a row from a deck of 52 cards *without replacement?* The probability that the first card is an ace is $\frac{4}{52}$, the second is $\frac{3}{51}$, and the third, $\frac{2}{50}$. The probability that these three events would occur in a row would therefore be found, as usual, by the product rule, or

$$\frac{4}{52} \times \frac{3}{51} \times \frac{2}{50} = 3/16,550.$$

It may be seen that calculating probabilities involving dependent events follows the same rules as those involving independent events. The difference lies in the way that probabilities are assigned to the separate events.

3.4 APPLICATIONS

Suppose that a woman with a hemophilic brother comes to us for an estimate of the probability that any son born to her will be hemophilic. Her parents are normal and she is married to a normal male.

We will start by assuming that the presence of the hemophilic brother implies that her mother is a carrier (Hh) of the recessive hemophilic gene. Since her father is normal, he is of the genotype YH. We may therefore assume that our counselee and her brother were produced by the following genetic cross:

$$YH \times Hh$$
$$F_2 \quad YH, \ Yh, \ HH, \ Hh$$

where Yh is the hemophilic brother. The lady in question could be either HH or Hh. Since she *is* a lady, she could hardly be YH or Yh. Therefore the probability she is a carrier (Hh) must be $\frac{1}{2}$. She is married to a normal male (YH); therefore, *if* she is a carrier (Hh), we again obtain YH, Yh, HH, and Hh for the offspring. The probability that a male resulting from this cross would be hemophilic is therefore $\frac{1}{2}$, since we can discount the female genotypes.

Now it may be seen that two events must occur in a row. First, she must be a carrier ($P = \frac{1}{2}$). Second, if she produces a male, he must be hemophilic ($P = \frac{1}{2}$). Applying the product rule, we obtain $\frac{1}{2} \times \frac{1}{2} = \frac{1}{4}$, which is the probability that a woman with her history will produce a hemophilic son. It should be noted that we ignored the possibilities involving female offspring since in dealing with hemophilia this would be of no concern.

As long as we are cast in the genetics counselor role, suppose that George and Mary come to us for some premarital advice. George has a brother with a form of mental retardation that is inherited as a simple recessive trait. George and his parents are all normal. Mary is also normal and has no history of this affliction in her family. Because of George's family situation, they are naturally concerned about having an afflicted child.

Calculations based on the Hardy-Weinberg law show that the probability that any individual, picked at random from the population, is a heterozygous carrier of this particular gene is $\frac{1}{100}$. Since Mary's family has no history of this form of mental retardation, we may assume the probability that she is a carrier is $\frac{1}{100}$.

Since George has an afflicted brother, we may assume that his parents, though normal, are both carriers. Thus

$$Ff \times Ff$$
$$F_2 \quad FF, Ff, Ff, ff$$

represents the cross that produced George and his brother (ff). Since George is normal, in his case we may disregard the ff genotype; therefore he must be FF or Ff. The probability that George is a carrier is therefore $\frac{2}{3}$.

Now, what is the probability that George and Mary are both carriers? This is analogous to two coins coming up heads, so we use the product rule; therefore $\frac{1}{100} \times \frac{2}{3} = \frac{2}{300}$. Also, if they *are* both carriers, what is the probability that any child they produce would be afflicted? Looking back at the results of a cross between two carriers, it is apparent that the probability of producing an afflicted child (ff) would be $\frac{1}{4}$.

Again, two events must occur in a row. First, they must both be carriers ($P = \frac{2}{300}$), and second, the roll of the genetic dice must produce an ff genotype in the child ($P = \frac{1}{4}$). Thus the probability that any child produced by George and Mary will be afflicted is the product of $\frac{2}{300}$ and $\frac{1}{4}$, or $\frac{1}{600}$.

It is interesting to note that if neither George nor Mary had an afflicted sibling, the probability would then have been $\frac{1}{100} \times \frac{1}{100} \times \frac{1}{4}$, or 1/40,000, which represents a drastic decrease in the probability they would have an afflicted child!

3.5 THE BINOMIAL DISTRIBUTION

In Chapter 2 we described measurement data as continuous, so that traits such as weight, length, temperature, etc., may assume values anywhere within given limits.

Suppose, however, that we once again apply our better mousetrap to a large population of field mice. This time, as we catch each mouse, we record the animal's sex. If we discount rare abnormalities, it is obvious that the character, sex, in a population of diecious animals *must* fall into one of two categories—male and female!

Many attributes of living organisms fall into this dichotomous, "*A*, non-*A*" type of classification. A child either has blue eyes or he does not; a rat treated with a drug either survives or does not; a sperm either carries the *X*-chromosome or does not, and so on. Traits such as these are distributed according to the *binomial distribution*.

To illustrate, let's return to our coin-tossing exercise. The probability that a coin will turn up either heads or tails is 1, or certainty. If p represents the probability of a head and q the probability of a tail, then $p + q = 1$. The probable distribution obtained from many tosses of a single coin can therefore be represented by $(p + q)^1$. The distribution resulting from tossing two coins would then be represented by $(p + q)^2$, and the distribution based on n tosses by $(p + q)^n$.

As an example, suppose that we toss five pennies a large number of times, recording the number of heads resulting from each toss. What distribution of heads could we expect? Expanding the expression $(p + q)^n$, or in this case $(p + q)^5$, we obtain

$$p^5 + 5p^4q + 10p^3q^2 + 10p^2q^3 + 5pq^4 + q^5.$$

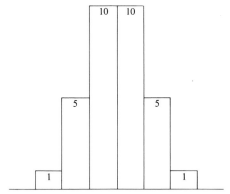

Fig. 3.1 Histogram based on expansion of binomial $(p + q)^5$.

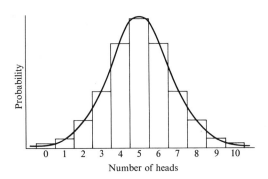

Fig. 3.2 Histogram based on repeated tossings of 10 pennies.

Keeping in mind that p represents the probability of obtaining a head in any one toss of a single coin, the probability of obtaining exactly 5 heads is represented by p^5, or $(\frac{1}{2})^5$, or $\frac{1}{32}$. The probability of 4 heads in any toss is derived from the expression $5p^4q$, or $5(\frac{1}{2})^4(\frac{1}{2})$, or $\frac{5}{32}$. Three heads is given by the expression $10p^3q^2$, or $10(\frac{1}{2})^3(\frac{1}{2})^2$, or $\frac{10}{32}$, and so on. The expression q^5 represents the probability of obtaining 0 heads, and at the same time represents the probability of obtaining 5 tails.

The result of the binomial expansion in the preceding example shows a definite symmetry, which is illustrated by the histogram in Fig. 3.1. Figure 3.2 shows a distribution of heads resulting from repeated tosses of 10 pennies. Note that as n increases, the binomial distribution becomes smoother and approximates the normal curve.

The degree of symmetry of the binomial distribution depends on the values of p and q. If p is $\frac{1}{2}$, and q is $\frac{1}{2}$, the resulting histogram and approximated curve will be symmetrical, as illustrated by Figs. 3.1 and 3.2. Figure 3.3 shows a histogram resulting from a distribution of p when p is $\frac{1}{4}$. This is a skewed distribution, which is not surprising since we would expect a greater

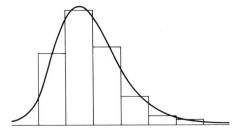

Fig. 3.3 Skewed distribution when $p = \frac{1}{4}$, $q = \frac{3}{4}$.

density of q's. As p becomes less and q increases, the skewness also increases so at very small values of p we encounter a different distribution, called the Poisson distribution, which is based on small values of p. This will be considered in detail in a later chapter.

3.6 THE FACTORIAL METHOD

It is not necessary to expand the binomial in order to calculate probabilities. Each coefficient found in the binomial expansion simply represents the number of possible combinations that can produce a given event. These coefficients can be easily calculated using a simple mathematical trick from beginning algebra.

To illustrate, consider the probability of obtaining 6 heads in 10 tosses of a coin. First, we can see that 6 heads and 4 tails are represented by $p^6 q^4$, where p and q are each equal to $\frac{1}{2}$. But this event can occur through a number of different combinations, and it is necessary to calculate this number before we can proceed. Using the formula,

$$\frac{n!}{x!\,(n-x)!},$$

where the exclamation point is read "factorial," we can substitute 10! for $n!$, 6! for $x!$, and 4! for $(n-x)!$, or

$$\frac{10!}{6!\,4!}.$$

This is another way of expressing

$$\frac{10\cdot 9\cdot 8\cdot 7\cdot 6\cdot 5\cdot 4\cdot 3\cdot 2\cdot 1}{(6\cdot 5\cdot 4\cdot 3\cdot 2\cdot 1)(4\cdot 3\cdot 2\cdot 1)}.$$

Cancelling and multiplying, we obtain 210 as the number of possible combinations that could produce 6 heads and 4 tails in 10 tosses of a coin. Then $210p^6 q^4$, or $210(\frac{1}{2})^6(\frac{1}{2})^4$, yields $\frac{210}{1024}$, or 0.205.

In using the factorial method, remember that 1! equals 1, and 0! is also considered 1.

3.7 CALCULATING PROBABILITY WITH A CURVE

It was fairly simple to calculate the probability of obtaining 6 heads in 10 tosses of a coin by the factorial method, but suppose this problem were extended to 600 heads in 1000 tosses? The mechanics of such a calculation would be laborious, to say the least. In this section we shall consider a simpler approach to calculating probabilities when n is large.

Looking again at Fig. 3.2, it may be seen that if 10 coins are tossed a very large number of times, a very few tosses will yield 0 heads, and at the other end of the scale, an equally small frequency of 10 heads will be produced. The greatest frequency of tosses will cluster around the *mean* number of heads, or 5.

It may also be seen that even with an n as small as 10, the resulting binomial distribution is a rather good approximation of a normal curve. This means that we can use the normal curve as a basis for calculating the probability of obtaining 6 heads in 10 tosses.

First, we calculate the mean of the binomial distribution by a formula based on the expression $(p + q)^n$,

$$\overline{X} = np = \tfrac{1}{2} \times 10 = 5.$$

Second, we calculate the variance of the distribution by

$$S^2 = npq = \tfrac{1}{2} \times \tfrac{1}{2} \times 10 = 2.50.$$

The standard deviation is found as usual by taking the square root of the variance; thus 2.50 yields 1.58 as the standard deviation.

Figure 3.4 shows the curve which is approximated by the binomial distribution of heads. Note that the area representing exactly 6 heads is bounded by the perpendiculars erected at 5.50 and 6.50, which are the lower and upper limits of 6. Knowing that the mean of the distribution is 5, and the standard deviation is 1.58, we can now use the procedures from Section 2.4 to calculate the area bounded by 5.5 and 6.5. Thus

$$Z = \frac{5.50 - 5.00}{1.58} = 0.32, \qquad Z = \frac{6.50 - 5.00}{1.58} = 0.95.$$

From Table IV, 0.95 is equivalent to 0.3289, and 0.32 is equivalent to 0.1255. Since we want to know the shaded area in Fig. 3.4, we subtract 0.1255 from 0.3289 and obtain 0.2034. This is the probability of obtaining 6 heads in 10 tosses of a coin. Comparing this with the value 0.205 obtained in Section 3.6, we can see that the difference is negligible even when working with a small n.

This method allows very simple and rapid calculation of the probabilities involving large n's, since the principle stays the same regardless of the number of coins, etc.

Suppose that we wish to know the probability of obtaining *at least* 6 heads in 10 tosses. This condition could be satisfied by 6, 7, 8, 9, *or* 10

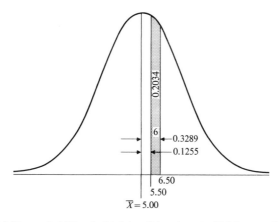

Fig. 3.4 The probability of obtaining 6 heads out of 10 tosses of a coin.

heads. The probability of *at least* 6 heads would therefore be represented by all the area above the lower limit of 6, or 5.50, as shown in Fig. 3.5. Thus

$$Z = \frac{5.5 - 5}{1.58} = 0.32.$$

Since 0.32 is equivalent to 0.1255 in terms of the normal curve area, subtracting this from 0.5000 yields 0.3745 as the probability of obtaining at least 6 heads. As might be expected, this is a greater probability than that connected with *exactly* 6 heads, since the *possibilities* of obtaining at least 6 heads are greater.

What is the probability of tossing 1000 coins in the air and obtaining *exactly* 500 heads? At this point the uninitiated is likely to shout "one-half!" since the probability of any single coin turning up heads is ½. Looking at the

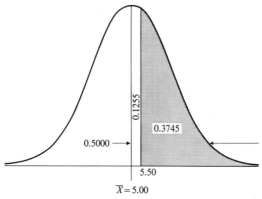

Fig. 3.5 The probability of obtaining *at least* 6 heads out of 10 tosses of a coin.

situation intuitively, how much would you be willing to bet that *exactly* 500 out of 1000 coins would turn up heads? Carrying this further, how would you like to stake your life's savings on *exactly* 500,000 coins out of a million turning up heads? We can see intuitively that the probability of obtaining *exactly* the mean diminishes as n grows larger.

Calculating the probability of 500 heads in 1000 tosses, we have

$$\overline{X} = np = \tfrac{1}{2} \times 1000 = 500,$$

and

$$S = \sqrt{npq} = \sqrt{\tfrac{1}{2} \times \tfrac{1}{2} \times 1000} = \sqrt{250} = 15.80.$$

In Fig. 3.6, the area representing the probability of obtaining exactly the mean, or 500 heads, is the area bounded by 499.50 and 500.50. Again, calculating the standard scores, we have

$$Z = \frac{500.5 - 500}{15.8} = 0.032, \qquad Z = \frac{499.5 - 500}{15.8} = -0.032.$$

Since 0.032 is equivalent to an area of approximately 0.0120, we *add* 0.0120 and 0.0120, obtaining 0.0240 as the probability of obtaining exactly 500 heads in 1000 tosses. This is a far cry from 0.5000!

Taking yet another example, suppose that we cross normal-winged fruit flies that are carriers of the recessive gene for vestigial wings. Our cross is therefore

$$Vv \times Vv$$
$$F_2 \quad VV, \; Vv, \; Vv, \; vv$$

The probability that any single offspring has vestigial wings is therefore $\tfrac{1}{4}$, and the probability of its having normal wings is $\tfrac{3}{4}$. Since these probabilities

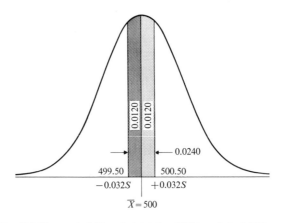

Fig. 3.6 The probability of obtaining 500 heads in 1000 tosses.

differ from $\frac{1}{2}$, we could expect the distribution to be skewed. What effect would this skewness have on our calculations if we used the curve method to determine probability?

We will test this by calculating the probability of obtaining exactly 6 vestigial-winged flies out of a total of 12, assuming the genetic cross demonstrated above. By the more laborious factorial method,

$$\frac{12!}{6! \, 6!} \, p^6 q^6,$$

where $p = \frac{1}{4}$ and $q = \frac{3}{4}$, we obtain 0.0400 as the required probability figure.

Using our skewed curve, we first calculate the mean,

$$\bar{X} = np = \frac{1}{4} \times 12 = 3,$$

and the standard deviation,

$$S = \sqrt{npq} = \sqrt{\tfrac{1}{4} \times \tfrac{3}{4} \times 12} = \sqrt{2.25} = 1.50.$$

Since the lower and upper limits of 6 are 5.5 and 6.5, we calculate the standard scores:

$$Z = \frac{5.5 - 3}{1.50} = 1.67, \qquad Z = \frac{6.5 - 3}{1.50} = 2.33.$$

Since 1.67 is equivalent to an area of 0.4525 and 2.33 is equivalent to 0.4901, we subtract and find the area representing 6 vestigial-winged flies to be 0.0376. This is sufficiently different from the previously calculated probability of 0.0400 to make us very cautious where skewed distributions are concerned. Actually, if n were larger, say around 40 or so, this discrepancy would be considerably reduced.

To summarize, if p and q differ from $\frac{1}{2}$, we should use the normal curve approximation only if n is large. If p is extremely small, we must go to another distribution—the Poisson distribution—which will be considered in a later chapter.

In the next chapter we shall apply what we have learned about probability and distributions to a consideration of inference—a concept which is really the essence of experimental statistics.

PROBLEMS

3.1 A fair coin is tossed three times. Compute the probability of obtaining:

    a) A tail first, then two heads.

    b) Two heads and a tail, with order of occurrence unspecified (see Section 3.2).

3.2 A die is rolled three times. Compute the probability of obtaining a 5 on the first roll, a 6 on the second roll, and anything but a 3 on the third roll (see Section 3.2).

3.3 A pair of dice is rolled twice. What is the probability of rolling either a 7 or an 11 on each roll? In other words, what is the probability of winning twice in a row? (See Section 3.2.)

3.4 PKU is inherited as a simple autosomal recessive trait. What is the probability that two normal persons will produce a PKU child if we know that both sets of grandparents are carriers? (See Section 3.2.)

3.5 Assume that the couple in Problem 3.4 has 3 children. What is the probability that at least one of the three will be afflicted with PKU? (See Section 3.2.)

3.6 Brachydactyly (short fingers) is inherited as a simple autosomal dominant trait. A man who has brachydactyly, but whose mother was normal, marries a normal woman. If they have three children, what is the probability that all three will have brachydactyly? (See Section 3.2.)

3.7 What is the probability of drawing 3 cards of the same suit from a deck, one at a time, without replacement? (See Section 3.3.)

3.8 From a box containing 3 white balls and 2 black balls, find the probability of drawing 2 black balls in a row if

    a) each ball is drawn with replacement,

    b) each ball is drawn without replacement.

(See Sections 3.2 and 3.3.)

3.9 If a coin is tossed 8 times, what is the probability of obtaining at least 6 heads? (See Section 3.6.)

3.10 If a coin is tossed 6 times, what is the probability of obtaining at most 2 heads? (See Section 3.6.)

3.11 A certain disease has a mortality rate of 75%. Two patients suffering from the disease are selected at random. What is the probability that at least one of them will recover? (See Section 3.2.)

3.12 A dihybrid cross between *AaBb* and *AaBb*, where *A* and *B* are dominant, produces 3 offspring. What is the probability that at least two of the three will be of the genotype *aabb*? (See Section 3.2.)

3.13 A flower of genotype *Bb* is self-fertilized and produces 100 seeds. What is the probability that at least 60 of the seeds are of genotype *Bb*? (See Section 3.7.)

3.14 Referring to Problem 3.13, what is the probability that, at most, 35 of the seeds will be of genotype *bb*? (See Section 3.7.)

4
INFERENCE

4.1 THE MEANING OF INFERENCE

The objective of many scientific investigations is to permit the investigator to make general statements based on specific and relatively limited observations. A biologist interested in the effect of a certain drug on rat metabolism may try the drug on a few rats, using the data thus obtained to make an "educated guess" concerning the drug's effectiveness on rats in general. In doing so, he makes use of an important statistical concept known as *inference*.

Essentially, the methods of inferential statistics enable the experimenter to make limited statements concerning some characteristic of a *population*, based on data derived from only a part of that population. The term "population" as used here, refers to all possible observations that can be made on a specific characteristic. In our example above, this could mean all rats now living and all rats yet unborn. Or it could conceivably mean all rats of a certain species now living in a specific area, or simply all rats of a certain species. Essentially, the definition of what constitutes a population is up to the experimenter, and depends on the nature of the problem under investigation.

From a practical viewpoint, a population is usually a group so large that it precludes making direct observations. Instead, observations are made on a small segment of the population. This small segment is called a *sample*, and conclusions or estimates concerning the population are derived on the basis of the sample observations.

As an illustration, suppose that we wish to know the mean height of all adult males in the United States. We can now say that all adult males in the

United States constitute our population. We can also see that to measure the height of each and every adult male in the United States is a practical impossibility, and the only way we will ever be able to make any statements concerning the mean of the population is through the use of inferential statistics.

4.2 SAMPLING

Our first step in attacking the problem is to draw a sample from our population of adult males. Now, it should be obvious that if our sample is to yield valid data concerning the population, the sample itself must be a fairly accurate cross section of the population. In other words, it is essential that a sample be *representative* of the population from which it is drawn.

Suppose that we visit racetracks around the country and measure all the jockeys we can find. Suppose further that we use the statistics gathered from this sample to estimate the true mean height of all adult males in the United States. Obviously we would be in error, with the error definitely on the short side! Or, suppose we draw our sample from the ranks of professional basketball players. Again, our estimate of the population value would be way off, this time in the upward direction.

Both the jockeys and the basketball players illustrate the chief ingredient of a statistician's nightmare, i.e., the *biased* sample. Obviously, a biased sample is *not* representative of the population from which it was drawn. Furthermore, it is apparent that if we are to make reasonably valid estimates of population values based on samples, every attempt must be made to use samples which are representative of the population of interest.

Actually, we may never be *certain* that a sample is unbiased. If we could be sure of this, it would mean that we would know the exact nature of the population and would have no problem in the first place. In practical terms, we can only increase the chances of obtaining an unbiased sample by the way in which we select the individuals or measurements that comprise it. Usually, this involves selecting the sample randomly. *A random sample may be defined as a sample drawn in such a way as to insure that every member of the population has an equal chance of being included.* Note that in the preceding illustration only jockeys or basketball players could be included; obviously these samples were no more random than they were representative.

A word of caution is in order at this point. A random sample is not *necessarily* always representative. For example, although the probability of doing so is small, by chance alone we could still draw a sample composed of basketball players! It is important to note that the term "random" as applied to a sample refers only to how it was drawn, and does not guarantee how representative it is. The terms random and representative are too often considered to be synonymous, when, in fact, they are not. Random sampling procedure increases the chances that a sample will be unbiased, and one of its major purposes is to minimize possible bias on the part of the experimenter.

Most experimenters are naturally going to be happier if they "prove" their hypotheses than if they fail to do so. No one is likely to gain fame and fortune for developing a drug that doesn't work or a hypothesis that proves untenable! The traditional "objectivity" of the scientist is probably more myth than fact, and scientific procedure demands that the experimenter show evidence that he has selected his samples and designed his experiment in order to avoid error through conscious or subconscious bias.

As a further illustration of the importance of randomness, let us suppose that we have 100 mice that we wish to divide into two groups of 50 each in order to test a drug for its effect on heart rate. We might be tempted to close our eyes, reach into the cages, and "randomly" select 50 mice which would be assigned to the experimental group. The second 50, or those left, would become the control group.

What is wrong with this procedure? The major objection involves the fact that our experimental group is composed of the first 50 mice we were able to catch! Apparently they were not as lively as their brothers in the control group. Could this have anything to do with metabolic rate, and therefore have a profound effect on an experiment involving heart rate?

How could we have avoided this basic error in selecting our samples? For one thing, we could have assigned a number to each of the 100 mice, put corresponding numbers on slips of paper, mixed them up in a hat, and randomly selected the first 50 numbers; we would then assign these mice to either the control or experimental group as determined by a flip of a coin. All 100 mice would then have had an equal chance to be included in the sample drawn, and we would have reduced the possible bias introduced by the experimenter or by the condition of the animals themselves.

The preceding example represents a rather simple problem in sampling. Unfortunately, obtaining a satisfactory random sample is not always so simple, especially for the biologist in the field. How does one collect a random sample of fish from a lake? Are the fish that allow themselves to be caught somehow different from the rest of the population? Similar problems arise in collecting samples of other fauna, whether by trapping, shooting, or other means. Actually, in cases like these it is probably well to admit that complete randomness in sampling is an ideal toward which the investigator must strive, but which he will probably never fully achieve. Collecting plants from a particular locality in a random fashion is also a problem, but it is easier than collecting animals randomly since plants stand still! Although some of the methods of field collecting are discussed later in conjunction with examples of statistical tests, a detailed account of this very complex area is beyond the scope of this book. The interested student is urged to consult the references cited in the bibliography.

4.3 SAMPLE SIZE

How does the size of the sample affect the accuracy of a generalization? Obviously, the larger the sample, the closer we are to measuring the population itself. Therefore, we may make the general statement that large samples are more useful than small samples *if* the large sample is *unbiased*. We can see that no matter how large a sample of jockeys we might have, any generalization based on it regarding the mean height of all United States adult males would be in error.

Essentially, a small unbiased sample is infinitely more useful than a large biased one. Logically, the *single* most important characteristic of a sample is not its size, but the extent to which it accurately represents the population from which it is drawn. Also, it will later be apparent from the logic of mathematics that the time and expense involved in increasing sample size beyond certain limits may result in diminishing returns.

4.4 STATISTICS AND PARAMETERS

Values such as means and standard deviations gained from samples are called *statistics*. In other words, sample attributes are statistics, and we speak of a sample mean as a *sample statistic*. Population values, on the other hand, are called *parameters*. Thus, in statistical inference, we draw samples from populations, derive sample statistics, and use these sample statistics as a basis for estimating unknown population parameters.

Although the symbols associated with these concepts are not used as uniformly as one might like, statisticians generally use Greek letters to designate parameters and Roman letters to designate statistics. Thus the population mean is usually μ (mu), and the variance (σ^2) and standard deviation (σ) are symbolized by sigma. The sample mean is given the symbol $\bar{X}$, and the sample variance and standard deviation are written as S^2 and S, respectively.

4.5 THE SAMPLING DISTRIBUTION

In order to understand the logical basis of inference, it is very important to grasp the concept of the sampling distribution. It is likely that no other single concept is as basic to the procedures of experimental statistics. Before investigating sampling distributions, however, it might be helpful to review a couple of items considered previously. Figure 4.1(a) shows a population distribution, and (b) shows a sample distribution. Note the symbols used to designate the mean and standard deviation in each case. Recalling the procedures of inference discussed earlier, we can visualize the sample distribution as representing a sample of measurements drawn from a population of measurements which are represented by the population distribution. Since the population is too large or is in some other way impossible to measure directly, we can assume that we do not know μ, and we probably do not know σ^2. Our problem, then, is to estimate on the basis of our sample statistics, $\overline{X}$ and S^2.

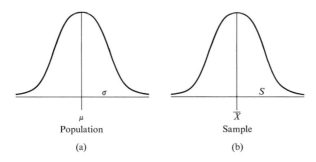

$$\sigma$$

$$\mu$$

Population

(a)

$$S$$

$$\overline{X}$$

Sample

(b)

Fig. 4.1 Symbols used in describing populations and samples.

Before we become too involved in the actual estimation procedure, we should take a look at $\overline{X}$ and S^2 as estimators of population parameters. The sample mean, $\overline{X}$, is called an *unbiased estimate of μ*. This is so, because if we were to draw an infinite number of samples of a certain number N from the population, with replacement, *the mean of these sample means would equal μ.* If the word "infinite" bothers you, a billion billion samples will probably do about as well.

On the other hand, the mean of all the S^2's of an infinitude of samples would *not* equal σ^2. In fact, it would tend to be smaller than σ^2. For this reason, S^2, the sample variance, is called a *biased* estimate of σ^2. We are beginning to see that the word "biased," as used in statistics, means "you can't depend on it"!

Let us look at the biased nature of S^2 from a logical viewpoint. If we return to our overworked example of United States adult males, and assume a sample of 50 such males randomly drawn from the population, could we logically expect the degree of dispersion around $\overline{X}$ to be as great as it would be around μ? Obviously not; we would probably be surprised if our sample of 50 contained a man 4' 8" tall and another man 6' 8" tall! In other words, we are not as likely to find the various extremes of the population adequately represented in the sample.

If, therefore, we are going to use S^2 as an estimate of σ^2, it is apparent that we need to do something about making S^2 unbiased.

Remember that the basic formula for variance is

$$S^2 = \frac{\sum x^2}{N}.$$

If 1 is taken away from N in the denominator, the value of S^2 would be increased, bringing it more in line with the population σ^2. Mathematical proof of this can be found in a book on mathematical statistics. It is actually rather simple, and is based on a principle found in Chapter 1; that is, the sum of the deviations from the true mean of a distribution will always equal zero, but the sum of the deviations from some number other than the mean will not equal zero. One does not have to be a mathematician, however, to see that this $N - 1$ factor is more important when using small samples; changing the denominator from 500 to 499 will hardly make an earth-shaking difference in S^2. In general, however, if we want to use statistics derived from a sample as estimates of population parameters, S^2 should be calculated as

$$S^2 = \frac{\sum x^2}{N - 1}.$$

Taking the square root of S^2 calculated in this manner will yield an estimate of σ which is more reliable.

Now, we return to our infinitude (or billion billion) samples drawn from our hypothetical population. Suppose that we were careful to record the mean of every sample drawn. *This would yield a distribution of sample means which would take the form of a normal distribution.* In other words, a few of these sample means would be extreme and would be found in the tails of the distribution. Most of the $\overline{X}$'s, however, would tend to cluster around μ, the mean of the population from which the samples were drawn! This is sometimes called the *central limit theorem*, and is one of the most basic and important principles in statistics.

It is highly unlikely that very many of our sample means would be exactly equal to the population mean, but we could probably expect that most of them would not deviate by too great an extent. A few, by chance alone, would be extreme deviates and be "way out" in the tails.

This distribution of *sample means* is called a *sampling distribution*, and is of critical importance to inferential statistics. Before someone thinks about all the work involved in drawing an infinite number of samples and decides to give up biometrics altogether, we should hasten to point out that the sampling distribution is a purely hypothetical concept, existing only in the minds of statisticians (and biologists interested in statistics). Like many such concepts in science, we shall shortly see that it is an extremely useful one.

It was pointed out previously that the mean of our sample means would equal μ. Therefore the mean of a sampling distribution and the mean of the population on which it is based are one and the same. Therefore μ may refer to either the mean of a population *or* its sampling distribution.

Having identified the mean of our sampling distribution as μ, we now need to calculate the second important characteristic of any distribution—the variance, or standard deviation. This will require some explaining, but if you understand this very important concept, you will later agree it was worth the effort.

4.6 THE STANDARD ERROR

Suppose that a sample consisting of one individual or measurement were drawn from a population. The mean of such a sample would be the same as the value of the measurement itself and it could obviously vary around the mean of a sampling distribution of samples of $N = 1$ to the same extent it could vary around the mean of the population from which it was drawn. In other words, the variance of the sampling distribution in this case would be equal to the population variance, σ^2.

To illustrate, suppose a Martian is sent here to look over the situation preparatory to invading Earth. By chance, as he steps out of his flying saucer the first Earth man he happens to run into is a man 7' 6" tall! Immediately he rushes back to Mars and reports that Earth is populated by a race of giants! The invasion will likely be called off unless a little green man with a knowledge of statistics points out that a conclusion of this kind cannot be drawn on the basis of a sample of one.

On the other hand, suppose (and just suppose, for we are not likely to do it) that we draw a sample from a population that consists of *all* individuals or measurements in that population. Now, if we calculate our sample mean, it will obviously be equal to the population mean, and will not vary around μ at all. In other words, the variance of a sampling distribution based on samples with N numbers equal to the population N will be zero! This, of course, assumes another unlikely event; it assumes that all measurements were made with absolute accuracy.

From the foregoing, it is apparent that the extent to which a sample mean varies around the sampling distribution mean will decrease as the sample size increases. We can also look at it in another way. If an infinitude of samples consists of large samples, we are not so likely to obtain extreme means as with samples that are smaller. Also, we note from our case of the nervous Martian that a small sample yields more room for error than a large one. If he had examined a reasonable sample of Earthlings, he would have been able to report on the size of Earth men in general with less chance for error.

Figure 4.2 shows how the shape of the sampling distribution becomes narrower as the sample size grows larger.

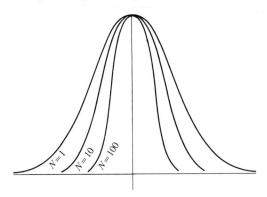

Fig. 4.2 Relationship between sample size and variance of sampling distribution.

Now we are ready to demonstrate a critically important basic formula. Recall that we said the variance of samples of $N = 1$ would be the same as σ^2, or the variance of the population itself. If we let $\sigma^2_{\bar{X}}$ stand for the variance of the sampling distribution, then

$$\sigma^2_{\bar{X}} = \frac{\sigma^2}{1} \qquad \text{or} \qquad \sigma^2_{\bar{X}} = \sigma^2.$$

On the other hand, we said that if sample size approaches the actual size of the population from which it is drawn, $\sigma^2_{\bar{X}}$ diminishes toward zero.

Thus it becomes apparent that

$$\sigma_{\bar{X}}^2 = \frac{\sigma^2}{N}.$$

Taking the square root of both sides yields

$$\sigma_{\bar{X}} = \frac{\sigma}{\sqrt{N}},$$

which is the formula for the standard deviation of a sampling distribution of means. Since it is the standard deviation of a distribution of means, it is given the special designation *standard error of the mean*. Remember, however, that $\sigma_{\bar{X}}$ *is* a standard deviation, and its relationship to the normal distribution is the same as we learned in Chapter 2. It is simply a standard deviation of sample means in a sampling distribution, instead of in a distribution of individual measurements. Figure 4.3(c) adds this third distribution to the other two previously discussed.

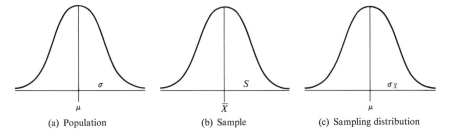

| (a) Population | (b) Sample | (c) Sampling distribution |

Fig. 4.3 Population, sample, and sampling distributions.

Now that we hopefully understand the sampling distribution concept, what can we do with it? For one thing, we can now perform an important and useful kind of inference called *estimation*.

4.7 ESTIMATION

Suppose that a sample is drawn from a population with an unknown μ and an unknown σ^2. Observations made on this sample yield the following statistics:

$$N = 100, \qquad \bar{X} = 50, \qquad S = 5.$$

Since we want to estimate μ on the basis of our sample statistics, we have derived S from an unbiased estimate of σ^2.

Next we will assume a sampling distribution based on an infinitude of samples of $N = 100$, drawn from our population.

Now the standard error of the mean can be calculated as follows, with the sample standard deviation substituted for the unknown σ, and $S_{\bar{X}}$ therefore substituted for $\sigma_{\bar{X}}$:

$$S_{\bar{X}} = \frac{S}{\sqrt{N}} = \frac{5}{\sqrt{100}} = 0.50.$$

Once again, remember that 0.50 represents a standard deviation of our sampling distribution of means. Therefore, one $S_{\bar{X}}$ up from the mean (μ) of the sampling distribution, and one $S_{\bar{X}}$ down from the mean will encompass about 68% of the total area. Since our sample mean is 50, and since this is an unbiased estimate of μ, 68% *of the time the population mean would fall between* 49.50 and 50.50. Or, in estimating on the basis of our sample statistics, we could say that the unknown parameter falls between 49.50 and 50.50, and we could further say we are 68% *confident* that we are correct in this estimate!

Unfortunately, this is not confident enough for scientific circles. Our estimation would be looked upon with more favor by our critical colleagues if we could say we are 95% or 99% confident. This change is simple to make. When we stated our 68% *confidence limits*, as they are called, we said that μ would range between ± 1 standard error 68% of the time. In more symbolic form, we said that

$$\mu = \bar{X} \pm S_{\bar{X}}(1) = 50 \pm 0.50(1) = 49.50\text{--}50.50.$$

If we want to change the confidence limits to 95% in order to maintain a proper aura of respectability, we must think in terms of 95% of the total area, or 47.50% on each side of μ. Looking at Table IV, it may be seen that an area of 47.50% is equivalent to a standard score of 1.96. Therefore, to maintain 95% confidence, we should say that

$$\mu = \bar{X} \pm S_{\bar{X}}(1.96) = 50 \pm 0.50(1.96) = 50 \pm 0.98.$$

Our new confidence interval is 49.02–50.98. It is immediately apparent that this new confidence interval is larger than before. Logically, this makes sense because if we are more confident that μ falls within a certain interval we must compensate by making the interval larger! In other words, we have lowered the *precision* of the estimate.

Since $S_{\bar{X}}$ is equal to S divided by $\sqrt{N}$, it can be seen that as N increases, $S_{\bar{X}}$ decreases. A look at the estimation formula reveals that as $S_{\bar{X}}$ decreases, the confidence interval must also decrease. Thus, as N increases, our estimate of μ becomes more precise. Again, this is logical since the larger the sample, the closer we come to the "truth," or the actual population value.

It is therefore apparent there are two ways to *increase* the precision of an estimate. First, we can use a lower confidence limit, and second, we can increase the sample size.

Note that we said *precision*, not *accuracy*. If we may once more trot out our now exhausted jockeys, we can easily see that if we used a large sample of jockeys, a very precise but highly inaccurate estimate of μ would be obtained! Precision, therefore, depends only on the sample size and confidence limits used; accuracy depends on proper sampling as well as the care and skill used in performing experiments from which data are derived.

4.8 AN EXAMPLE

As a summary of estimation procedure, let us consider the following example:

A sample of 35 female students is drawn randomly from an undergraduate college population of 2000 female students. The pulse rates of the 35 students are checked following one hour of complete rest. From the collected data, estimate μ with 95% confidence.

Table 4.1 Pulse Rates of 35 Female Students

X	X_c	x_c	x_c^2	X	X_c	x_c	x_c^2	X	X_c	x_c	x_c^2
75	0	−1	1	88	13	12	144	78	3	2	4
81	6	5	25	75	0	−1	1	71	−4	−5	25
74	−1	−2	4	70	−5	−6	36	76	1	0	0
73	−2	−3	9	81	6	5	25	76	1	0	0
79	4	3	9	79	4	3	9	75	0	−1	1
83	8	7	49	68	−7	−8	64				
69	−6	−7	49	74	−1	−2	4				
74	−1	−2	4	65	−10	−11	121				
81	6	5	25	75	0	−1	1				
64	−11	−12	144	80	5	4	16				
72	−3	−4	16	78	3	2	4				
76	1	0	0	77	2	1	1				
82	7	6	36	75	0	−1	1		$\bar{X} = 76$		
80	5	4	16	79	4	3	9		$\bar{X}_c = 1$		
77	2	1	1	80	5	4	16		$\sum x_c^2 = 870$		

Now, we will go through the problem step by step:

1. First, we code the raw data, X, by subtracting 75 from each raw measurement.

2. Adding the coded data, X_c, yields 35. Dividing this by $N = 35$ results in 1, which added back to 75 yields $\bar{X} = 76$.

3. We subtract the mean of the coded data from each coded pulse rate, X_c. This yields x_c, the deviation of the coded measurement from the coded mean.

4. Squaring all x_c values and summing the squares yields $\sum x_c^2 = 870$.

5. Now we can calculate the *unbiased* variance of the sample as

$$S^2 = \frac{\sum x_c^2}{N - 1} = \frac{870}{34} = 25.59.$$

6. Taking the square root of 25.59 yields the sample standard deviation, 5.06.

7. Using the sample standard deviation, we calculate the standard error as

$$S_{\bar{X}} = \frac{S}{\sqrt{N}} = \frac{5.06}{\sqrt{35}} = \frac{5.06}{5.92} = 0.85.$$

8. To calculate 95% confidence limits, we need $\bar{X}$, $S_{\bar{X}}$, and the standard score equivalent to 47.50%. From the normal curve table, we find this to be 1.96.

9. $\mu = \bar{X} \pm S_{\bar{X}}(1.96) = 76 \pm 0.85(1.96) = 76 \pm 1.67$.

10. The confidence interval is therefore 75.33–77.67.

An interesting question now arises. May we infer from our sample of 35 only to the college population of 2000 from which it was drawn, or may we infer to the population consisting of *all* females in the same age group? The answer depends on our willingness to assume that in terms of pulse rate, our sample of 35 is truly representative of all females in the 18 to 21 age bracket. The fact that various selective factors make girls go to college in some ways makes them a biased sample of the general population as far as some things are concerned, but does it affect pulse rate? Probably not, but unless we are certain of this we would be safer to infer only to our specific college population from which our sample was randomly drawn. Another possibility, of course, is to infer to the population consisting of *all college girls* in the 18 to 21 bracket.

Our conclusion might be stated something like this: "On the basis of our sample statistics, we estimate that the mean pulse rate in our defined population falls in the interval 75.33–77.67, and we are 95% confident that this is correct."

In the next chapter we will see how the ideas presented here can be extended to another statistical procedure of extreme importance to the experimental biologist—hypothesis testing.

PROBLEMS

4.1 Given the following distribution, calculate (a) the biased variance, and (b) the unbiased variance (see Section 4.5):

$$20, 19, 4, 8, 30, 24, 6, 18, 8, 19, 14, 10.$$

4.2 Given the following distribution, compute (a) the unbiased variance, and (b) the standard deviation (see Section 4.5):

$$142, 189, 172, 120, 198, 202, 150, 155, 168, 160, 145, 172, 162, 190, 150.$$

4.3 Compute the standard error of the mean of a sampling distribution based on a sample of 144, where the sample estimate of σ is 18 (see Section 4.6).

4.4 Compute the standard error of the mean of a sampling distribution based on a sample of 49, where the sample standard deviation is 14 (see Section 4.6).

4.5 Fifty C.O.D. measurements, in milligrams/gram, are taken at a specific location in a river. The mean C.O.D. is 95.50 and the sample S is 6. Estimate μ with 95% confidence (see Section 4.7).

4.6 Given the following sample data, compute

    a) the mean;
    b) the unbiased sample variance;
    c) the standard error of the mean;
    d) the 95% confidence limits of μ.

(See Sections 4.5, 4.6, and 4.7.)

| 72 | 75 | 77 | 79 | 86 | 89 | 92 | 40 | 65 | 54 | 55 | 42 | 52 | 63 | 40 | 36 | 62 | 96 |
| 48 | 51 | 49 | 54 | 55 | 59 | 64 | 95 | 46 | 62 | 48 | 51 | 55 | 78 | 38 | 92 | 46 | 66 |

4.7 A sample of 30 is drawn from a population. The sample mean is 60, and the unbiased sample variance is 25. Compute (a) the 95% confidence limits of μ, and (b) the 99% confidence limits of μ (see Section 4.7).

4.8 A sample of 36 is drawn from a population. The sample mean is 82.50, and the sample standard deviation is 12. Estimate μ with 99% confidence (see Section 4.7).

4.9 A sample of 225 is drawn from the same population referred to in Problem 4.8. Assume that the sample mean and the standard deviation are the same. Compute the 99% confidence limits of μ. How does the precision of your

estimation compare with the precision of the estimation of μ in Problem 4.8?
(See Section 4.7.)

4.10 A sample is drawn from a population where σ is known to be 13. What minimum sample size would have to be drawn in order to ensure a maximum range of 3.92 between the limits when estimating μ with 95% confidence? (See Section 4.7.)

4.11 A sample is drawn from a population where σ is known to be 18. What minimum sample size would have to be drawn in order to ensure a maximum range of 7.74 between the limits when estimating μ with 99% confidence? (See Section 4.7.)

4.12 From a sample of 64, the 95% confidence is computed as $\bar{X} \pm 6.80$. Determine the standard deviation of the sample (see Section 4.7).

4.13 A sample of 30 mice was drawn from a population. The adrenals were removed and weighed to the nearest tenth of a milligram. From the following raw data, representing weights of adrenals in milligrams, establish the 95% confidence limits for μ (see Section 4.7):

2.7, 8.4, 7.1, 6.3, 3.4, 4.0, 4.0, 4.3, 4.4, 4.4, 4.5, 7.0, 6.3, 5.6, 4.9, 4.1, 4.9, 4.8, 4.0, 2.6, 3.3, 5.8, 3.2, 2.8, 8.2, 5.6, 6.2, 4.5, 4.3, 4.4.

5
HYPOTHESIS TESTING

5.1 DECISION MAKING

The experimental biologist is often required to make decisions or judgments concerning differences of various kinds. The taxonomist may wish to know if certain morphological differences between populations are large enough to suggest subspeciation processes. The physiologist or clinician may be interested in the effectiveness of a specific drug on some variable such as heart rate or blood pressure. Furthermore, it is usually necessary to make these judgments on the basis of samples, drawn from populations which are too large to measure directly.

What constitutes a meaningful, or *significant* difference? Someone has defined a significant difference as "a difference that is large enough to make a difference"! This is not as silly as it may sound, since it is essentially the kind of judgment we have to make when dealing with certain kinds of experimental data.

It might be wise to point out a possible distinction between practical significance and statistical significance. As we shall see, statistical significance is determined in part by the experimenter and in part by the results of the statistical test. It is essentially arbitrary, and is mechanically determined. Practical significance, on the other hand, is determined by the biological knowledge and insight of the investigator as he interprets the statistical results in terms of the experimental setting. We should never forget that the statistical test is a tool, to be used judiciously by the competent biologist. Statistical results will certainly help him make valid judgments, but they should never be allowed to blind him to various possibilities inherent in a specific experimental situation. Statistics is a useful slave, but it should never be permitted to become the master!

5.2 DECISION MAKING—AN EXAMPLE

Suppose that we toss a coin 100 times, and record the number of heads obtained. Suppose that we repeat this procedure for a very large number of trials. What would be the expected mean number of heads?

Recalling the binomial distribution, the expected mean would be

$$\bar{X} = np = 100 \times \tfrac{1}{2} = 50.$$

Figure 5.1 shows the normal curve approximation resulting from many trials involving 100 tosses of an honest coin. Note that in such a distribution there is a possibility of zero heads and a possibility of 100 heads turning up, since these unlikely and unlooked for events *could* happen by chance.

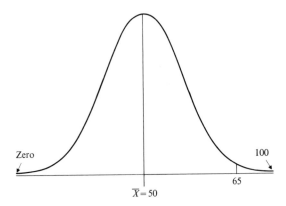

Fig. 5.1 Normal curve approximation based on 100 tosses of an honest coin.

Now, suppose that when we toss our coin, we obtain 65 heads. We are probably not too surprised, since we know that chance deviations from the mean would be the expected, rather than the unusual. Still, the more skeptical among us might wonder if a difference this large is due to chance alone. We might even harbor a dark suspicion that a difference this large could be due to a *causative factor*, such as a dishonest coin which is somehow biased in favor of heads!

Thus we have a problem. Is our coin a fair coin or is it biased in favor of heads? While we may never know the answer to this question, at least for certain, we can use statistical principles to help us arrive at an intelligent decision.

First of all, we must admit that it *is* possible to obtain even as many as 100 heads from 100 tosses of an honest coin by chance alone! We must therefore admit that 65 heads could possibly turn up without *necessarily* implying sinister machinations by a gambling syndicate. Still, you argue, the probability that 100 heads would turn up is no doubt so small as to be practically negligible, and you are willing to state *almost* without fear of contradiction that 100 heads out of 100 tosses would indicate a biased coin. Therefore, our problem really involves *finding the probability that an honest coin would produce 65 or more heads out of 100 tosses by chance alone*! Once this probability is determined, we can then make a decision about the fairness of the coin.

From Section 3.7, we are already familiar with this computation, and we can proceed to calculate the mean as 50, and the standard deviation as

$$S = \sqrt{npq} = \sqrt{\tfrac{1}{2} \times \tfrac{1}{2} \times 100} = \sqrt{25.00} = 5.00.$$

Now, we place our value, 65 heads, on the distribution as illustrated in Fig. 5.2. Calculating the Z-value, using the lower limit of 65, we obtain

$$Z = \frac{X - \bar{X}}{S} = \frac{64.50 - 50.00}{5} = 2.90,$$

which is equivalent to a normal curve area of 0.4981. The probability of obtaining 65 or more heads out of 100 tosses of an honest coin is therefore represented by the area *remaining* in the right-hand tail: 0.5000 − 0.4981 yields 0.0019 (see Fig. 5.2). Thus we find that the probability of obtaining 65 or more heads by chance alone is 0.0019, or 19/10,000. Even the less conservative must admit that this is a pretty small probability, since we would expect to obtain 65 or more heads only about once in 500 trials!

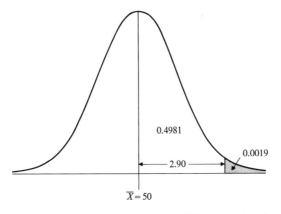

Fig. 5.2 Probability of 65 or more heads from 100 tosses of an honest coin.

What, therefore, is our most logical decision concerning the fairness of the coin? Since it has been established that the probability of an event "this bad or worse" occurring with an *honest* coin is only 0.0019, we may well be justified in deciding that our coin is indeed biased in the direction of heads!

Can we make this decision with complete confidence that we are correct? The answer is definitely no! Questions involving statistical decision making cannot be answered with certainty; the purpose of statistical hypothesis testing is to help us make intelligent judgments in the face of ever present uncertainty. We have one distinct advantage, however; we can estimate the degree of uncertainty! In our example, the possibility of obtaining 65 or more heads with an honest coin *does* exist, and the probability of that possibility is 0.0019. Therefore, the probability that we have made an incorrect decision is 0.0019.

From the foregoing, it should be apparent that the word "prove" should be eliminated from the experimental biologist's vocabulary. He can never be *certain* his conclusions are correct, since he will always be haunted by a probability, however small, that an observed difference occurred by chance and not because of an assumed causative factor.

5.3 HYPOTHESIS TESTING

In the preceding section, we used statistical principles to reach a decision concerning the fairness of a coin. In doing so, we determined whether the difference between the number of heads expected and the number actually observed was statistically significant. In biological research, we often need to make decisions concerning differences, and we are aided in this by an important procedure called *hypothesis testing*. In this section, we shall go through a step-by-step procedure involving a typical hypothesis-testing situation, explaining each step as we go along.

Statement of the Problem

Suppose that a great many measurements taken over a long period of time indicate that the mean blood hemoglobin content in the adult human male is 15.80 g/100 ml. Now further suppose that we have randomly drawn a sample of 64 adult males from a locality 5000 ft above sea level, and we wish to test the hypothesis that prolonged exposure to lowered oxygen pressure produces a significant increase in the blood hemoglobin level. Appropriate tests performed on the sample yield a mean hemoglobin content of 16.50 g/100 ml with a standard deviation of 2.00 g/100 ml.

Our data may then be summarized as follows:

Population	Sample
$\mu = 15.80$ g/100 ml	$N = 64$ $\bar{X} = 16.50$ g/100 ml $S = 2.00$ g/100 ml

The Null Hypothesis

In performing statistical tests of significance, the hypothesis is always stated in the null form. A *null hypothesis* is therefore simply a statement of "no difference." Thus in our hemoglobin problem, we state that "no statistically significant difference exists between the population mean and the sample mean." Using H_0 as the symbol for null hypothesis, this statement can be expressed symbolically as

$$H_0: \quad \mu = \bar{X}, \quad \text{or} \quad H_0: \quad \mu - \bar{X} = 0.$$

In dealing with the results of most biological experimentation, we would like to show that a significant difference *does* exist. Naturally, no one wants to spend years developing a drug, only to demonstrate that it is not effective! If we state our hypothesis in the null form, our objective is then to statistically reject it, thus lending support to the claim that a significant difference is involved. Note the absence of the word "prove" in the preceding statement.

The use of the null hypothesis is logically sound, since it is difficult, if not impossible, to "prove" a hypothesis. No matter how much evidence is gathered in support of a specific hypothesis, one can never be certain that this same body of evidence would not equally support any number of unknown alternative hypotheses! On the other hand, it *is* logically possible to reject a hypothesis, since this can be done by finding evidence which contradicts it.

Level of Significance

In our coin problem in Section 5.2, it was established that the probability of obtaining, by chance alone, a difference "as large or larger" than the observed difference was 0.0019. We decided that this probability was too small to justify concluding that the observed difference was due to chance alone. Essentially, our decision at this point was to reject the null hypothesis that "no statistically significant difference exists between the observed and expected numbers of heads."

In formal hypothesis-testing procedures, we should establish, *prior* to performing the test, the *maximum* probability of a "chance alone" difference at which the null hypothesis will be rejected. In doing so, we are also stating the maximum acceptable probability that we will be wrong in rejecting the hypothesis.

The maximum probabilities, or *levels of significance*, that have been more or less arbitrarily established as acceptable rejection points are 0.05 and 0.01. In our hemoglobin-content problem we will set the level of significance at 0.05. Therefore

$$\text{L.S.} = 0.05.$$

General principles involving levels of significance will be taken up in more detail in Section 5.5.

The Sampling Distribution

Our next step is to assume that this experiment has been performed an infinitude of times, yielding an infinitude of samples. From Chapter 4, we recall that the means of these samples would be normally distributed, and would constitute a sampling distribution of means as shown in Fig. 5.3.

From the experimental data and from the null hypothesis, we assume that the mean of this sampling distribution is μ, or 15.80 g/100 ml. Our sample mean, $\bar{X}$, is 16.50 g/100 ml, and therefore falls on the distribution somewhere to the right of μ. Now we need to determine just how far to the

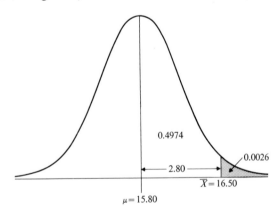

0.4974

0.0026

2.80

$\bar{X} = 16.50$

$\mu = 15.80$

Fig. 5.3 Sampling distribution of means for the blood hemoglobin problem.

right, or how "far out" it is. This requires that we compute the standard error of our hypothetical sampling distribution.

In computing the standard error, we use the procedure developed in Section 4.6. Since we are working with a fairly large sample (64), we can use S as a good estimate of the unknown σ. It may be assumed that S^2 has been computed as the *unbiased* estimate of σ^2 (Section 4.5). Thus we have

$$S_{\bar{X}} = \frac{S}{\sqrt{N}} = \frac{2.00}{\sqrt{64.00}} = \frac{2.00}{8.00} = 0.25.$$

Our next step is again a familiar one. In order to place our sample statistic, $\bar{X}$, on the sampling distribution, we calculate a Z-value in the usual manner (Section 2.4). Thus

$$Z = \frac{\bar{X} - \mu}{S_{\bar{X}}} = \frac{16.50 - 15.80}{0.25} = 2.80.$$

Having obtained 2.80 as the Z, or standard score, we now turn to Table IV and determine how much of the curve area is found between μ and our statistic $\bar{X}$. Since a Z-value of 2.80 is equivalent to 0.4974, we note from Fig. 5.3 that 0.0026 is left in the right-hand tail. Thus the probability of obtaining a difference as large or larger than the observed difference by chance alone is 0.0026.

The Decision

Originally, we stated 0.05 as the maximum probability that we would accept as a basis for rejecting the null hypothesis. Since 0.0026 is considerably less than our self-imposed limit of 0.05, our decision is to reject the hypothesis, H_0: $\mu - \bar{X} = 0$. Another approach is to note that an area of 0.05 in the right-hand tail would leave 0.4500 between μ and $\bar{X}$. This is equivalent to a Z-value of 1.64. Therefore, if our Z-value turned out to be 1.64 or above, it would have indicated rejection (see Fig. 5.4). Since our Z-value is actually 2.80, we are obviously justified in rejecting the null hypothesis.

Since 0.0026 is not only less than 0.05, but is also less than 0.01, we can state our decision as follows: "The null hypothesis is rejected with significance beyond the 0.01 level."

Since the probability of rejecting a true hypothesis is quite low (0.0026), we can feel reasonably safe in having made the decision to reject it. However, so we do not become overconfident and given to statements containing the word "prove," we should remind ourselves that although the possibility of having made the wrong decision is small, it nevertheless exists!

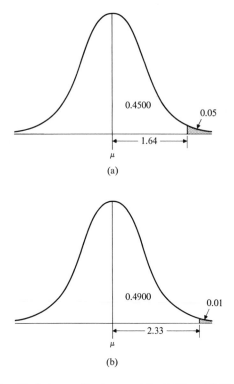

Fig. 5.4 Relationship between Z-values and the 0.05 and 0.01 rejection points.

In the case in point, we were able to reject the null hypothesis. If, on the other hand, we had obtained a Z-score of *less* than 1.64, an area *greater* than 0.05 would have been left in the tail. In that case, we would have *failed to reject* the null hypothesis. Note that we say "fail to reject" rather than "accept," since to accept a null hypothesis implies that no alternative hypotheses exist which would fit the situation equally well. This may be considered to be a bit of statistical pinhead polishing, and many respectable statistics references unashamedly use the word "accept"!

Verbalizing Conclusions

Having rejected the null hypothesis, $\mu - \bar{X} = 0$, we have ostensibly provided support for our contention that the sample mean differs significantly from the population mean. In other words, by demonstrating statistical significance, we have laid a foundation for arguing the existence of practical significance.

In the most practical terms, we are now prepared to suggest, based on the data derived from this specific experiment, and within the limitations and assumptions underlying this experiment, that adult males living for prolonged periods at high altitudes are likely to have a blood hemoglobin content significantly higher than the general population of adult males.

Note the extensive use of "weasel" words in the preceding statement. The careful investigator hesitates, particularly on the basis of limited data, to make sweeping and positive statements. The phrase "beyond the shadow of a doubt" may be appropriate for the courtroom, but it has no place in the laboratory or field.

5.4 ONE- AND TWO-TAILED TESTS

In the decision problem described in Section 5.2, and again in the hypothesis testing situation in Section 5.3, we were interested in whether our sample statistic was significantly *above* the mean of the distribution. In both cases, therefore, we were concerned with the area remaining in the right-hand tail only. This is called a one-tailed test and is appropriate if the *direction* of the difference is important or specified.

On the other hand, there are many situations where the investigator is concerned only with the significance of a difference, regardless of direction. If, for example, we were interested only in the question of whether $\bar{X}$ differed significantly from μ, and were not concerned with its being larger (or smaller) than μ, a two-tailed test would be appropriate. Figure 5.5(a) and (b) shows a two-tailed test situation. Note that since we will allow our statistic to go in either direction from the mean, the 0.05 probability of a "chance alone" difference is divided between the two tails, so we have 0.025 in the left tail and 0.025 in the right tail comprising the total rejection region. Since this means that an area of 0.4750 or more must exist between the mean of the sampling distribution and the sample statistic, we note from Table IV that a minimum Z-value of 1.96 is necessary to reject the null hypothesis at the 0.05 level. Similar reasoning applied to the 0.01 level (0.005 in each tail) shows that a Z-value of 2.58 or more would be required for rejection with significance at or beyond the 0.01 level.

Since it requires a minimum Z-score of 1.96 to reject a two-tailed test at the 0.05 level, as opposed to the 1.64 required for rejection of a one-tailed test, it would appear to be more difficult to reject a null hypothesis when using a two-tailed test. Theoretically this is not really true, since in performing a two-tailed test we have two alternatives, or routes, to rejection. In the

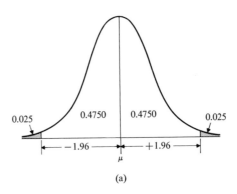

(a)

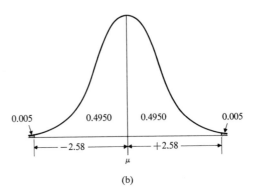

(b)

Fig. 5.5 Rejection areas and Z-values in two-tailed tests.

one-tailed test, on the other hand, we may reject only if our sample statistic falls in the area of rejection in one specific direction.

5.5 LEVELS OF SIGNIFICANCE

In Section 5.3 we described the level of significance as the probability of obtaining, by chance alone, a difference as great or greater than the observed difference. We also said that the experimenter should preset the maximum probability that he will accept as justification for rejecting a null hypothesis.

Why did we select 0.05? Actually, there is nothing magical about it; in general, 0.05 and 0.01 are accepted as traditional levels and are considered compatible with sound experimental procedure. In a sense they are arbitrary, but they may also be said to have a basis in experience and logic.

Figure 5.5 illustrates the 0.05 and 0.01 levels of significance. Using normal curve relationships, it may be seen that ± 1.96 or more is the Z-value necessary to reject at the 0.05 level, using a two-tailed test. To reject at the 0.01 level, however, a Z-value of at least ± 2.58 is required, again assuming a two-tailed test. Thus it is more difficult to reject a null hypothesis at the 0.01 level than at the 0.05 level. Therefore, assuming that rejection of a specific null hypothesis is likely to lead the investigator to fame and fortune, it is obvious that the 0.01 level provides the more rigorous test and places the greatest "burden of proof" on the investigator. Setting a level of significance of 0.001 would quite obviously establish even greater rigor, but this is unsound since it would be more likely to lead to failure to. reject null hypotheses when practical significance is actually present.

In the hemoglobin content problem described in Section 5.3, we rejected the null hypothesis "beyond the 0.01 level," actually at 0.0026. The probability that we were wrong in our decision to reject is therefore 0.0026, or "less than 0.01." If we were indeed wrong, then we were guilty of rejecting a hypothesis when it was true, and we committed a *Type I Error*. The probability of a Type I error is specified by the level of significance resulting from the test; in the case in point it turns out to be 0.0026, or "less than 0.01." Note that it is *not* 0.05, since 0.05 was simply the *maximum* probability of making such an error that we were willing to accept.

Suppose, however, that we had failed to reject the null hypothesis. Suppose further that we should have rejected it; i.e., the hypothesis was false. We would then have been guilty of committing a *Type II Error*.

Table 5.1   Type I and Type II Errors

	Reject	Fail to reject
Hypothesis true	Type I (α)	
Hypothesis false		Type II (β)

Table 5.1 shows the relationship involving Type I and Type II errors. Note that the letters alpha (α) and beta (β) are used to denote the probabilities of Type I and Type II errors, respectively. As we have seen, alpha is specified by the level of significance obtained from the statistical test. The determination of beta is more complicated, but since failure to reject the null hypothesis usually implies an absence of practical significance, beta is not computed directly. "Success," in biological research situations, usually

involves rejection of the null hypothesis; therefore, the investigator (and his critics!) is more interested in the probability of a Type I error.

Figure 5.6(a) and (b) shows a rather obvious relationship between Type I and Type II errors. As the probability of a Type I error increases, the probability of a Type II error decreases, and vice versa. Thus, one approach to decreasing beta is to increase alpha. A better approach to decreasing beta, however, is demonstrated in Fig. 5.7. We know from Section 4.6 that the shape of a sampling distribution becomes "narrower" as the sample size increases and the standard error decreases. Figure 5.7 shows that the "failure to reject" region becomes smaller, and beta thus decreases as the sample size increases.

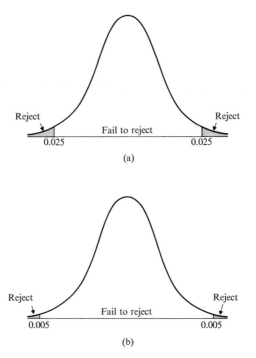

Fig. 5.6 Relationship between curve areas and probabilities of Type I and Type II errors.

To summarize, we would say that the "best" experimental procedure would involve a reasonably low level of significance in order to minimize the probability of a Type I error, and a sufficiently large sample to minimize the probability of a Type II error.

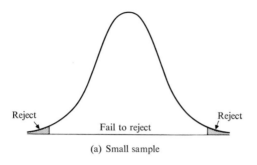

Reject

Fail to reject

Reject

(a) Small sample

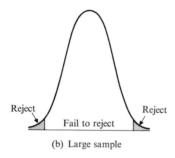

Reject

Fail to reject

Reject

(b) Large sample

Fig. 5.7 Relationship between sample size and the probability of a Type II error.

In practice, the investigator must work with what is available and in the best experimental setting that can be devised within the limitations of the situation. This is clearly no excuse, however, for experiments that pointedly ignore the basic principles of statistical procedures, but are still presented with claims of significance. Research projects that are reported in the literature along with apologies for sample size and sampling procedures should be viewed critically, to say the least!

5.6 TWO-GROUP HYPOTHESES

A common problem in biological research involves differences between sample means. As an illustration of this type of problem, suppose that we wish to test a newly developed drug in order to determine whether it is effective in changing the heart rate of the Norway rat.

Following the random procedures described in Chapter 4, we would divide our sample into two groups. One group would be given the drug and the other group would serve as a control. In order to make certain that as many variables as possible are kept constant, we will administer a placebo (a harmless inert substance) to the control group. In this way, we will reduce any difference due to the injection procedure itself. Following an appropriate time interval, the heart rate of each rat is measured, and we establish the following data:

Drug group	Control group
$N_D = 37$	$N_C = 40$
$\bar{X}_D = 290$	$\bar{X}_C = 287$
$S_D^2 = 196$	$S_C^2 = 144$

We will now go through the hypothesis-testing procedure step by step:

1. We state the null hypothesis as $H_0: \mu_D - \mu_C = 0$. Note that we do *not* say $\bar{X}_D - \bar{X}_C = 0$, since we are interested in generalizing our conclusions to *all* Norway rats. Therefore we use parametric symbols in stating the null hypothesis.

2. We set a level of significance at 0.05. This now becomes our preset maximum level of rejection.

3. We assume the sampling distribution shown in Fig. 5.8. In this case we are hypothesizing a sampling distribution based on the statistic, $\bar{X}_D - \bar{X}_C$, which would be obtained if this experiment were performed an infinitude of

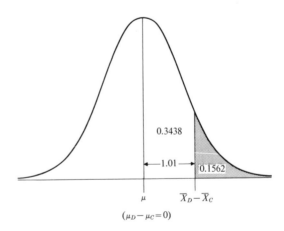

0.3438

—1.01—→ 0.1562

μ $\bar{X}_D - \bar{X}_C$

$(\mu_D - \mu_C = 0)$

Fig. 5.8 Sampling distribution of differences between means, showing a Z-value of 1.01.

times. It is therefore a distribution of *differences between means*. Since our null hypothesis maintains that *no* significant difference exists between the parameters of these means, we are assuming a sampling distribution with a mean "difference between means" of *zero*.

4. We then place the sample statistic, $\bar{X}_D - \bar{X}_C$, on the sampling distribution. To do this, we need to compute the standard error of the distribution. Since this is a standard error of a distribution of *differences between means*, we compute it as

$$S_{\bar{X}_D - \bar{X}_C} = \sqrt{\frac{S_D^2}{N_D} + \frac{S_C^2}{N_C}} = \sqrt{\frac{196}{37} + \frac{144}{40}} = \sqrt{8.90} = 2.98.$$

Note that the above formula is a simple algebraic extension of $S_{\bar{X}} = S/\sqrt{N}$, and pools the data obtained from both groups. The sample statistic is now located on the sampling distribution by calculating the Z-value as

$$Z = \frac{\bar{X}_D - \bar{X}_C}{S_{\bar{X}_D - \bar{X}_C}} = \frac{290 - 287}{2.98} = 1.01.$$

5. We make the decision concerning rejection of the null hypothesis. Since we are interested only in the question as to whether our drug will *change* heart rate, and we are not at this time concerned with the *direction* of change, we will use a two-tailed test. Reviewing Fig. 5.5, it may be seen that a Z-value of ± 1.96 or more is necessary to reject at the 0.05 level. We therefore fail to reject the hypothesis, $\mu_D - \mu_C = 0$, since our obtained Z-value is 1.01.

6. We verbalize conclusions. Having failed to reject the null hypothesis, we have not found statistical evidence to support our contention that our drug is effective in changing heart rate in the Norway rat. Statistically, we must conclude that the observed difference occurred by chance. Remember, however, the point made previously concerning the fact that statistics is a tool, not a substitute for the biological knowledge and skill of the experimenter. In this case, although the observed difference was not statistically significant, we might decide to try new experiments, possibly with different drug concentrations, dosages, etc.

In this chapter, we have attempted to present the basic theory and logic of hypothesis testing. In subsequent chapters we will take up special techniques for testing hypotheses in practical situations. The first of these will be the

t-test, which is of considerable practical importance to the experimental biologist.

PROBLEMS

5.1 A pair of dice is rolled 150 times, and a total of 40 sevens appear. On the basis of these data, would you conclude that the dice are honest? (See Section 5.2.)

5.2 A cross between a vestigial-winged fruit fly (vv) and a heterozygous normal-winged fly (Vv) resulted in 20 offspring, 12 of which were of the vestigial pheno-type. By using the normal curve approximation, determine the probability of obtaining 12 or more vestigial-winged flies from such a cross. What is your decision concerning the validity of the genetic model? (See Section 5.2.)

5.3 Serum haptoglobin is known to have an approximate mean value of 100 mg/100 ml in the normal population, with a population standard deviation of 40 mg/100 ml. A sample of 64 cancer patients is found to have a mean haptoglobin value of 113 mg/100 ml. Determine whether the sample mean value is significantly greater than the population mean (see Section 5.3).

5.4 The mean level of prothrombin in the normal population is known to be approximately 20 mg/100 ml of plasma. A sample of 40 patients showing a vita-min K deficiency has a mean prothrombin level of 18.50 mg/100 ml. The sample standard deviation is 4 mg/100 ml. Is the sample mean significantly lower than the population mean? (See Section 5.3.)

5.5 Thirty measurements of total solids in milligrams/liter were made in a lake at location "A" and 36 measurements were made at location "B." From the resulting data, determine whether there is a statistically significant difference between the concentrations of total solids at locations "A" and "B" (see Section 6.6):

$$\bar{X}_A = 184 \qquad \bar{X}_B = 190$$
$$S_A^2 = 144 \qquad S_B^2 = 196$$
$$N_A = 30 \qquad N_B = 36$$

5.6 A sample of males was drawn from each of two geographically isolated populations of *Rana pipiens*, and their body lengths were measured to the nearest millimeter. From the data below, determine whether there is a statistically signi-ficant difference between the males of the two populations in terms of body length (see Section 5.6):

$$\bar{X}_2 = 74 \qquad \bar{X}_2 = 78$$
$$S_1^2 = 225 \qquad S_2^2 = 169$$
$$N_1 = 42 \qquad N_2 = 56$$

5.7 Two different food media were compared in order to determine whether there was any difference in effect on the length of the larval stage in *Drosophila*.

Analyze the following data for significant difference between the two media. The length of the larval stage is given in days. (See Section 5.6.)

Medium I	Medium II
$\bar{X}_1 = 5.20$	$\bar{X}_2 = 7.50$
$S_1^2 = 16$	$S_2^2 = 25$
$N_1 = 40$	$N_2 = 42$

5.8 A drug which was believed to hasten blood clotting time was tested by comparing a drug group with a placebo group. Analyze the following data in order to determine whether the mean clotting time of the drug group is significantly lower than the mean clotting time of the placebo group. The clotting time is given in minutes. (See Section 5.6.)

Drug	Placebo
$\bar{X}_D = 6.30$	$\bar{X}_P = 7.45$
$S_D^2 = 10.24$	$S_P^2 = 12.96$
$N_D = 64$	$N_P = 64$

6
TWO-GROUP COMPARISONS—STUDENT'S *t*

6.1 STUDENT'S *t*

So far we have seen that the hypothesis-testing procedure basically involves (1) the location of a sample statistic on an appropriate sampling distribution, and (2) the determination of the statistic's relative distance from the mean of that distribution. We have also seen that this requires the computation of the standard deviation, or *standard error*, of the sampling distribution. Significance may then be determined by interpretation of the results of the relationship,

$$\frac{\text{Sample statistic} - \text{Distribution mean}}{\text{Standard error}}.$$

In previous examples of hypothesis testing, this resulted in a Z-value, since we were working with the normal distribution described by Table IV.

Now, it will be recalled that the standard error of the mean is computed by

$$\sigma_{\bar{X}} = \frac{\sigma}{\sqrt{N}},$$

where σ is the population standard deviation. By now it should be obvious that in most cases we do *not* know σ, but can only estimate it, using the square root of the unbiased version of our sample S^2 as the estimator.

This use of S as an estimate of σ is legitimate only in cases where the sample from which S is derived is sufficiently large. What is "sufficiently large" may be open to some debate, but most references consider a sample of

30 or more as providing a sample standard deviation which is a sufficiently reliable estimate of σ.

Unfortunately, the realities of biological research situations often restrict the experimenter to smaller samples. The sample S is *not* a reliable estimate of σ in such cases, even when derived from an unbiased estimate of σ^2. Therefore if we compute

$$S_{\bar{X}} = \frac{S}{\sqrt{N}},$$

where S is derived from a small sample, we are in danger of rejecting null hypotheses that should *not* be rejected!

Fortunately for small-sample experimentation, a statistician by the name of W. S. Gosset, writing under the pseudonym "Student," developed a family of distributions which contain a "built-in" recognition of the limitations imposed by small samples. These "Student's t" distributions are based on the relationship

$$\frac{S}{\sqrt{N-1}},$$

where $N - 1$ represents "degrees of freedom." Putting it simply, the degrees of freedom associated with a distribution are determined by the number of variates that can be entered in that distribution before the values of the remainder of the variates are fixed by the necessity to produce a certain total. This somewhat elusive concept may be clarified by considering the following distribution of five numbers.

$$
\begin{array}{c}
X \\
6 \\
5 \\
3 \\
8 \\
3
\end{array}
$$

It may be easily seen that the sum of this distribution is 25 and the mean is 5. Now, if we are to maintain these same sum and mean values, we may enter *four* numbers of *any* value, but the value of the fifth number is fixed by the necessity to produce a sum of 25 and a mean of 5! Since we have "freedom to play around" with any *four* of these numbers, we say that this distribution has four degrees of freedom.

When putting on a pair of gloves, we have a choice as to which glove, right or left, we will put on first. Once the decision has been made, however, we have no further choices; the other glove is "fixed." We might therefore say that putting on gloves involves one degree of freedom!

A more basic discussion of degrees of freedom will be found in any good book on mathematical statistics. For now, it will suffice to understand that this concept is associated with sample size; i.e., the larger the sample, the more degrees of freedom.

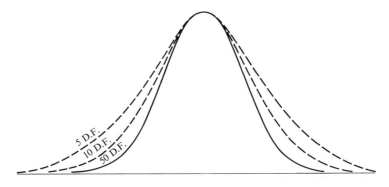

Fig. 6.1 Relation of shape of *t*-distribution to sample size.

Figure 6.1 shows how the shapes of *t*-distributions are related to sample size, or degrees of freedom. Note especially how the amount of room in the tails increases as the sample size becomes smaller. Also note that with increasing sample size, the curves increasingly approximate the normal distribution of *Z*-values. This is logical, since the larger the sample, the more we are justified in using *S* as an estimate of *σ*.

Figure 6.2 shows that as *N* decreases we must work with curves having proportionately more room in the tails. Note that with a sample of 50, the sample statistic must be located at least 1.96 standard errors from the mean in order to reject H_0 at the 0.05 level. But, with a sample of 12, the statistic must be located a minimum of 2.20 standard errors from the mean if we are to be justified in rejecting H_0 at the same 0.05 level! A glance at Table III in the appendix will show that the minimum, or *critical* value, required for rejection of the null hypothesis increases as degrees of freedom decrease.

The logic inherent in associating the *t*-curve's rejection values with sample size can be understood intuitively. If we are going to reject a null hypothesis on the basis of statistics gleaned from a small sample, then we need to demonstrate a larger critical value than would be necessary if our sample were large. In essence, the *t*-curves are telling us that small samples are not too

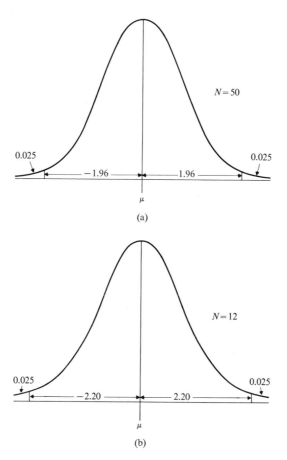

Fig 6.2 Relation of sample size to the *t*-value necessary for rejection of H_0.

reliable, and we must therefore go to greater lengths in order to justify rejecting a null hypothesis!

Referring again to Table III, it may be seen that when using this table, we need to consider critical values of *t* that are specifically associated with appropriate degrees of freedom as well as a specific level of significance. Thus if we were working with a sample, $N = 12$, and we wished to know the minimum, or critical value that must be attained for rejection at the 0.05 level, we would enter the table at $N - 1$, or 11 degrees of freedom. In the column labeled 0.05, we would find that the critical value is 2.20.

It is important to note that Table III has columns for both one- and two-tailed tests. Our value of 2.20 is the critical value for a two-tailed test at the 0.05

level. If a one-tailed test value is desired, then we must find the critical value in the next column to the left. In this case, look up the value associated with 11 degrees of freedom. This yields a one-tailed critical value of 1.80.

It is sometimes said that the *t*-distribution permits the effective use of small samples; i.e., as long as the *t*-test is used, small samples may be considered just as reliable as large samples. This is not really true! Large samples are still better than small ones, and the major advantage of the *t*-distribution lies in the reduction of Type I errors that might otherwise result from the use of small samples. This, of course, is a useful advantage, but it still does not justify earth-shaking conclusions drawn from 7 or 8 specimens collected in a dubiously random manner! Perhaps at this point we need to again remind ourselves that statistical tests are no substitute for the common sense and biological knowledge of the investigator.

The following example illustrates how the *t*-distribution helps us to exercise caution when drawing conclusions based on small samples.

Example. A sample of $N = 81$ was drawn from a population and yielded an $\bar{X}$ of 50 and an S of 3. Assume that we wish to use this sample as a basis for estimating μ, the population mean, with 95% confidence.

1. Recalling the procedure of estimation, we first compute the standard error of the mean as

$$S_{\bar{X}} = \frac{S}{\sqrt{N}} = \frac{3}{9} = 0.33.$$

2. Then μ is estimated by

$$\mu = \bar{X} \pm S_{\bar{X}}(1.96) = 50 \pm 0.33(1.96)$$
$$= 50 \pm 0.65 = 49.35\text{--}50.65.$$

3. Now, instead of a sample of 81, suppose that we draw a sample, $N = 10$, from the same population, and assume the same mean of 50 and standard deviation of 3.

4. Again we find the standard error of the mean by

$$S_{\bar{X}} = \frac{S}{\sqrt{N}} = \frac{3}{3.16} = 0.95,$$

noting that the standard error associated with a sample of 10 is considerably larger than the 0.33 value associated with the sample of $N = 81$.

5. Now we find the *t*-value associated with a two-tailed test at the 0.05 level, and at $N - 1$, or 9 degrees of freedom, we find the value 2.26. This value of

2.26 must now be used in the estimation formula in place of the 1.96 value which we were permitted to use with a sample as large as 81. Thus we have

$$\mu = \bar{X} \pm S_{\bar{X}}(t_{0.05}) = 50 \pm 0.95(2.26)$$
$$= 50 \pm 2.15 = 47.85\text{–}52.15.$$

6. Thus with a sample of $N = 81$ we were able to compute a confidence interval of 1.30, but with a sample of $N = 10$, this confidence interval became 4.30, which is a considerably less precise estimation of μ than that obtained from the larger sample!

From the foregoing example, it may be seen that, when working with small samples, use of the t-distribution essentially provides a realistic estimate of the precision, or lack of it, that is associated with small sample inference. This is *not* the same as permitting inference from small samples with efficiency equalling that which is possible with large samples!

At this point it should be emphasized that the t-distribution test is "open on both ends"; that is, it may be used with large as well as small samples. Table III in the appendix shows that as the sample size grows larger, the critical values decrease until they have become the same values associated with the normal distribution. In practice, therefore, it is convenient to consult the t-table directly rather than bother with the normal curve table.

In the next section, we shall discuss some of the fundamental principles associated with two-group experimental comparisons. Following this, we shall apply Student's t to data obtained from fundamental two-group designs.

6.2 TWO-GROUP EXPERIMENTAL DESIGN

Suppose that we wish to test the hypothesis that a specific drug significantly elevates pulse rate in human subjects. Suppose further that we select an adult female, measure her pulse rate prior to injection of the drug and again fifteen minutes after the drug is injected. This yields the following data:

Before	After
75	85

Now, just as we are about to set up a cheer for our drug, someone wonders if the injection itself, and not the drug, could have possibly caused the increase in pulse rate. This brings up the need for a *control*, so we change our plan a bit and search around for another subject to act as a control. It so happens that we select a male for this purpose. This time, we inject the female with the drug and the male receives a placebo, which is an inert substance having no effect on pulse rate (we hope!), and after a fifteen-minute interval we obtain the following data:

Female (drug)	Male (placebo)
85	78

Now, while we are rushing to publish our results, someone reminds us that females have an inherently higher pulse rate than males. Consulting the literature, we find that females, as a group, do indeed tend to have higher pulse rates than males. We are thus guilty of a basic error in that we have *confounded* two factors, both of which have an effect on the variable of interest. In other words, the effects of the drug factor and the sex factor are so thoroughly confused that we cannot separate the effects of one from the other! Obviously, no conclusions may be drawn concerning the effect of the drug alone.

We now improve things by substituting an adult male for the female. Having learned of the dangers of confounding, we are more cautious this time and are careful to choose a control subject who is alike as possible to the experimental subject in age and size. This time we obtain

Drug (male)	Placebo (male)
86	78

Once again, at the height of our self-congratulations, our troublemaker spoils the celebration by asking an irritating question: "Is it not true that a considerable variation in pulse rate exists among human subjects, even when they are of the same sex, size, and age?"

Our results thus have doubtful validity when we consider that a considerable natural variation does occur in living systems. We think about this, and decide that if we could only repeat this experiment enough times, using different subjects, we could take this natural variation into consideration. This sounds like a good solution, but it is apparent that if this approach is to be valid, the experiment must be repeated under *exactly* the same conditions; in other words, the experiment must be *replicated*!

After some thought, we decide that the easiest and most economical way to effect this replication procedure is to treat several subjects at the same time. We therefore select 40 adult males of similar age and size to use as subjects. Having read Chapter 4, we recall how important it is to assign subjects to control and experimental groups in such a way as to avoid subconscious bias. We therefore turn to Table II in the appendix, which is a table of random numbers. This table may be used as follows:

1. Assign a number ranging from 1 to 40 to each of the 40 subjects in the group.

2. Drop a pencil point somewhere on the random numbers table. From the point of pencil contact, we proceed to underline succeeding two-digit groups which include the numbers 1–40. Thus we might have:

<u>26</u> 94 <u>03</u> 68 58 70 <u>29</u> 73 41 <u>35</u> 53 <u>14</u> 03 <u>33</u> <u>40</u>

and so on. Note that once a number is underlined it is subsequently ignored, as in the case of the number 03.

3. After 20 subjects have been selected in this way, these subjects now constitute one group and the remaining 20 comprise the second group. We can now toss a coin to see which group receives the drug and which group is given the placebo.

Now we have established two groups, and although they are composed of different subjects, we are hopeful that our "complete randomization" procedure produced two groups that are not significantly different in terms of variable response *before* treatment. In other words, any conclusions based on experimental results must include the assumption that both groups were drawn from the same statistical population. To use an example stated earlier, males and females are in different statistical populations—at least insofar as pulse rate is concerned.

We have just described a method which is sometimes called an "uncorrelated samples" comparison. There is another approach which will somewhat reduce error due to variability, provided we can assume that neither the drug nor the placebo will have a permanent effect on the subject's physiological state. If we are reasonably certain this assumption is valid, the *same subjects* can be used for both drug and placebo injections—at different times, of course. The placebo could be given first, the data collected, and then the drug could be given and its associated data collected. Or, with each subject, it might be randomly decided as to which shall be given first: the drug or the placebo. Yet another possibility would involve two separate experiments, using the same subjects, in which the order of drug and placebo administered is reversed. A comparison of results might then shed light on whether the order of administration of drug and placebo had any effect.

This procedure, known as a "matched-pair" design, has the obvious advantages inherent in using the same subject for both drug and placebo.

Since the same subject is involved with both treatments, there is a high probability that extraneous factors affecting the variable are kept relatively constant. Naturally, it can be used only in cases where the subject is not permanently altered by either treatment.

Matched-pair designs sometimes involve a matching, or attempted matching, of two different subjects which then makes up a replication. This is useful in diet experiments where pairs may be matched in terms of weight, sex, genetic background, etc. This procedure should be approached with caution, since it is not always easy to account for all the possible variables that could affect the validity of experimental results.

6.3 ANALYSIS OF "MATCHED-PAIR" DATA

In the preceding section we discussed the nature of the matched-pair design and its application to two-group comparisons. In this section we will see how the *t*-distributions may be used to analyze data derived from such a design. Suppose that we do this by presenting the following example, followed by a step-by-step solution.

Example. An investigator wished to determine whether epinephrine has the effect of elevating plasma cholesterol content in human subjects. Twelve adult males were selected, and the same subjects were given both the placebo and the drug. Blood samples were taken following injection of the placebo and again after injection of epinephrine. Analysis of the blood samples resulted in the data given below, where cholesterol content is expressed in milligrams/100 ml.

Subject	Placebo	Epinephrine
1	178	184
2	240	243
3	210	210
4	184	189
5	190	200
6	181	191
7	156	150
8	220	226
9	210	220
10	165	163
11	188	192
12	214	216

The Null Hypothesis

As usual, we test the hypothesis in its null, or "no difference" form. Since this is a matched-pair design, we are interested in the *mean difference, $\bar{D}$,* which is found by summing the differences between the placebo and drug responses for each replication and dividing by the number of pairs. Thus

$$\bar{D} = \frac{\Sigma D}{N}.$$

Since we are stating that no significant difference exists between the drug and the placebo in terms of effect on cholesterol content, our null hypothesis in symbolic form is

$$H_0: \bar{D} = 0.$$

The Sampling Distribution

Figure 6.3 shows the sampling distribution associated with this test. This is a distribution of $\bar{D}$'s obtained from a hypothetical infinitude of experiments performed on samples of 12 drawn from the same population. Since we have stated $H_0: \bar{D} = 0$, the mean of this distribution is the mean of all sample $\bar{D}$'s, and is assumed to be zero. Since it is a mean of means, it may be symbolized by $\bar{\bar{D}}$. We should also note that our sampling distribution is a *t*-curve based on 11 degrees of freedom, or 12 *pairs* minus 1.

Level of Significance

We will set the level of significance at 0.05. Since we are interested only in whether epinephrine will *elevate* cholesterol content, we shall assume a one-tailed test, as shown by Fig. 6.3.

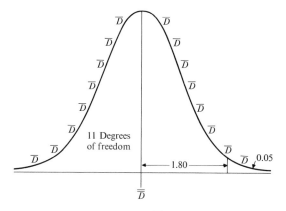

Fig. 6.3 Sampling distribution of $\bar{D}$ with 11 degrees of freedom.

Computations

1. Our first step consists of finding the difference, D, between the measurements taken on each replication. Note that this is a signed difference, and is $(+)$ if the drug response is larger, and $(-)$ if the placebo response is larger. Actually, it could be done the other way around, but a casual examination of the data listed in Table 6.1 indicates a trend toward larger values as we go from placebo to drug, so this way we simply avoid working with minus signs.

Table 6.1

Subject	Placebo	Epinephrine	D	$(D - \bar{D})$	$(D - \bar{D})^2$
1	178	184	+ 6	+ 2	4
2	240	243	+ 3	− 1	1
3	210	210	0	− 4	16
4	184	189	+ 5	+ 1	1
5	190	200	+10	+ 6	36
6	181	191	+10	+ 6	36
7	156	150	− 6	−10	100
8	220	226	+ 6	+ 2	4
9	210	220	+10	+ 6	36
10	165	163	− 2	− 6	36
11	188	192	+ 4	0	0
12	214	216	+ 2	− 2	4

$$12\overline{)48} = 4 \qquad \sum(D - \bar{D})^2 = 274$$
$$\bar{D} = 4$$

2. Next, we determine the mean difference. This yields $\bar{D} = 4.00$.

3. Since we need to compute S_D, the standard deviation of the differences, we now obtain the deviation of each difference from $\bar{D}$, and then proceed to square each deviation. This yields the column $(D - \bar{D})^2$, and summing this column yields $\sum(D - \bar{D})^2$. The standard deviation of the differences can now be computed by applying a familiar formula,

$$S_D = \sqrt{\frac{\sum(D - \bar{D})^2}{N - 1}} = \sqrt{\frac{274.00}{11.00}} = 4.99.$$

4. Now we compute the standard error of the mean difference, $S_{\bar{D}}$, by

$$S_{\bar{D}} = \frac{S_D}{\sqrt{N}} = \frac{4.99}{3.46} = 1.44.$$

5. Now that we have the standard error of our sampling distribution, we can place our sample statistic, $\bar{D} = 4.00$, on this distribution by computing t. This is done by

$$t = \frac{\bar{D} - 0}{S_{\bar{D}}} = \frac{4.00 - 0}{1.44} = 2.78.$$

The Decision

We now enter the t-table at $N - 1$, or 11 degrees of freedom. We look for the critical value in the column for one-tailed tests with a level of significance of 0.05. This indicates that a value of 1.80 or above is necessary to reject the null hypothesis at the 0.05 level. Since our experimentally obtained t-value is 2.78, the table shows that it is significant beyond the 0.01 level.

Thus, as far as this experiment is concerned, our contention that epinephrine produces a significant elevation of cholesterol content has been statistically supported.

6.4 ANALYSIS OF UNCORRELATED GROUP DESIGN

Another approach to two-group comparison involves assigning *different* subjects to each of the two groups. This may be done randomly, as in the drug-placebo situation discussed in Section 6.2, or each group may consist of subjects drawn randomly from a specific population, where the objective is to compare the two populations from which the samples were drawn. The following example will illustrate the statistical analysis of this kind of design.

Example. A taxonomist suspects that a significant difference in bill length exists between an eastern population of a certain bird species and a western population of the same species. He hopes to use this difference, if significant, as part of a general morphological picture on which to base a claim of subspeciation.

A total of 14 specimens were collected from the eastern population and 18 specimens were obtained from the western population. The bill length of each specimen was measured to the nearest hundredth of a millimeter, resulting in the following data:

Eastern	Western
$\bar{X}_E = 8.57$	$\bar{X}_W = 8.40$
$\sum (X_E - \bar{X}_E)^2 = 2.39$	$\sum (X_W - \bar{X}_W)^2 = 2.74$
$N_E = 14$	$N_W = 18$

Note that the figures 2.39 and 2.74 represent the sum of squared deviations from the mean in each case. This could be found very quickly with a
desk calculator by

$$\sum X^2 - \frac{(\sum X)^2}{N}.$$

The Null Hypothesis

Since the investigator wants to know if a significant difference in bill length
exists between the *populations* from which the samples were drawn, the null
hypothesis is stated as

$$H_0: \mu_E - \mu_W = 0.$$

Note that we are now concerned with a *difference between means*, which is
not the same thing as the *mean difference* considered in Section 6.3.

The Sampling Distribution

Our sample statistic in this case is $\overline{X}_E - \overline{X}_W$, so we construct a hypothetical
sampling distribution of "differences between means" as shown by Fig. 6.4.
As usual, this is based on an infinitude of samples drawn from the populations of interest. Since our null hypothesis implies a parameter of zero
difference, the sampling distribution mean is assumed to be zero.

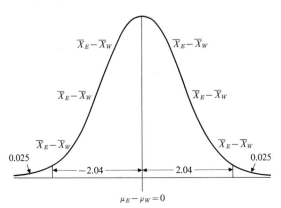

Fig. 6.4 Sampling distribution of differences between means.

Level of Significance

We shall preset the level of significance at 0.05. Since we are interested only
in whether a difference exists, and not the direction of the difference, a two-
tailed test is appropriate. Figure 6.4 therefore shows a rejection region of
0.025 in each tail.

Computations

1. The first step involves the calculation of a *pooled variance*. This procedure takes into consideration all information that is obtained from both samples. The pooled variance, S_p^2, is computed by an application of the familiar formula for variance. Thus

$$S_p^2 = \frac{\sum (X_E - \bar{X}_E)^2 + \sum (X_W - \bar{X}_W)^2}{N_E + N_W - 2}$$

$$= \frac{2.39 + 2.74}{14 + 18 - 2} = \frac{5.13}{30} = 0.17.$$

Note that in the above formula we are using the sums of squared deviations from two means, one from each sample. Since this involved the calculation of two separate means, or two parameter estimates, we lose one degree of freedom for each parameter estimated. This accounts for the expression, $N_E + N_W - 2$.

2. Next, we use the pooled variance, S_p^2, to compute the standard error of differences between means. Again, we utilize an algebraic extension of the basic formula for the standard error of the mean. Thus

$$S_{\bar{X}_E - \bar{X}_W} = \sqrt{\frac{S_p^2}{N_E} + \frac{S_p^2}{N_W}} = \sqrt{\frac{0.17}{14} + \frac{0.17}{18}}$$

$$= \sqrt{0.021} = 0.15.$$

3. Now, having obtained the standard error, we proceed as usual to place our statistic, $\bar{X}_E - \bar{X}_W$, on the sampling distribution. This is done by computing the *t*-value as

$$t = \frac{\bar{X}_E - \bar{X}_W}{S_{\bar{X}_E - \bar{X}_W}} = \frac{8.57 - 8.40}{0.15} = 1.13.$$

The Decision

Recalling that the number of degrees of freedom associated with this design is $N_1 + N_2 - 2$, we enter Table III at $14 + 18 - 2$, or 30 degrees of freedom. We look for the critical value in the 0.05 column for a two-tailed test and we find the value of 2.04 (Fig. 6.4).

Since our experimentally derived *t*-value is 1.13, we fail to reject the null hypothesis. We have thus failed to demonstrate that a significant difference in bill length exists between the two populations.

6.5 SUMMARY

We have discussed two basic methods for making two-group comparisons, and we have seen the appropriate statistical procedure for each case. There are variations on these designs, of course, and there are accompanying variations on the statistical procedures. These will be found in more advanced texts found in the bibliography.

We have also seen that the use of small samples in two-group experimentation requires the application of Student's *t*-distributions. It should also be recalled that Student's *t* may be used for large-sample as well as small-sample comparisons.

In the next chapter we will consider the analysis of data known as *enumeration data*.

PROBLEMS

6.1 A sample of 9 measurements yields a mean of 45 and a standard deviation of 8. Estimate the population mean with 95% confidence (see Section 6.1).

6.2 A sample of 14 measurements yields a mean of 50 and a standard deviation of 5. Estimate the population mean with 99% confidence (see Section 6.1).

6.3 An estimation based on a sample of 16 measurements yields a 95% confidence interval of 26.80–33.20. What is the standard deviation of the sample? (See Section 6.1.)

6.4 A group of mice were placed in a series of stress situations which elicited a fear response. After a period of time under these conditions, the mice were compared to those of a control group which had not been put under stress. Analyze the following data to determine whether a significant difference in adrenal gland weight exists between the two groups. The adrenal weight is expressed in milligrams (see Section 6.4).

Experimental	Control	Experimental	Control
3.8	4.2	3.9	3.6
6.8	4.8	5.9	2.4
8.0	4.8	6.0	3.2
3.6	2.3	5.7	4.9
3.9	6.5	5.6	
4.5	4.9	4.5	

6.5 Nine samples were taken from each of two different locations on a river, and the measurements of the total solids, in milligrams/liter, were determined. Analyze the following data and determine whether the total solids content is significantly higher at location II than at location I (see Section 6.4):

Location I	Location II	Location I	Location II
222	211	191	206
176	244	239	218
207	226	228	215
194	270	184	207
227	251		

6.6 An investigator tests a drug which he has reason to believe will increase hemoglobin content in grams/100 ml. The hemoglobin content of 8 subjects is measured before and after administration of the drug. Analyze the following data in terms of the effectiveness of the drug (see Section 6.3):

Subject	Before	After	Subject	Before	After
1	10	12	5	8	9
2	9	11	6	7	10
3	11	13	7	12	12
4	12	14	8	10	14

6.7 Two groups of plants were used to test the effect of an auxin on height. One group was treated with the auxin and the other group, grown under identical conditions, was left untreated as a control. On the basis of the following data, test the hypothesis that no significant difference, in terms of height, exists between the experimental and control groups (see Section 6.4):

Experimental	Control
$N_E = 12$	$N_C = 15$
$\bar{X}_E = 260$ mm	$\bar{X}_C = 250$ mm
$\sum x_E^2 = 460$	$\sum x_C^2 = 450$

6.8 Two varieties of peas were compared in terms of ascorbic acid content, measured in milligrams/100 g. From the following data, which were derived from

10 samples drawn from each variety, determine whether a significant difference in ascorbic acid content exists between the two varieties (see Section 6.4):

Variety I	Variety II	Variety I	Variety II
39	42	28	34
40	39	26	27
34	41	21	25
32	36	19	31
29	28	22	22

6.9 The effect of a nutrient solution on plant growth was tested using 12 plots, each plot containing two plants. In each plot, one plant was treated with the solution and the other plant was left untreated as a control. Analyze the following data to determine whether the treated plants show significantly greater height than the untreated plants. Height is recorded in centimeters. (See Section 6.3.)

Plot	Treated plants	Untreated plants	Plot	Treated plants	Untreated plants
1	24.8	22.6	7	22.4	19.5
2	21.6	21.0	8	26.7	21.6
3	27.8	23.4	9	23.8	20.3
4	29.9	27.5	10	22.8	18.5
5	30.0	39.0	11	26.6	26.0
6	23.0	20.0	12	24.0	21.0

6.10 Two different methods were used to determine the concentration of prothrombin in plasma. Both determinations were made on the same subject, using 8 subjects in all. On the basis of the following data, where prothrombin is expressed in milligrams/100 ml, determine whether a significant difference exists between the two methods (see Section 6.4):

Subject	Method I	Method II	Subject	Method I	Method II
1	17	18	5	22	23
2	17	17	6	17	15
3	18	20	7	23	25
4	21	24	8	23	22

6.11 A sample of male subjects and a sample of female subjects were tested for fibrinogen concentration, measured in μg/100 ml. On the basis of the following data, test the hypothesis that fibrinogen concentration is not higher in women than in men (see Section 6.4):

Men	Women	Men	Women
0.27	0.34	0.27	0.29
0.30	0.27	0.28	0.27
0.23	0.38	0.25	0.28
0.35	0.35	0.35	0.35
0.27	0.41	0.33	0.39

7
ENUMERATION DATA—CHI-SQUARE
AND POISSON DISTRIBUTIONS

7.1 ENUMERATION DATA

As the term implies, *enumeration data* result from a counting process. This usually involves the assignment of experimental units to specific categories in accordance with certain attributes, and then counts are taken on the units in each category. This is obviously different from measurement data, which, ideally, can take any value at all between two extremes on a continuum.

To illustrate, suppose that we administer a therapeutic drug to twenty patients suffering from a disease which is usually fatal. Discounting the added possibility of varying degrees of improvement, there are two possible alternatives that can happen in each case: either the patient will recover, or he will not recover! Counting the number of patients who recover and the number who die yields an example of enumeration data.

There are many examples of these "*A*, non-*A*" kinds of data. People either have blue eyes or they do not, a fruit fly either has vestigial wings or it has normal wings, a gentleman prefers blondes or he does not, and so on. There are many situations in biological science, and most especially in genetics, where experimental data are of this enumeration variety.

7.2 CHI SQUARE WITH A PRIORI HYPOTHESIS

One of the most familiar and useful statistical tests is the technique known as chi square (χ^2). In order to illustrate how this technique can be used to treat enumeration data, we shall return briefly to the coin problem of Section 5.2.

A review of this problem shows that, based on 100 tosses of an unbiased coin, the probability of obtaining 65 or more heads by chance alone was only

0.0019. We therefore rejected the null hypothesis of "no difference" between 65 heads and the expected 50 heads, and concluded that the coin was not fair, but biased in favor of heads. In Section 5.2 this decision was based on the use of the normal-curve approximation to the binomial.

Now we shall use chi square to determine whether 65 heads and 35 tails is a significant departure from the 50 heads and 50 tails that one would expect from 100 tosses of an honest coin. By now, we are much too sophisticated about these things to really expect *exactly* 50 heads and 50 tails every time a coin is tossed 100 times, but based on the probability value of $\frac{1}{2}$ that is attached to a fair coin, we should certainly be suspicious if the deviation of the observed frequencies from the expected frequencies is unusually large!

Note that the *observed* frequencies are those actually derived from observations made on experimentally produced data. The *expected* frequencies, on the other hand, are based on some preconceived notion, or *a priori hypothesis*, which in this case is simply the fact that the probability of an honest coin coming up heads in any single toss is $\frac{1}{2}$! Thus the expected frequencies in our case in point are 50 heads and 50 tails.

These observed and expected frequencies are now organized in the form of a table:

	Heads	Tails	
Observed	65	35	100
Expected	50	50	100
	115	85	

It may be seen that in this 2 × 2 table we could enter any value in any given cell, but the values to be entered in the three remaining cells would then be fixed by the marginal totals. In other words, one and only one cell frequency may be entered with any freedom as to its value. We therefore say that a 2 × 2 chi-square table has *one* degree of freedom. Thus, like the *t*-test, the chi-square test is based on a family of distributions, where the shape of the distribution is based on degrees of freedom. In general, degrees of freedom associated with chi square may be determined by the formula

(rows − 1)(columns − 1) = degrees of freedom,

and since a 2 × 2 table has 2 rows and 2 columns, the degrees of freedom are computed by $(2 - 1)(2 - 1) = 1$.

The chi-square formula is now applied to the data as they appear in the table. This formula involves a *summation of the squared differences between each observed frequency and its associated expected frequency, divided by the expected frequency.* Thus

$$\chi^2 = \sum \frac{(O - E)^2}{E}.$$

It should be obvious that the size of the obtained chi-square value will be determined by the magnitude of the differences between the observed and expected frequencies. Large differences will produce a large value of chi square; smaller differences will produce smaller chi-square values, and if no differences at all exist, then $\chi^2 = 0$.

In our present example, we will need to slightly modify the basic formula. Chi square is based on a discrete, not a continuous variable. We therefore need to "correct for continuity" by subtracting 0.50 from the absolute difference between each observed and expected frequency combination. This is called the Yates correction factor, and is to be used with 2 × 2 tables only. It should also be mentioned here that although the literature is confusing on this point, it would be well to use the Yates correction factor with *all* 2 × 2 table situations, regardless of the size of cell values.

In our present example we therefore compute chi square by

$$\chi^2 = \sum \frac{[(O - E) - 0.50]^2}{E}$$

$$= \frac{[(65 - 50) - 0.50]^2}{50} + \frac{[(35 - 50) - 0.50]^2}{50}$$

$$= \frac{14.5^2}{50} + \frac{14.5^2}{50} = 8.40.$$

If we enter Table V (located in the appendix) at the row associated with one degree of freedom, we move across the chi-square values to 6.635. This is the critical value for the 0.01 level. In the next column we find 7.879, which is the critical value for the 0.005 level. Our obtained value of 8.40 is therefore significant well beyond the 0.005 level, and it appears to correspond to the probability of 0.0019 obtained in Section 5.2 by normal-curve approximation. The probability that this large a difference between the observed and expected frequencies could have occurred by chance alone is therefore so small that we once again suspect that our coin is biased in favor of heads.

In the following example, the a priori hypothesis, on which the expected frequencies are based, is derived from a genetic model.

Example. There is a genetic model which assumes that black coat color in mice is inherited as a simple dominant trait, and that brown color is inherited as a recessive trait. A cross between pairs of heterozygous black mice produced an F_2 generation consisting of 220 black mice and 60 brown mice.

1. According to our genetic model, a cross between heterozygous black mice would produce offspring as follows:

$$Bb \times Bb$$
$$F_2 \quad BB, Bb, Bb, bb$$

which represents a phenotype ratio of 3 black mice to 1 brown.

2. Now, if the total of 280 offspring occurred in exactly a 3:1 phenotype ratio, as *expected* from our genetic model, we would have $\frac{3}{4}$ (280) and $\frac{1}{4}$ (280), or 210 black and 70 brown mice. The *observed* ratio of 220:60 obviously differs from the expected, but is this difference large enough to be significant? In other words, can we accept this difference as being due to chance alone, or is it large enough to lead us to suspect a causative factor, which might possibly cast doubt on the validity of the original genetic model?

3. Our next step involves setting up a chi-square table as follows:

	Black	Brown	
Observed	220	60	280
Expected	210	70	280

4. Note that the row totals must be equal. Now, using the Yates correction factor, we apply the chi-square formula:

$$\chi^2 = \frac{[(220 - 210) - 0.50]^2}{210} + \frac{[(60 - 70) - 0.50]^2}{70}$$

$$= \frac{9.5^2}{210} + \frac{9.5^2}{70} = 0.42 + 1.28 = 1.70.$$

5. If we look at Table V with one degree of freedom, we find that a chi-square value of 1.70 is too small to indicate significance at the 0.05 level.

6. We have therefore failed to demonstrate that the observed offspring ratio was significantly different from the expected ratio. We therefore conclude that the observed difference was due to chance alone and have no reason to doubt the validity of the genetic model on which the expected frequencies were based.

When using chi square, we are not limited to only two categories. This is illustrated by the following example.

Example. Suppose that two dihybrids are crossed in a situation where complete dominance is assumed. It is further assumed that no linkage or other complicating factors are present. We therefore have the genetic model

$$AaBb \times AaBb$$
$$F_2 \quad 9 \ A\text{--}B\text{--}, \ 3 \ A\text{--}bb, \ 3 \ aaB\text{--}, \ 1 \ aabb$$

which is the classic 9:3:3:1 phenotype ratio. Now, suppose that the actual F_2 generation shows frequencies of 85 A–B–, 28 A–bb, 35 aaB–, and 12 $aabb$. Is this result significantly different from the expected frequencies as dictated by the genetic model?

1. As the first step, we set up the chi-square table as follows:

	A–B–	A–bb	aaB–	$aabb$	
Observed	85	28	35	12	160
Expected	90	30	30	10	160

2. In this case, since we have a chi-square table larger than 2×2, we apply the chi-square formula *without* the Yates correction factor. Thus

$$\chi^2 = \frac{(85-90)^2}{90} + \frac{(28-30)^2}{30} + \frac{(35-30)^2}{30} + \frac{(12-10)^2}{10}$$

$$= \frac{25}{90} + \frac{4}{30} + \frac{25}{30} + \frac{4}{10} = 1.63.$$

3. Since our chi-square table has four columns and two rows, we enter Table V at $(4-1)(2-1)$, or three degrees of freedom. With three degrees of freedom, the critical value at the 0.05 level is 7.815. Since our obtained chi-square value does not equal or exceed this critical value, we have failed to provide statistical evidence that the assumed genetic model is not operating as expected.

The following example illustrates the use of chi square as a tool in genetic detective work when establishing genetic models.

Example. In fowls, the creeper gene (producing deformed legs) is dominant over the gene for normal leg development. A series of crosses between heterozygous creepers (Cc) produce a phenotype ratio of 164 creepers to 76 normal birds.

1. Simple inspection of the obtained phenotype ratio reveals an obvious deviation from the 3:1 ratio expected from a $Cc \times Cc$ cross. Is it different enough to lead us to suspect a causative factor which would render the 3:1 model invalid? Application of the chi-square test shows

	Creeper	Normal	
Observed	164	76	240
Expected	180	60	240

$$\chi^2 = \frac{[(164 - 180) - 0.50]^2}{180} + \frac{[(76 - 60) - 0.50]^2}{60}$$

$$= \frac{15.5^2}{180} + \frac{15.5^2}{60} = 1.33 + 4.00 = 5.33.$$

2. Entering Table V at the level of one degree of freedom, we find our chi-square value of 5.33 to be significant beyond the 0.05 level. We now have statistical support for the suspicion that the observed genetic ratio does not conform to the 3:1 model!

3. Inspection of the 164:76 observed ratio of creepers to normal birds suggests a proximity to a 2:1 model. We therefore test this new idea with chi square by

	Creeper	Normal	
Observed	164	76	240
Expected	160	80	240

$$\chi^2 = \frac{[(164 - 160) - 0.50]^2}{160} + \frac{[(76 - 80) - 0.50]^2}{80}$$

$$= \frac{3.5^2}{160} + \frac{3.5^2}{80} = 0.230.$$

4. Table V shows that a chi-square value of 0.230 is not significant, and we may conclude that the observed 164:76 ratio fits a 2:1 model much better than it conforms to a 3:1 model.

5. On this basis, we now look for a genetic mechanism other than that of simple dominance with no complicating factors. A look at the observed ratio suggests that if 76 homozygous recessive (normal) birds were produced, 3×76, or 228 creepers should have been produced. In other words, from an uncomplicated cross between Cc and Cc we should, theoretically, obtain

CC, Cc, Cc, and cc as the F_2 generation. Now, if we were to assume that CC is lethal in the homozygous condition, this might account for obtaining what appears to be Cc and cc genotypes only, and could therefore explain the missing creepers. As a matter of fact, further investigation would confirm this lethal gene hypothesis!

The foregoing example once again reminds us of the paramount importance attached to the investigator's knowledge of the *biological* aspects of a problem. The statistician can provide us with tools of inference, but the important answers will always be provided by insights derived from familiarity with the principles. It has been said that research does not solve problems; research provides data with which the trained mind can then attack a specific problem.

7.3 CHI SQUARE WITHOUT A PRIORI HYPOTHESIS

In the preceding section we dealt with situations where some kind of expected frequencies were either known or assumed. Now we will need to consider the application of chi-square techniques to cases in which there are no a priori expected frequencies. The following example will illustrate the basic procedure in a simplified fashion by the use of contrived values.

Example. Suppose that we wish to know if an association exists between the factors sex and hair color. We proceed to check the first 50 men and the first 50 women who come down the street, noting in each case whether the individual is blonde or brunette. In order to keep our illustration simple, we will ignore the question of whether the ladies are blonde as a result of hereditary or environmental influences.

1. As the first step, we will organize the data in the form of the following table:

	Hair color		
Sex	Blonde	Brunette	
Men	20	30	50
Women	24	26	50
	44	56	100

This is called a contingency table, and we are, in effect, asking if hair color is *contingent* upon sex.

2. Note that we have no a priori expected frequencies. We must therefore compute the expected frequencies, using the marginal totals as a basis for the calculations. The rationale underlying the computation of expected frequencies is a form of null hypothesis wherein we assume that hair color is *not* contingent upon sex. If this is true, then we should observe no tendency for one sex or the other to contain a preponderance of blondes (or brunettes). Since we have established a table with nice round figures, it may easily be seen that $\frac{1}{2}$ the total sample are men and $\frac{1}{2}$ are women. Therefore, if *no* special relationship exists between sex and hair color, we could *expect* that $\frac{1}{2}$ the blondes in the sample would be men and $\frac{1}{2}$ would be women! The same reasoning then applies to the brunettes. Working with the marginal totals, we therefore have

$$\tfrac{50}{100} \times 44 = 22, \qquad \tfrac{50}{100} \times 44 = 22,$$

$$\tfrac{50}{100} \times 56 = 28, \qquad \tfrac{50}{100} \times 56 = 28.$$

The completed table, with computed expected frequencies, then becomes

	Blonde	Brunette	
Men	20/22	30/28	50
Women	24/22	26/28	50
	44	56	100

3. Now the chi-square value is computed, and since we are dealing with a 2×2 table, we will use the Yates correction factor. Thus

$$\chi^2 = \frac{[(20 - 22) - 0.50]^2}{22} + \frac{[(30 - 28) - 0.50]^2}{28}$$

$$+ \frac{[(24 - 22) - 0.50]^2}{22} + \frac{[(26 - 28) - 0.50]^2}{28}$$

$$= 0.102 + 0.080 + 0.102 + 0.080 = 0.364.$$

4. Entering Table V at one degree of freedom, we find that 0.364 is not significant at the 0.05 level. We have therefore not shown that the observed frequencies and those computed on the basis of a "no relationship" hypothesis are significantly different, and we are led to the conclusion that hair color is not associated with sex. In other words, the two factors appear to be independent.

As before, this form of chi-square test may be used where more than two categories are involved, as in the following example.

Example. A therapeutic drug was tested against a placebo in terms of three subjectively evaluated patient categories: (1) much improved, (2) slightly improved, and (3) not improved. A total of 120 patients were assigned to the drug group and 90 other patients were given the placebo. All were judged to be in approximately the same initial condition. Physician evaluation was then made without knowing which treatment the patient received. The resulting data were organized in the following 2 × 3 table:

	Much improved	Slightly improved	Not improved	
Drug	60	32	28	120
Placebo	28	17	45	90
	88	49	73	210

1. This time, we base our calculations of expected frequencies on the hypothesis that no significant difference in degree of improvement exists between the drug and the placebo groups. Therefore since $\frac{120}{210}$ of the sample consists of the drug group, we should expect $\frac{120}{210} \times 88$ to yield the expected frequency associated with "drug—much improved"; $\frac{90}{210} \times 88$ is then the expected frequency associated with "placebo—improved," and so on. The computed expected frequencies are therefore:

$$
\begin{aligned}
\text{Drug—Much improved:} & \quad \tfrac{120}{210} \times 88 = 50.28 \\
\text{Placebo—Improved:} & \quad \tfrac{90}{210} \times 88 = 37.71 \\
\text{Drug—Slightly improved:} & \quad \tfrac{120}{210} \times 49 = 28.00 \\
\text{Placebo—Slightly improved:} & \quad \tfrac{90}{210} \times 49 = 21.00 \\
\text{Drug—Not improved:} & \quad \tfrac{120}{210} \times 73 = 41.71 \\
\text{Placebo—Not improved:} & \quad \tfrac{90}{210} \times 73 = 31.28
\end{aligned}
$$

We may now organize the data in the form of columns as follows:

$O - E$	$(O - E)^2$	$(O - E)^2/E$
60 − 50.28	94.48	1.88
32 − 28.00	16.00	0.57
28 − 41.71	187.96	4.51
28 − 37.71	94.28	2.50
17 − 21.00	16.00	0.76
45 − 31.28	188.24	6.02
		$\chi^2 = 16.24$

Entering Table V with $(3 - 1)(2 - 1)$, or two degrees of freedom, we find that a chi-square value of 16.24 is significant beyond the 0.005 level. We therefore have statistical evidence that a significant difference in degree of improvement does indeed exist between the placebo group and the drug group.

7.4 CAUTIONS IN THE USE OF CHI SQUARE

It is important to remember that only *frequency* data may be analyzed by chi square. It is not appropriate to apply this technique to data existing in the form of percentages or proportions. In many cases, however, it is possible to convert proportions to frequencies and chi square may then be applied.

We have already discussed the wisdom of using the Yates correction factor in all 2×2 table analyses. Even with large samples, the difference between chi-square values obtained with and without this correction factor may be important enough to affect values of borderline significance.

Finally, it is important to note that each cell in a chi-square table must contain a minimum expected frequency of 5. Tables containing expected frequencies of less than five may produce results of doubtful validity. Discussions of how to handle situations where one or more expected frequencies are less than 5 are found in references listed in the bibliography, but the best approach is to try to avoid such problems by careful planning when designing experiments.

7.5 THE POISSON DISTRIBUTION

Suppose that we survey a certain stretch of highway in order to determine the incidence of dead wildlife found by the roadside and presumably killed by automobiles. Suppose further that as we go along the highway, we glance at any randomly selected spot beside the road. What is the probability of finding a dead animal at that specific location? Assuming that the roadside is not littered with dead animals, it should be obvious that the probability is exceedingly small—so small, in fact, as to approach zero! In other words, the probability (p) of finding an animal in a specific location is very small compared to the probability (q) of *not* finding an animal in the same specific location.

In cases such as this it makes no sense to count "A's" and "non-A's." For example, how many "nonfish" would be located in a pond if we assume that a "nonfish" is simply a space where a fish is not found? Or, how many "nonclicks" are heard from a Geiger counter in a unit of time?

In situations such as these we are dealing with isolated events as they occur in time or space. The number of clicks produced by a counter in a unit of time, the number of tadpoles in a pond, and the number of yeast cells per cubic millimeter in a suspension are examples of situations involving a certain kind of isolated event in a time or space continuum.

Since p is therefore very small and q is very large, application of the binomial distribution is not appropriate, and we therefore need to consider the *Poisson* distribution.

The Poisson distribution is based on a relationship obtained from the calculus. It may be shown that if we have a series,

$$\frac{1}{0!} + \frac{1}{1!} + \frac{1}{2!} + \frac{1}{3!} + \frac{1}{4!} + \cdots,$$

and if the members of this series are summed, we obtain a number approximating 2.718. This number is given the symbol e and is an important value in mathematics, since it is the base of the natural, or Naperian logarithms. It is similar to pi in that it is an apparently endless, nonrepeating decimal.

Now, if e is raised to any power, which we will symbolize by λ (lambda), $e^\lambda = 2.718^\lambda$ and therefore

$$e^\lambda = \frac{\lambda^0}{0!} + \frac{\lambda^1}{1!} + \frac{\lambda^2}{2!} + \frac{\lambda^3}{3!} + \frac{\lambda^4}{4!} \cdots$$

Since $e^\lambda \times e^{-\lambda}$ is equal to 1, and since e^λ is equal to the above series, we may substitute the above series for e^λ and obtain

$$1 = e^{-\lambda} \times e^\lambda = e^{-\lambda}\left(1 + \lambda + \frac{\lambda^2}{2!} + \frac{\lambda^3}{3!} + \frac{\lambda^4}{4!} \cdots\right)$$

$$= e^{-\lambda} + e^{-\lambda}\lambda + \frac{e^{-\lambda}\lambda^2}{2!} + \frac{e^{-\lambda}\lambda^3}{3!} + \frac{e^{-\lambda}\lambda^4}{4!} \cdots$$

which is the Poisson distribution, and which describes the occurrence of an isolated event in a time or space continuum; λ is used to represent the observed mean occurrence of that event.

It should be noted that $e^{-\lambda}$ represents the probability of zero events, $e^{-\lambda}\lambda$ the probability of one event, $e^{-\lambda}\lambda^2/2!$ the probability of two events, and so forth.

7.6 VARIANCE OF THE POISSON DISTRIBUTION

It will be recalled that the mean and variance of the binomial distribution $(p + q)^n$ are, respectively,

$$\bar{X} = np \quad \text{and} \quad S^2 = npq.$$

Now, it may be seen that if p approaches zero, and q therefore approaches 1, the variance of the Poisson distribution is practically $np(1)$, or np, and therefore approximates the mean! The mean and variance values of the Poisson distribution are thus considered to be equal, and this is a useful and simplifying aspect of this distribution.

7.7 DETERMINING THE PROBABILITY OF ISOLATED EVENTS

As indicated previously, the Poisson distribution may be used to determine the probabilities of 0, 1, 2, 3, etc., events occurring in a given continuum. Consider the following example.

Example. A survey was made along a 20-mile stretch of highway to determine the incidence of dead wildlife found on or near the road. The total number of dead animals counted was 15. Assuming the distribution over the 20-mile distance to be relatively uniform, λ is computed as

$$\lambda = \tfrac{15}{20} = 0.75 \text{ animals/mile.}$$

What is the probability of finding no dead animals in any randomly selected mile along this stretch of highway? What is the probability of finding one animal? Two animals?

1. Since $\lambda = 0.75$, we will first need to determine the value of $e^{-\lambda}$. This may be done by consulting Table VI in the appendix, where we find that for $\lambda = 0.75$, $e^{-\lambda} = 0.472$.

2. Since the probability for zero events is given by the Poisson distribution as $e^{-\lambda}$, the probability of finding *no* animals in a one-mile stretch is 0.472.

3. The probability of finding one animal is found by $e^{-\lambda}\lambda$. Therefore

$$(0.472)(0.75) = 0.354.$$

4. Since the probability of finding two animals is given by $e^{-\lambda}\lambda^2/2!$, we have

$$\frac{(0.472)(0.563)}{2 \times 1} = 0.133.$$

5. The probabilities associated with finding three, four, five, or more animals may be easily found by using the corresponding values in the Poisson distribution.

7.8 THE CONFIDENCE INTERVAL OF A COUNT

In Chapter 5 we saw that sample statistics can be used to estimate a population parameter with certain confidence limits. It will be recalled that the general method for such estimation involves the relationship

$$\mu = \bar{X} \pm 1.96(S_{\bar{X}}).$$

Using the Poisson distribution, we may make estimations involving counts, again using a sample statistic as a basic for inference about a population value. Such estimations might be applied to a red blood cell count in terms of cells per cubic millimeter, or to bacterial counts, yeast cell counts, etc. An estimation of the density of a certain type of organism in a pond is another example.

Naturally, estimations of organism density assume a uniform distribution. This underlines the importance of careful sampling as well as careful counting techniques.

The following example will illustrate the procedure of estimation, using the Poisson distribution.

Example. A sample of blood was removed from a patient and diluted 1:200. A total of 250 platelets were counted in a counting chamber having a volume of 0.2 mm³. What is the 95% confidence interval for the patient's true platelet count per cubic millimeter?

1. The sample count yielded a total of 250 platelets/0.2 mm; this was based on a blood sample which had been diluted 1:200. Our sample count is therefore 250, and we will symbolize this by C.

2. Keeping in mind that the variance of the Poisson distribution is equal to the mean, we can find the standard deviation of C by $\sqrt{C}$.

3. Using λ to symbolize the true platelet count, we then have

$$\lambda = C \pm 1.96\sqrt{C} = 250 \pm 1.96\sqrt{250}$$
$$= 250 \pm 1.96(15.81) = 250 \pm 30.99$$
$$= 219.01\text{–}280.99/0.2 \text{ mm}^3.$$

4. Since the blood sample represented a 1:200 dilution, we need to multiply the above figures by 200 and then multiply the product by 5 to obtain the estimated true platelet count per cubic millimeter. Thus we have

$$\lambda = (219.01\text{–}280.99) \times 200 \times 5$$
$$= 219,010\text{–}280,990$$

as the 95% confidence-limit estimate of the true platelet count per cubic millimeter in the patient's circulatory system.

7.9 DETERMINING RANDOMNESS

A useful application of the Poisson distribution involves the determination of randomness. An ecologist may wish to determine whether a particular plant is distributed randomly over a given area, or whether the plant has a tendency toward clumping. A bacteriologist may wish to know if bacterial growth on plates is random, or if unusual growth has occurred on certain plates. A radiation biologist may want to determine whether the counts produced by a Geiger counter are random, since nonrandomness might indicate a defective instrument.

These and other problems may be approached with a method which combines the Poisson distribution with an application of chi square. The following example illustrates the procedure.

Example. An ecologist wants to determine whether goldenrod plants containing one or more galls tend to be randomly distributed or clumped. He reasons that clumping might suggest that the wasps which produce the galls range only short distances from the point of emergence. He therefore selects a field in which goldenrod plants are uniformly distributed and randomly throws 100 quadrats throughout the field. Counting the number of gall-bearing plants in each quadrat results in the following data:

60 quadrats contain zero plants with galls.
24 quadrats contain one plant with galls.
11 quadrats contain two plants with galls.
 3 quadrats contain three plants with galls.
 2 quadrats contain four plants with galls.
_____
100 quadrats, Total

1. Multiplying the quadrat number times the number of plants per quadrat, we have

$$60 \times 0 = 0, \quad 24 \times 1 = 24, \quad 11 \times 2 = 22,$$
$$3 \times 3 = 9, \quad 2 \times 4 = 8,$$

yielding a total of 63 plants counted.

2. Thus we have $\frac{63}{100}$, or 0.63 plants/quadrat. Therefore $\lambda = 0.63$.

3. Table VI indicates that when λ is 0.63, $e^{-\lambda}$ has the value, 0.533.

4. Our next step is to determine the probabilities that any single quadrat thrown at random will contain zero, one, two, three plants, etc. Thus

$$(P) \text{ zero plant} = e^{-\lambda} = 0.533,$$

$$(P) \text{ one plant} = e^{-\lambda}\lambda = (0.533)(0.63) = 0.336,$$

$$(P) \text{ two plants} = \frac{e^{-\lambda}\lambda^2}{2 \times 1} = \frac{(0.533)(0.397)}{2} = 0.106,$$

$$(P) \text{ three plants} = \frac{e^{-\lambda}\lambda^3}{3 \times 2 \times 1} = \frac{(0.533)(0.250)}{6} = 0.022,$$

$$(P) \text{ four plants} = \frac{e^{-\lambda}\lambda^4}{4 \times 3 \times 2 \times 1} = \frac{(0.533)(0.158)}{24} = 0.003.$$

5. Now we can determine the numbers of quadrats that would be *expected* to contain zero, one, two, three, or four plants with galls *if* random conditions were obtained. This is done simply by multiplying the appropriate probability values by 100, or the total number of quadrats. Thus

$$100 \times 0.533 = 53.3 \text{ quadrats,}$$
$$100 \times 0.336 = 33.6 \text{ quadrats,}$$
$$100 \times 0.106 = 10.6 \text{ quadrats,}$$
$$100 \times 0.022 = 2.2 \text{ quadrats,}$$
$$100 \times 0.003 = 0.3 \text{ quadrats.}$$

6. Now we use chi square to determine the probability that the difference between the observed quadrat frequencies and the expected quadrat frequencies occurred by chance alone. Thus

Plants	0	1	2	3	4
Observed	60	24	11	3	2
Expected	53.3	33.6	10.6	2.2	0.3

$$\chi^2 = \frac{(60 - 53.3)^2}{53.3} + \frac{(24 - 33.6)^2}{33.6} + \frac{(11 - 10.6)^2}{10.6}$$

$$+ \frac{(3 - 2.2)^2}{2.2} + \frac{(2 - 0.3)^2}{0.3} = 12.69.$$

7. We enter the chi-square table with *three* degrees of freedom, since one degree of freedom is considered lost because of the estimation of λ. Since the critical value of chi square at the 0.05 level is 7.81, we conclude that the differences between expected and observed quadrat frequencies did *not* occur by chance alone; this therefore suggests that the gall-bearing goldenrod plants have a tendency to be clumped rather than distributed randomly throughout the area.

Further applications of this technique to ecological work will be found in references listed in the bibliography. It is interesting to note, for example, that judicious variation of quadrat size together with the application of chi square will even provide an estimate of clump size.

PROBLEMS

7.1 When pink 4 o'clocks are crossed, it is expected that the F_2 frequencies will be on the order of 1 red : 2 pink : 1 white. An investigator obtains an actual ratio of 30 red : 48 pink : 27 white. Are these results consistent with the genetic model? (See Section 7.2.)

7.2 The F_2 generation resulting from crosses between heterozygous red owls contained 16 red and 8 grey owls. Are these results consistent with the genetic theory that red is dominant over grey? (See Section 7.2.)

7.3 A vaccine was developed which was supposed to protect mice against a particularly virulent bacterium. A group of 55 mice was given the vaccine and then challenged with a heavy dose of the bacterium. Another group of 55 mice, which had not been vaccinated, was challenged with the same dose. Twenty-nine mice in the vaccine group contracted the disease, and thirty-five in the control group became ill. Test these data in terms of the effectiveness of the vaccine (see Section 7.3).

7.4 A number of samples were taken from a lake in order to determine whether two species of *Oligochaetes* are associated, that is, tend to occur together. The results of an examination of 135 samples are organized in the table below. Test the hypothesis that species A and B are not associated (see Section 7.3).

		Species B		
		Present	Absent	
Species A	Present	40	35	75
	Absent	28	32	60
		68	67	135

7.5 An experiment was performed to determine the degree to which the isopod *P. laevis* can acclimate to different temperatures. Of 50 specimens held at 10°C,

32 died. Meanwhile, of 50 specimens held at 20°C, 20 died. Analyze the data for the difference in their abilities to acclimate to the two temperatures (see Section 7.3).

7.6 A group of 500 Germans living in Germany was analyzed with respect to blood types. Another group of 476 persons of German origin, but living in Hungary, was also analyzed for blood types. Analyze the following data for possible difference between the two groups in terms of blood-type frequencies (see Section 7.3):

	AB	A	O	B	Totals
Group I (Germany)	25	215	200	60	500
Group II (Hungary)	15	207	194	60	476

7.7 An investigator set up an experiment involving the effect of a light gradient on the gastropod *Littorina*. The gradient was established with three zones of light intensity, and of a sample of 33 gastropods, 15 were noted in zone 1, 12 in zone 2, and 6 in zone 3. Test the hypothesis that the light gradient had no effect on the distribution of the organism (see Section 7.2).

7.8 Analyze the following contingency table to determine whether color in a certain variety of mice depends on, or is associated with sex (see Section 7.3).

	Male	Female
Black	26	15
Brown	17	24
White	15	18

7.9 A drug believed to have teratogenic properties was given to a group of 65 pregnant female rats, and it was later noted that 23 females of this group produced litters containing at least one malformed offspring. From a group of 85 females used as a control, 12 litters contained at least one malformed offspring. On the basis of these data, what conclusion might be drawn relative to the teratogenic properties of the drug? (See Section 7.3.)

7.10 An antimalarial drug was given to 1500 men, and 15 individuals showed an anaphylactic reaction. Of 1400 women given the same drug, 40 individuals had a similar reaction. Analyze these data to determine whether an association exists between sex and an allergic reaction to the drug (see Section 7.3).

7.11 An urn contains nine black marbles and one white marble. Ten marbles are drawn from the urn, one by one, with replacement. By using the binomial distribution, find the probability that exactly two of the ten marbles will be white (see Section 3.6).

7.12 Solve Problem 7.11 by using the Poisson distribution. Is there a discrepancy between the results obtained by the binomial and the Poisson distribution? (See Section 17.) [*Hint:* $\lambda = np$.]

7.13 In testing a new antibiotic, it was found that 5 out of 5000 patients suffered an allergic reaction. On the basis of these data, compute the probability that out of 1000 patients chosen at random,

    a) exactly one would suffer a reaction;

    b) exactly three would suffer a reaction;

    c) more than three would suffer a reaction.

(See Section 7.7.) [*Hint:* $\lambda = np$.]

7.14 In order to determine the mode of distribution of a certain species of cricket, a total of 200 quadrats were randomly thrown on a field. Each quadrat was examined for crickets, and the following data were obtained in terms of the cricket count:

Quadrats	Number of crickets/quadrat
98	0
52	1
28	2
22	3

Analyze these data to determine whether the crickets are randomly dispersed throughout the area (see Section 7.9).

7.15 A Geiger counter yields a total of 10,000 counts during a one-minute period when exposed to a radioactive source. Compute the 95% confidence interval in terms of counts per minute (see Section 7.8).

7.16 An investigator counted 256 yeast cells in a one milliliter sample taken from a culture. Compute the 95% confidence interval for the mean count per milliliter in the culture (see Section 7.8).

7.17 Fifty-five samples were randomly collected from a pond, using a plankton net, in order to determine the distribution of mayfly larvae. On the basis of the following data, are the larvae randomly distributed over the pond area or are they clumped? (See Section 7.9.)

Number of samples	Larvae per sample
30	0
10	1
8	2
5	3
2	4

8
MULTIPLE GROUP DESIGNS—
ANALYSIS OF VARIANCE

8.1 ANALYSIS OF VARIANCE

In Chapter 6 we considered two-group comparisons, using the Student's t distributions as a basis for data analysis. The use of the t-test is perfectly legitimate when comparing two groups, but there are many situations in biological experimentation which call for comparisons among three or more groups.

Comparing three or more groups with the t-test would entail certain difficulties. To begin with, in comparing groups A, B, C, and D, we would need to test for differences between pairs AB, AC, AD, BC, BD, and CD, requiring 6 separate t-tests in all. Not only would this be tedious, but even more important, the probability of error would increase with the number of tests, bringing the total error probability to a prohibitive level!

Fortunately, this problem is overcome by using a statistical tool called *analysis of variance*, which for this and other reasons is one of the most useful devices available for biological work. As we proceed, it will become clear that analysis of variance allows the use of a variety of experimental designs which provide a maximum of information.

Recalling our discussion of the need for replications, we know that the responses of experimental subjects to specific treatments depend on the effectiveness of the treatment *and* the natural variation among the subjects. Thus if two entirely homogeneous groups were compared, any differences between groups could be assumed to be due to treatment differences provided we could discount measurement errors. The nature of living systems, however, is such that observed differences between groups inevitably consist of

(1) a component due to any differential treatment effects that exist, and (2) a component resulting from natural variation.

This natural variability among experimental units is an important source of *error*. In this case, "error" is not synonymous with "mistake," since variability among biological units is natural and expected. The total error involved with an experiment may also, of course, contain measurement errors, but these can at least be minimized and controlled by careful procedures.

If the total variability between groups consists of the components contributed by treatment effects and by natural variation (error), it is apparent that we need to somehow separate, assess, and compare these two components. If in so doing we find that natural variability within the groups is as great or greater than the variability between the groups, we would have to conclude that the treatment effects are nonsignificant. On the other hand, if between-group variability is significantly greater than the random variability within groups, we might suspect that a major part of the variability between groups was produced by the effects of differential treatment.

A so-called linear model of this situation would be

$$X = \bar{\bar{X}} + T + e,$$

where any individual measurement (X) consists of (1) the grand mean of all measurements ($\bar{\bar{X}}$), (2) the effect due to the treatment (T), and (3) the effect due to error (e). It is assumed that the error is randomly distributed, and to increase the probability that this is so, it is essential to carry on thorough randomization procedures when assigning experimental units to treatment groups. Recalling an example from Chapter 4, if we assign more active mice to one group and the sluggish mice to the other, the error due to natural variability would not be random, but would be *systematic*. This, of course, would definitely bias the results.

Measurement errors are also assumed to be random, and one hopes that such errors will tend to cancel out. Naturally, a defective measuring device could produce systematic measurement errors, and the validity of the results would be doubtful.

8.2 PARTITIONING THE TOTAL VARIABILITY

Table 8.1 contains three groups of measurements—A, B, and C—together with the data derived from these measurements. Note that k is used to symbolize the number of measurements in a specific group, N represents the total

Table 8.1

A	B	C	
2	9	10	
3	6	6	
1	8	9	$\overline{\overline{X}} = 6$
5	7	7	$N = 15$
4	5	8	$\sum X^2 = 640$
$k_A = 5$	$k_B = 5$	$k_C = 5$	$\sum X = 90$
$\overline{X}_A = 3$	$\overline{X}_B = 7$	$\overline{X}_C = 8$	$\sum X_A = 15$
			$\sum X_B = 35$
			$\sum X_C = 40$

number of all three groups combined, and $\overline{\overline{X}}$ denotes the grand mean, or mean of all X's.

In order to partition the total variability of the data in Table 8.1, we need to first compute the total sum of squares. We will recall that the "sum of squares" refers to the sum of squared deviations of all members of a distribution from the mean of that distribution. In previous chapters this concept was symbolized by $\sum (X - \overline{X})^2$, or $\sum x^2$. In this chapter we will use the more convenient symbol, S.S.

Referring to the data in Table 8.1, we will compute the total S.S. as the sum of squared deviations of all measurements (X) from the grand mean $(\overline{\overline{X}})$. Thus

$$\begin{aligned} \text{S.S.}_{\text{total}} &= \sum (\overline{\overline{X}} - X)^2 \\ &= (2 - 6)^2 + (3 - 6)^2 + (1 - 6)^2 + (5 - 6)^2 + \cdots + (8 - 6)^2 \\ &= 100. \end{aligned}$$

Next, we compute the S.S. between groups. The term "between groups" is traditionally used. This process involves summing the squared deviations between each group mean and the grand mean, making sure that we multiply each squared deviation by the number (k) in each group. Thus

$$\begin{aligned} \text{S.S.}_{\text{between}} &= k_A(\overline{\overline{X}} - \overline{X}_A)^2 + k_B(\overline{\overline{X}} - \overline{X}_B)^2 + k_C(\overline{\overline{X}} - \overline{X}_C)^2 \\ &= 5(6 - 3)^2 + 5(6 - 7)^2 + 5(6 - 8)^2 \\ &= 45 + 5 + 20 = 70. \end{aligned}$$

Finally, we compute the within-group (error) S.S., by first summing the squared deviations between each measurement in a specific group and the mean for that group, then summing the within squares of all three groups.

Thus

A	$(\bar{X}_A - X)^2$	B	$(\bar{X}_B - X)^2$	C	$(\bar{X}_C - X)^2$
2	1	9	4	10	4
3	0	6	1	6	4
1	4	8	1	9	1
5	4	7	0	7	1
4	1	5	4	8	0
	10		10		10

$$\text{S.S.}_{\text{within}} = 10 + 10 + 10 = 30.$$

We have now partitioned the total variability of the data in Table 8.1 into a "between-group" component and a "within-group," or error component. Our next step is to compute the two variances involved and compare them.

First we arrange the data as shown in Table 8.2.

Table 8.2

Source	Degrees of freedom	Sum of squares	Mean square
Between	2	70	35.00
Within (error)	12	30	2.50
Total	14	100	

The total for the degrees of freedom is found as usual by $N - 1$. Since there is a total of 15 variates, the total for the degrees of freedom is 14. The number of between-group degrees of freedom is found by subtracting 1 from the total number of groups; since there are 3 groups, the number of between-group degrees of freedom is $3 - 1$, or 2. Therefore the within-group degrees of freedom make up the difference between the total degrees of freedom and the between-group degrees of freedom. The "within" degrees of freedom could also be estimated from the fact that we computed three means in arriving at the "within" sum of squares; therefore we have $15 - 3$, or 12 degrees of freedom associated with the within-group sum of squares.

By dividing the sum of squares found for the between-group component by the degrees of freedom associated with that component, we obtain the "mean square," which is another term for variance. The same operation applied to the within-group sum of squares yields the within-group mean square, or the within-group variance.

Thus we have

$$M.S._{between} = \tfrac{70}{2} = 35.00$$

and

$$M.S._{within} = \tfrac{30}{12} = 2.50.$$

The final step in the analysis involves a comparison of the between-group variance with the within-group variance in order to determine whether the between-group variance is significantly larger. In other words, we want to know if the treatment effects are significant, or if differences between groups can be explained simply on the basis of random variation.

To make this comparison, we use a distribution of variance ratios known as the F-distribution. Appropriate use of Table VII in the appendix will help determine whether the mean square in the numerator of a variance ratio is significantly greater than the mean square in the denominator. Turning to Table VII, we see that the F-table is similar to the mileage chart on a road map. Note that the columns are headed by the degrees of freedom associated with the numerator, and rows are labeled with the degrees of freedom associated with the denominator. In our case in point, we have

$$F_{2,12} = \frac{M.S._{between}}{M.S._{within}}$$

$$= \frac{35.00}{2.50} = 14.00.$$

In performing the F-test for simple cases of analysis of variance, the "within" or error mean square will always be placed in the denominator. Recalling the fact that the between-groups mean square contains both the treatment variance component *and* the error component, in performing the F-test we are essentially setting up a ratio:

$$F = \frac{\sigma_e^2 + \sigma_T^2}{\sigma_e^2}.$$

Having established that $F_{2,12}$ is 14.00, we refer to Table VII. Since two degrees of freedom are associated with the numerator and 12 degrees of freedom with the denominator, we go down the second column to the twelfth row. Where the column and row intersect, we locate 3.88 as the critical F-value for the 0.05 level and 6.93 as the critical value for the 0.01 level. Since the obtained F-value is 14.00, it is clearly significant well beyond the 0.01 level. We may therefore conclude that the treatment effect produced statistically significant differences among the groups.

From the foregoing, it should be obvious that F-values of 1 or less are automatically nonsignificant, since the numerator in the variance ratio would be smaller than the denominator. Any F-value larger than one, however, should be checked by using Table VII.

8.3 MACHINE COMPUTATIONS

In the preceding section, the computation of the appropriate S.S. was demonstrated by using the basic arithmetic associated with the theory. As is often the case, the definition formulas are difficult and tedious to use in practice, especially where large amounts of data are involved. Recalling the machine formula for computing variance, it may be seen that the total sum of squares may be computed by applying part of that formula. Thus

$$S.S._{total} = \sum X^2 - \frac{(\sum X)^2}{N},$$

where X refers to each measurement and N refers to the total number of measurements. Referring back to Table 8.1, we may compute the total S.S. by

$$S.S._{total} = 640 - \frac{(90)^2}{15} = 640 - 540 = 100.$$

The S.S. for between groups is then computed as

$$S.S._{between} = \frac{(\sum X_A)^2}{k_A} + \frac{(\sum X_B)^2}{k_B} + \frac{(\sum X_C)^2}{k_C} - \frac{(\sum X)^2}{N},$$

where the quantity $(\sum X)^2/N$ is called the correction factor, and has already been found when the total S.S. was computed. Therefore, from Table 8.1,

$$S.S._{between} = \frac{(15)^2}{5} + \frac{(35)^2}{5} + \frac{(40)^2}{5} - 540$$

$$= 610 - 540 = 70.$$

Now, since the total sum of squares is equal to the $S.S._{between}$ plus the $S.S._{within}$, we can use a shortcut method for computing the within-group sum of squares. Thus

$$S.S._{within} = S.S._{total} - S.S._{between}$$
$$= 100 - 70 = 30.$$

8.4 ASSUMPTIONS UNDERLYING THE ANALYSIS OF VARIANCE

There are certain basic assumptions that must be considered if the analysis of variance is to be valid.

First, the analysis of variance is a so-called parametric test, and its use therefore assumes that the variable in question is normally distributed in the population from which the samples are drawn. A moderate deviation from complete normality will not have significant effects on the results, but serious deviations may throw doubt on the reliability of the F-value, particularly when there is a borderline significance.

Second, it is assumed that treatment effects are constant and additive. This is a somewhat difficult concept to explain and may be better understood from the following illustration.

Suppose that we have a distribution such as

$$
\begin{array}{ll}
2 & \\
3 & \\
1 & \\
5 & \bar{X} = 3 \\
4 & \sum (X - \bar{X})^2 = 10
\end{array}
$$

The mean of this distribution is 3. Now, if we sum the squared deviations of all members of the distribution from the mean, we obtain an S.S. of 10. This, divided by $N = 5$, yields a variance of 2.

Now, let's *add* a constant, say 3, to each member of the original distribution. This results in a new distribution,

$$
\begin{array}{ll}
2 + 3 = 5 & \\
3 + 3 = 6 & \\
1 + 3 = 4 & \\
5 + 3 = 8 & \bar{X} = 6 \\
4 + 3 = 7 & \sum (X - \bar{X})^2 = 10
\end{array}
$$

which has a mean of 6. Again, we determine the S.S. and obtain 10, which divided by $N = 5$ yields a variance of 2. Thus it may be seen that adding a constant to a distribution produces a new distribution with a greater mean but with the *same* variance.

If we now *multiply* each member of the original distribution by 3 we will obtain a new distribution,

$$
\begin{array}{ll}
2 \times 3 = 6 & \\
3 \times 3 = 9 & \\
1 \times 3 = 3 & \\
5 \times 3 = 15 & \bar{X} = 9 \\
4 \times 3 = 12 & \sum (X - \bar{X})^2 = 90
\end{array}
$$

which has a mean of 9. This time, when we compute the S.S., we obtain a total of 90. Dividing this by 5, we obtain a variance of 18. The variance of the new distribution is considerably different from the variance of the original distribution, and the mechanics of analysis of variance cannot be legitimately applied. Therefore, if the treatment effects are multiplicative rather than additive, it is not proper to apply the analysis of variance, at least to the raw data.

It could also happen that treatment effects are additive but not constant, as in the following example:

$$2 + 3 = 5$$
$$3 - 1 = 2$$
$$1 + 2 = 3$$
$$5 - 3 = 2 \quad \bar{X} = 4$$
$$4 + 4 = 8 \quad \sum (X - \bar{X})^2 = 26$$

The mean of the new distribution in this case is 4, and after computing the sum of squares, we obtain 5.20 as the variance. Again, this deviates from the variance of 3 which was associated with the original distribution.

Now, in actual experimental situations we would be surprised if treatment effects were *exactly* constant, and some differences among group variances are therefore expected. This is not of concern as long as group variances are relatively homogeneous. The degree to which group variances differ may be easily determined provided only two groups are involved. This is accomplished by setting up a variance ratio, with the larger variance in the numerator, and checking the significance of the resulting quotient in the F-table. If it is significant, caution should be exercised in interpreting the F-values obtained from the analysis, especially when such F-values have borderline significance.

When three or more groups are involved, Bartlett's test for homogeneity of variance may be used. This test may be found among the references appearing in the bibliography.

8.5 THE LOGARITHMIC TRANSFORMATION

When multiplicative, rather than additive treatment effects are present, it is sometimes possible to save the situation by using a logarithmic transformation.

Given the following two groups,

A	B	A	B
40	80	15	30
20	40	25	50
30	60		

it may be seen that the treatment effect is multiplicative, since each variate in A is multiplied by a factor of 2. Now, since the $\log xy$ is equivalent to $\log x + \log y$, converting the raw data to equivalent logarithms will change multiplicative effects to additive effects, as follows:

A	$(X - \bar{X}_A)$	$(X - \bar{X}_A)^2$	B	$(X - \bar{X}_B)$	$(X - \bar{X}_B)^2$
1.602	0.212	0.044944	1.903	0.212	0.044944
1.301	0.089	0.007921	1.602	0.089	0.007921
1.477	0.087	0.007569	1.778	0.087	0.007569
1.176	0.214	0.045796	1.477	0.214	0.045796
1.398	0.008	0.000064	1.699	0.008	0.000064
6.954		0.106294	8.459		0.106294
$\bar{X}_A = 1.390$			$\bar{X}_B = 1.691$		

Computing the variance on the basis of the sums of squares obtained above, we have

$$\sigma_A^2 = \frac{\sum (X - \bar{X}_A)^2}{5} = \frac{0.106294}{5} = 0.021258$$

and

$$\sigma_B^2 = \frac{\sum (X - \bar{X}_B)^2}{5} = \frac{0.106294}{5} = 0.021258.$$

Thus the variances have been made equal by the log transformation, and we may proceed with the analysis of variance, using the transformed data. Since in our example we worked with contrived data, we obtained textbook results, but with actual experimental data we would be satisfied if we obtained variances showing an acceptable degree of homogeneity.

8.6 THE ARCSIN TRANSFORMATION

Biological data may occasionally take the form of percentages or proportions. Such data may not be appropriately treated with analysis of variance until they are changed to a different form. This may be done by a mathematical device known as the *arcsin or arc sine transformation*.

For example, a percentage value such as 74% is first converted to the decimal form, 0.74. We then find the square root of that decimal, or

$$\sqrt{0.74} = 0.86.$$

We now look in a table of natural sines for an angle, the sine of which is 0.86. This turns out to be slightly more than 59° 20″. Expressing 20″ as a decimal, we arrive at 59.34° as the arcsin transformation of 74%.

While this procedure is not difficult, it could be quite tedious when dealing with large quantities of data. Happily, the mathematicians have once more come to our rescue by providing Table VIII, which may be used to find the transformed values directly.

The following example will illustrate the arcsin transformation:

Example. An experiment was performed to determine significant differences, if any, among the effects of three inhibitors, A, B, and C, on cellular uptake of epinephrine labeled with C^{14}. The data below are expressed in percent uptake per milligram dry weight of cells. Each treatment was replicated 8 times.

A		B		C	
%	Degrees	%	Degrees	%	Degrees
65	53.73	68	55.55	70	56.79
72	58.05	67	54.94	74	59.34
59	50.18	70	56.79	60	50.77
69	56.17	66	54.33	74	59.34
70	56.79	63	52.53	71	57.42
68	55.55	57	49.02	69	56.17
70	56.79	71	57.42	66	54.33
73	58.69	68	55.55	71	57.42

Each of the percent values in the original data was first converted to the decimal form, and the decimal was then transformed to degrees by the use of Table VIII. Having transformed the data, analysis of variance may now be performed in the usual manner.

8.7 SINGLE CLASSIFICATION ANALYSIS OF VARIANCE

Single classification analysis of variance is a relatively simple operation involving a comparison of two or more groups. The following example will serve to illustrate the procedure.

Example. An ornithologist divides a certain bird species into three populations, A, B, and C. The division is based on geographic barriers, and the investigator wants to know if isolation mechanisms have caused significant morphological differences. From population A, he collects 10 specimens, from population B, he collects 12 specimens, and from population C, he obtains 15 specimens. The variable, wing length, is measured to the nearest millimeter, and the following data are collected:

A	B	C
69	71	71
72	75	74
71	72	72
72	72	70
72	74	75
73	76	74
71	73	73
68	70	68
69	75	73
75	76	75
	73	74
	74	74
		72
		70
		74

We will now proceed to analyze these data by an orderly, step-by-step procedure.

1. First, we note that N, the total number of specimens, is 37. The number of specimens from each of the three populations is represented by

$$k_A = 10, \qquad k_B = 12, \qquad k_C = 15.$$

2. We now compute the various pieces of working data. This results in

$$\sum X_A^2 = 50{,}734 \qquad \sum X^2 = 194{,}576$$
$$\sum X_A = 712 \qquad \sum X = 2682$$
$$\sum X_B^2 = 64{,}721 \qquad \bar{X}_A = 71.20$$
$$\sum X_B = 881 \qquad \bar{X}_B = 73.41$$
$$\sum X_C^2 = 79{,}121 \qquad \bar{X}_C = 72.60$$
$$\sum X_C = 1089$$

3. Before proceeding further, we compute the variances of the individual groups. For group A, we have

$$S_A^2 = \frac{\sum X_A^2 - (\sum X_A)^2/k_A}{k_A}$$

$$= \frac{50,374 - 50,694.40}{10} = 3.96.$$

Applying the same procedure to groups B and C, we obtain

$$S_B^2 = 3.41, \qquad S_C^2 = 3.97.$$

Comparing the variances of the three groups, it may be seen without further testing that these data conform nicely to the assumption concerning homogeneity of variances.

4. We now compute the total sum of squares by

$$\text{S.S.}_{\text{total}} = \sum X^2 - \frac{(\sum X)^2}{N} = 194,576 - \frac{(2682)^2}{37}$$

$$= 194,576 - 194,408.75 = 167.25.$$

5. Next, we compute the between-groups sum of squares by

$$\text{S.S.}_{\text{between}} = \frac{(\sum X_A)^2}{k_A} + \frac{(\sum X_B)^2}{k_B} + \frac{(\sum X_C)^2}{k_C} - \frac{(\sum X)^2}{N}$$

$$= \frac{(712)^2}{10} + \frac{(881)^2}{12} + \frac{(1089)^2}{15} - 194,408.75$$

$$= 194,435.88 - 194,408.75 = 27.13.$$

6. Finally, we compute the within-group, or error sum of squares by

$$\text{S.S.}_{\text{within}} = \text{S.S.}_{\text{total}} - \text{S.S.}_{\text{between}}$$
$$= 167.25 - 27.13 = 140.12.$$

7. The data may now be set up in the analysis of variance table below:

Source	D.F.	S.S.	M.S.
Between groups	2	27.13	13.56
Within groups	34	140.12	4.12
Total	36	167.25	

Note that the degrees of freedom for between groups are one less than the number of groups compared. The within-groups degrees of freedom must then be 34 in order to add to a total of 36. The total degrees of freedom are taken as $N - 1$, or $37 - 1$.

8. We now perform an F-test to determine whether differences in wing length among groups A, B, and C are significant. This is done as follows:

$$F_{2,34} = \frac{\text{M.S.}_{\text{between}}}{\text{M.S.}_{\text{within}}}$$

$$= \frac{13.56}{4.12} = 3.29.$$

Consulting Table VII, we find that with 2 and 34 degrees of freedom, an F-value of 3.29 is significant at the 0.05 level. It should also be noted that it is *not* significant at the 0.01 level.

9. We may now conclude that a significant difference in wing length exists among populations A, B, and C. Such a conclusion should obviously be drawn cautiously, since our F-value has borderline significance, and there is always doubt that specimens such as these are drawn in a truly random manner, despite the good intentions of the collector.

8.8 RANDOMIZED BLOCK DESIGN

An advantage of the analysis of variance as a statistical technique lies in the fact that it permits a variety of experimental designs which provide maximum efficiency as well as maximum information.

One such design involves the use of randomized blocks, and provides an excellent approach to reducing the variability error discussed in Section 8.1. It will be recalled that the term "error" applies primarily to the uncontrolled variation which exists among experimental subjects, and which thereby "contaminates" the treatment effects. Naturally, the more this error can be reduced, the more precise the experimental outcomes will be.

The technique of randomized blocks originated with agricultural research, since it provided an excellent way to reduce error resulting from heterogeneity of soil. If, for example, we wish to test for differences in yield among four varieties of corn, we could establish blocks in the experimental field and randomly plant plots of the four varieties in each block. Figure 8.1 shows such an arrangement. Here we are assuming that the soil within each block will have maximum homogeneity, but the soil between blocks, particularly at widely different parts of the field, will tend to show the greatest differences. In other words, we arrange the design so as to have minimum variation within blocks and maximum variation between blocks. This allows a reduction in total error due to random variation by the simple expedient of removing that part of the error due to variation between blocks. Thus it

C	A	D	B	A	C	B	D
B	D	A	C	C	B	D	A
A	B	C	D	C	D	B	A
B	D	C	A	A	C	D	B
A	B	D	C	C	B	D	A
A	D	B	C	C	A	D	B

Fig. 8.1 Randomized block design; twelve blocks, four varieties randomly planted in each block.

may be seen that proper blocking procedure involves making the experimental units within each block as *alike* as possible, leaving the greatest amount of variation *between* the blocks.

The following example demonstrates how this design can be applied to a laboratory situation:

Example. An investigator tested the effects of drugs A and B on the lymphocyte count in mice by comparing A, B, and a placebo, P. In designing the experiment, he assumed that mice from the same litter would be more homogeneous in their responses than would mice from different litters. He arranged the experiment in the form of randomized blocks, with three littermates forming each block. There was a total of seven blocks, thus there were seven replications per treatment. In each block the littermates were assigned randomly to the three treatments, resulting in the following arrangement, where lymphocyte counts are expressed in thousands per cubic millimeter of blood.

Treatments	Blocks (litters)							Treatment totals
	1	2	3	4	5	6	7	
P	5.4	4.0	7.0	5.8	3.5	7.6	5.5	38.8
A	6.0	4.8	6.9	6.4	5.5	9.0	6.8	45.4
B	5.1	3.9	6.5	5.6	3.9	7.0	5.4	37.4
Block totals	16.5	12.7	20.4	17.8	12.9	23.6	17.7	121.6

1. Computing the means, we obtain

$$\bar{X}_P = 5.54, \qquad \bar{X}_A = 6.48, \qquad \bar{X}_B = 5.34.$$

2. The total sum of squares is computed as usual by

$$S.S._{total} = \sum X^2 - \frac{(\sum X)^2}{N}$$

$$= (5.4)^2 + (6.0)^2 + (5.1)^2 + \cdots + (6.8)^2 + (5.4)^2 - \frac{(121.6)^2}{N}$$

$$= 734.40 - 704.12 = 37.34.$$

3. The sum of squares for blocks is computed by using the block totals and the number of measurements per block as follows:

$$S.S._{blocks} = \frac{(\sum X_1)^2}{b_1} + \frac{(\sum X_2)^2}{b_2} + \cdots + \frac{(\sum X_7)^2}{b_7} - \frac{(\sum X)^2}{N}$$

$$= \frac{(16.5)^2}{3} + \frac{(12.7)^2}{3} + \cdots + \frac{(17.7)^2}{3} - 704.12$$

$$= 734.40 - 704.12 = 30.28.$$

4. The sum of squares for treatments is computed by using the treatment totals and the number of replications per treatment. Thus

$$S.S._{treatment} = \frac{(\sum X_A)^2}{k_A} + \frac{(\sum X_B)^2}{k_B} + \frac{(\sum X_C)^2}{k_C} - \frac{(\sum X)^2}{N}$$

$$= \frac{(38.8)^2}{7} + \frac{(45.4)^2}{7} + \frac{(37.4)^2}{7} - 704.12$$

$$= 709.33 - 704.12 = 5.21.$$

5. The sum of squares for error can now be computed by removing the sum of squares for treatment *and* the sum of squares for blocks from the total sum of squares. Thus

$$S.S._{error} = S.S._{total} - (S.S._{blocks} + S.S._{treatment})$$
$$= 37.24 - (30.28 + 5.21) = 1.75.$$

6. We may now establish an analysis of variance table as follows:

Source	D.F.	S.S.	M.S.
Blocks	6	30.28	
Treatment	2	5.21	2.60
Error	12	1.75	0.14
Total	20	37.24	

Note that the degrees of freedom for blocks are found by the number of blocks minus one. For treatment the degrees of freedom are found by the number of treatments minus one, and the error degrees of freedom represent the difference between the total (20) and the sum of the blocks plus treatment degrees of freedom (8).

7. The F-test for treatment differences is now performed as

$$F_{2,12} = \frac{2.60}{0.14} = 18.57.$$

Consulting Table VII, we find that for 2 and 12 degrees of freedom, the critical value at the 0.05 level is 3.88. Our F-value is therefore significant at the 0.05 level. Since it also exceeds the value of 6.93 established at the 0.01 level, we should report significance beyond the 0.01 level.

It is important to remember that the theory of blocking assumes that experimental units within blocks are as homogeneous as possible—at least as far as any specific response variable is concerned. This obviously calls for careful planning on the part of the experimenter, and the assumption of homogeneity within blocks should have a logical basis.

The principle of blocking may be applied to a large variety of experimental problems, and is one of the most useful basic designs in biological work. A single animal may constitute a block, provided two or more treatments can be applied to it without residual effects resulting from any one treatment. This will be recognized as an extension of the matched-pair design discussed in Section 6.2.

8.9 FACTORIAL DESIGNS

The varieties of factorial designs that may be encountered in biological experimentation are quite extensive, and much of this topic is beyond the scope of this book. In this section, we will examine a simple two-factor design which is very useful in many experimental situations.

Essentially, a factorial design permits the separation and evaluation of the effects of each of two (or more) factors operating in a single experimental setting. In addition, this design permits the detection of *interaction* effects between two (or more) factors. By interaction, we mean that factor A may have different effects when operating in the presence of factor B than when factor B is not present. To use a somewhat rough analogy, a young man may enjoy going to the movies, and he may enjoy going out with girls. Now, if he takes a girl to a movie, we might assume that his enjoyment of the entire evening is intensified due to the interaction between the two factors!

Or, suppose that we test the effects of pH on some variable while the temperature is held constant. Obviously, it will be more enlightening if we can determine whether the effects of pH are different at different temperatures!

Example. An experimenter wished to determine the effect of a drug versus a placebo relative to blood pressure in human subjects. He was also interested in the effect that would be produced by a possible interaction with the factor, sex. He therefore set up a two-factor factorial experiment with 5 replications per cell, as in Table 8.3.

Table 8.3

Sex Factor	Drug factor		
	Placebo	Drug	
Male	153 140 133 $\sum X_{mp} = 712$ 123 163	132 115 142 $\sum X_{md} = 668$ 125 154	$\sum X_m = 1380$
Female	164 150 134 $\sum X_{fp} = 766$ 144 174	142 155 167 $\sum X_{fd} = 726$ 133 129	$\sum X_f = 1492$

$$\sum X_p = 1478 \qquad \sum X_d = 1394$$
$$\sum X^2 = 417,322$$
$$\sum X = 2872$$

1. Our first step is to find the totals shown above. These include (a) cell totals, (b) total for males, (c) total for females, (d) totals for drug and placebo, and (e) the usual $\sum X^2$ and $\sum X$ which are found by utilizing all measurements found in the data. The symbols shown have appropriate subscripts which identify the particular factor level or combinations of levels represented.

2. We begin the analysis by computing the total sum of squares by

$$\text{S.S.}_{\text{total}} = \sum X^2 - \frac{(\sum X)^2}{N} = 417,322 - \frac{2872^2}{20}$$
$$= 417,322.00 - 412,419.20 = 4902.80.$$

3. Next, we compute the sum of squares for the drug factor by utilizing the total for the placebo and the total for the drug. Thus

$$S.S._{drug} = \frac{(\sum X_p)^2}{k_p} + \frac{(\sum X_d)^2}{k_d} - \frac{(\sum X)^2}{N}$$

$$= \frac{1478^2}{10} + \frac{1394^2}{10} - 412,419.20$$

$$= 412,772.00 - 412,419.20 = 352.80.$$

4. We now compute the sum of squares for the sex factor, using the male and female totals. Thus

$$S.S._{sex} = \frac{(\sum X_m)^2}{k_m} + \frac{(\sum X_f)^2}{k_f} - \frac{(\sum X)^2}{N}$$

$$= \frac{1380^2}{10} + \frac{1492^2}{10} - 412,419.20$$

$$= 413,046.40 - 412,419.20 = 627.20.$$

5. Our next step is the computation of the sum of squares for the effect of interaction. To do this we use the totals for the various cells, since each cell total represents a combination of a specific level of one factor with a specific level of the other. Thus

$$S.S._{interaction} = \frac{(\sum X_{mp})^2}{k_{mp}} + \frac{(\sum X_{md})^2}{k_{md}} + \frac{(\sum X_{fp})^2}{k_{fp}} + \frac{(\sum X_{fd})^2}{k_{fd}} - \frac{(\sum X)^2}{N}$$

$$= \frac{712^2}{5} + \frac{668^2}{5} + \frac{766^2}{5} + \frac{726^2}{5} - 412,419.20$$

$$= 413,400 - 412,419.20 = 980.80.$$

Since the sum of squares computed for interaction is "contaminated" by the separate effects due to the drug and sex factors, we must now remove these effects by removing the sums of squares previously computed for drug and sex. Thus

$$S.S._{interaction} = 980.80 - (352.80 + 627.20)$$
$$= 980.80 - 980.00 = 0.80.$$

6. Finally, the sum of squares for error may be computed by direct subtraction, such as

$$S.S._{error} = S.S._{total} - (S.S._{drug} + S.S._{sex} + S.S._{interaction})$$
$$= 4902.80 - (352.80 + 627.20 + 0.80)$$
$$= 4902.80 - 980.80 = 3922.00.$$

7. We may now set up an analysis of variance table as below:

Source	D.F.	S.S.	M.S.
Drug	1	352.80	352.80
Sex	1	627.20	627.20
Interaction	1	0.80	0.80
Error	16	3922.00	245.12
Total	19	4902.80	

Note that degrees of freedom for the main effects are found by the usual method. There is a new factor to consider—that of interaction. For interaction, the degrees of freedom are computed by multiplying together the degrees of freedom for the main effects. Thus, in this case, $1 \times 1 = 1$.

We may now perform the appropriate F-tests as follows:

$$F_{1,16(\text{treatment})} = \frac{352.80}{245.12} = 1.43,$$

$$F_{1,16(\text{sex})} = \frac{627.20}{245.12} = 2.55,$$

$$F_{1,16(\text{interaction})} = \frac{0.80}{245.12} = 0.0032.$$

8. Turning to Table VII, it may be seen that the F-value for the main effects, sex and drug, do not reach significance at the 0.05 level. The F-test for interaction is less than one and may therefore be automatically regarded as nonsignificant. We may therefore conclude that the results of this experiment indicate no statistical significance for the drug effect, the effect of sex, or the interaction effect.

In this chapter we have presented only a few of the more basic designs made possible by analysis of variance. There are a number of interesting and extremely useful extensions and variations on the basic experimental procedures examined here, and the reader should look to the bibliography for some excellent references on the subject.

PROBLEMS

8.1 The following data represent the height (in centimeters) of plants grown in 3 different nutrient media, 5 replications/medium. Analyze these data for significant difference among the media in terms of plant growth (see Section 8.7).

Media

A	B	C
10	15	19
14	17	15
18	21	11
15	17	13
12	14	16
$\overline{X}_A = 13.80$	$\overline{X}_B = 16.80$	$\overline{X}_C = 14.80$

8.2 Eight samples were taken from each of 3 locations in a river in order to determine whether a significant difference in total nitrogen content existed among the locations. Analyze the data below for significance. The total nitrogen content is expressed in milligrams/100 g (see Section 8.7).

Location

A	B	C
222	326	263
300	275	260
262	218	299
264	207	221
200	272	198
211	268	211
267	308	266
326	229	319
$\overline{X}_A = 256.50$	$\overline{X}_B = 262.88$	$\overline{X}_C = 254.63$

8.3 Three strains of rats were selectively bred for differences in blood pressure in order to determine the possible effect of heredity on the blood pressure variable.

Strain

A	B	C
84	87	89
82	84	94
86	84	92
89	92	91
85	88	92
85	89	91
92	92	95
80	89	89
79	87	87
83	88	91
$\overline{X}_A = 84.50$	$\overline{X}_B = 88.00$	$\overline{X}_C = 91.10$

The data in the table were collected from 10 replications/strain, and are expressed in millimeters Hg. Analyze these data with respect to significant differences among the strains (see Section 8.7).

8.4 Two different baits were tested for significant difference in terms of consumption by wild rats. The following data were obtained from 5 locations per bait, and are expressed in percentage consumption. Analyze these data for significance, applying the arc sine transformation for percentage data (see Section 8.6).

	Bait
A	*B*
10	15
15	20
12	16
20	25
14	20

8.5 Examination of the three sets of treatment data below reveals the presence of multiplicative effects. Compute the mean and variance of each set of raw data, then apply a log transformation and again compute the mean and variance of each set. Compare the variances with respect to homogeneity (see Section 8.5).

I	II	III
12	16	31
15	29	26
9	23	20
11	22	36
13	23	28

8.6 Three clinical methods of determination of hemoglobin content were tested for significant difference in results. Six subjects were used, each subject constituting a single block. Analyze the data below, where the figures represent grams/100 ml (see Section 8.8).

			Blocks			
Method	*A*	*B*	*C*	*D*	*E*	*F*
1	14	12	16	15	10	11
2	18	16	17	19	12	13
3	15	14	12	14	12	9

8.7 Two diets were tested, using hamsters, for significant difference in terms of final weight measured after a specified period of time. The subjects were blocked, two to a block, the blocking done on the basis of original, prediet weight. Test the following data for significant difference between diets. The weights are expressed in grams (see Section 8.8).

Blocks

	1	2	3	4	5	6	7	8	9	10
Diet *A*	105	101	103	108	106	109	105	106	104	103
Diet *B*	110	108	106	112	110	112	110	106	108	108

8.8 Five samples of plankton were taken from each of two locations on a lake during the month of May. This process, using the same locations, was repeated in early August. The data, expressed in thousands of plankton per liter, are given below. Test these data for significant difference between locations, between collection times, and also for interaction between location and time (see Section 8.9).

Location I August (*A*) 97, 103, 109, 98, 102
                May (*B*) 108, 113, 119, 109, 112

Location II August (*A*) 106, 110, 116, 105, 111
                May (*B*) 111, 116, 120, 111, 113

8.9 An experiment was performed to test the photoreactivation phenomenon found in bacteria that have been exposed to ultraviolet. A plate of bacteria was exposed to ultraviolet for five minutes. A sample was taken from the exposed plate, plated, exposed to visible light for five minutes, then incubated. A second sample was exposed to visible light for a ten-minute period before incubation. A third sample was incubated without prior exposure to visible light. After a specific incubation time, the colonies were counted. The following data represent colony counts from five replications per treatment. Analyze for significant difference in number of colonies (see Section 8.9).

No exposure to visible light—45, 40, 10, 23, 32
Five minutes exposure to light—72, 81, 53, 55, 48
Ten minutes exposure to light—90, 100, 75, 70, 64

8.10 Three strains of *Drosophila pseudoobscura* were bred for resistance to an insecticide. Three levels of concentration of the insecticide were tested with the three inbred strains. The data, expressed in percent of mortality over a period of time, are based on five replications per treatment combination. Analyze these data for significant differences in mortality rate among strains, among levels of insecticide, and for interaction between the strain and the insecticide. (*Note:*

Because the data fall between 30% and 80%, it will not be necessary to use the arcsin transformation.) (See Section 8.10.)

Insecticide level 1

    Strain A 60, 55, 52, 38, 31
    Strain B 58, 53, 50, 35, 30
    Strain C 37, 43, 57, 60, 66

Insecticide level 2

    Strain A 44, 37, 54, 57, 65
    Strain B 63, 59, 54, 38, 38
    Strain C 59, 51, 53, 62, 71

Insecticide level 3

    Strain A 46, 51, 63, 66, 74
    Strain B 63, 44, 46, 66, 71
    Strain C 51, 80, 68, 71, 55

9
NONPARAMETRIC TESTS

9.1 DISTRIBUTION-FREE METHODS

Up to now, we have been concerned with *parametric* tests of significance, where sample statistics have been used to infer parameters, or population values.

Parametric tests assume that the variable in question follows, or at least approximates, some kind of distribution (normal, binomial, Poisson, etc.) and this distribution is then a basis for sample to population inference. Therefore, underlying every parametric test is an assumption concerning the distribution of the population data.

Since it is not always possible to make this assumption, and indeed, in some examples of biological data it is obvious that it *cannot* be made, it is sometimes appropriate to analyze data with so-called *nonparametric*, or *distribution-free* methods.

Such tests do not require knowledge about the population distribution. Further, they are usually simple to perform, and require a minimum of calculations. However, nonparametric tests should not be used simply because they are quicker and easier than standard parametric tests. They should be used only where assumptions cannot be made relative to population distributions, or possibly as rapid tests on small amounts of data derived from small pilot studies. In the latter case, they should be considered as a prelude to more rigorous testing with standard parametric devices.

The investigator who indiscriminately substitutes a distribution-free method for a parametric test may be sacrificing *efficiency*. Efficiency is defined here as the ability of a test to detect false hypotheses, and parametric tests in general have a greater sensitivity to false hypotheses. In other words, the probability of making a Type II error is smaller when a standard parametric test is used.

The following are intended as general guidelines for making a choice between a parametric method and a nonparametric test:

1. If it is obvious that no assumption can be made concerning the type of distribution which a variable follows or approximates, a nonparametric test is indicated.

2. Nonparametric tests may be useful for obtaining rapid estimates on small amounts of trial data.

3. When making inferences and broad generalizations from sample data, parametric tests are indicated.

9.2 THE SIGN TEST FOR MATCHED PAIRS

A good example of the "quick and dirty" methods described in this chapter is the sign test. This test may be used as a substitute for the matched-pair t-test described in Section 6.3, particularly when there is ample reason to doubt the normality of the data. The computations are based on the binomial distribution, and they are very simple.

The following example will illustrate the sign test, and the data are contrived to show its major pitfall.

Example. Twenty dogs are tested for lymphocyte count before and after administration of a drug which is supposed to produce a decrease in circulating lymphocytes. The resulting data are expressed in thousands per cubic millimeter of blood in Table 9.1.

1. Note that each replication is assigned a $(+)$ or $(-)$, depending on whether the lymphocyte count increased or decreased following administration of the drug.

2. The two cases which did not change were assigned zeros. These are removed from the total N number and are not included in the calculations. The working N number is therefore 18.

3. If the drug has *no effect* on lymphocyte count, then the probabilities of obtaining a plus value and a minus value in any randomly selected case will be equal. Therefore, $P(+) = \frac{1}{2}$, and $P(-) = \frac{1}{2}$. We can ignore the probability of obtaining a zero, since zeros are removed from the computation.

Table 9.1

Animal	Before	After	Sign
1	2.5	2.6	+
2	1.2	1.5	+
3	2.9	2.9	0
4	3.1	2.0	−
5	3.1	2.3	−
6	1.1	1.3	+
7	1.5	1.6	+
8	4.1	3.1	−
9	2.1	1.4	−
10	2.4	2.5	+
11	1.3	1.4	+
12	2.8	2.8	0
13	3.5	2.4	−
14	3.6	2.1	−
15	1.1	1.3	+
16	1.6	1.7	+
17	4.2	3.2	−
18	2.2	1.5	−
19	2.5	2.1	−
20	1.3	1.1	−

4. We then have a binomial distribution of *minus* values. This is the distribution of interest, because we wish to know if the drug significantly *lowers* the lymphocyte count.

5. The distribution mean is *np*, and the standard deviation is $\sqrt{npq}$. Substituting, we have

$$\text{Mean} = \tfrac{1}{2}(18) = 9,$$
$$\text{Standard deviation} = \sqrt{\tfrac{1}{2} \times \tfrac{1}{2}(18)} = \sqrt{4.5} = 2.12.$$

6. Recall that we obtained 10 minus values. Now we need to compute the probability of obtaining *10 or more minus values by chance alone*. Taking 9.5 as the lower limit of 10, we obtain

$$Z = \frac{9.50 - 9.00}{2.12} = 0.235$$

as the Z-value. Since the sample is fairly large, we consult the table of normal curve values and find that a Z of 0.235 is considerably less than the 1.64 that is needed in order to reject the null hypothesis when a one-tailed test is assumed.

7. The probability of obtaining 10 or more minus values by chance alone is quite high; we have therefore found no statistical evidence that the drug is effective in reducing the lymphocyte count.

At this point we might try a matched-pair t-test and compare results. If we do, we will obtain a t-value of 2.91, which is significant beyond the 0.01 level! In other words, the t-test produces exactly the opposite of the results obtained from the sign test in the preceding example. Why the contradiction?

Looking back at the original data, it may be seen that a $(+)$ or $(-)$ sign merely represents a *direction* of change and does not take into consideration the *magnitude* of the change. A casual inspection of the data used in the example reveals that upward changes in lymphocyte count were usually quite small, while downward changes were substantially greater. The sign test is not sensitive to these differences in magnitude, but since the computations of the t-test incorporate absolute changes, it produced significant results.

Thus it may be seen that although the sign test has the advantage of simplicity, the careful investigator will do well to scan the data in order to determine whether absolute changes have reasonably similar magnitudes in both directions.

9.3 THE WILCOXON TEST FOR UNPAIRED DATA

The Wilcoxon test for unpaired data is a useful nonparametric substitute for the t-test considered in Section 6.4. As nonparametric tests go, the Wilcoxon test is reputed to have a high degree of efficiency.

This test is based on a ranking system, and the following simple example will serve to illustrate the basic computations.

Example. The pulse rates of 6 males were compared with the pulse rates of 6 females, and the following data were obtained:

Males	74	77	78	75	72	71
Females	80	83	73	84	82	79

1. As a first step, we rank *all* the above data in order of increasing magnitude. As we do so, we underline those values taken from the group with the *smallest* mean. By simple inspection, this is quite obviously the male group. Thus we have

$$\underline{71} \quad \underline{72} \quad 73 \quad \underline{74} \quad \underline{75} \quad \underline{77} \quad \underline{78} \quad 79 \quad 80 \quad 82 \quad 83 \quad 84$$
$$\underline{1} \quad \underline{2} \quad 3 \quad \underline{4} \quad \underline{5} \quad \underline{6} \quad \underline{7} \quad 8 \quad 9 \quad 10 \quad 11 \quad 12$$

2. Under each ordered value we also show a number indicating its rank, with the number 1 assigned to the lowest rank. Note that the rank numbers are underlined, or not, according to the raw data they represent.

3. Now, it may be seen that if there is actually no difference between the male and female groups, the values of the ranks should be such that the rank totals are approximately equal. In our case in point, we have

$$\text{Males} \quad \underline{1} + \underline{2} + \underline{4} + \underline{5} + \underline{6} + \underline{7} = 25,$$
$$\text{Females} \quad 3 + 8 + 9 + 10 + 11 + 12 = 53.$$

In this situation the rank total of the female group is much higher than that of the males, indicating that *larger* rank numbers make up that total.

4. We now compute the value U by

$$U = T_1 - \tfrac{1}{2}n_1(n_1 + 1),$$

where T_1 is always the total of the ranks assigned to the group with the *smallest* mean, n_1 is the number of cases in the group with the smallest mean, and n_2 is the number of cases found in the group with the largest mean. Thus

$$U = T_1 - \tfrac{1}{2}n_1(n_1 + 1)$$
$$= 25 - \tfrac{1}{2}(6)(7)$$
$$= 25 - 21 = 4.$$

5. Turning to Table IX in the appendix, we look down the "n_1-n_2" column to the point indicated by $n_1 = 6$, $n_2 = 6$. The $C_{n_1 n_2}$ column at this point shows the figure 924, which represents the number of possible combinations of ranks from a total of 12, taken 6 at a time. We now find the U-value, 4, along the top portion of the table, and going down the column headed by 4 to the point opposite 924, we find the value 12. This represents the number of possible rank totals that would be equal to or less than 25. The probability, therefore, of finding a rank total of 25 or less in this case is

$$\tfrac{12}{924} = 0.012.$$

6. If we assume a one-tailed test, we may conclude significance beyond the 0.05 level. If a two-tailed test were involved, we would need to double the probability, obtaining 0.024, and we could still claim significance beyond the 0.05 level.

What happens when there are two or more values alike, producing ties? The following example illustrates the procedure used to handle ties and also shows that n_1 does not have to be exactly equal to n_2.

Example. We are given the following set of data:

$$n_1:\quad 19\quad 14\quad 20\quad 17\quad 18\quad 20$$
$$n_2:\quad 24\quad 19\quad 33\quad 32\quad 21\quad 18\quad 20$$

1. We again arrange all units of data in the order of increasing value. Thus we have 13 pieces of data arranged as follows:

14 17 18 18 19 19 20 20 20 21 24 32 33

2. We again underline those values obtained from n_1, which is the set with the smallest mean. This time, however, the situation is complicated by a tie of three values (20) and two ties of two values each (18 and 19). We therefore assign to each member of a tie the *mean* value of the ranks that would normally be assigned if there were no tie! Thus we have

14	17	18	18	19	19	20	20	20	21	24	32	33
1	2	3.5	3.5	5.5	5.5	8	8	8	10	11	12	13

Note that the rank assigned to both 18's is the mean of 3 and 4, or 3.5. The rank assigned to both 19's is 5.5, which is the mean of 5 and 6. Each value of 20 is assigned the rank, 8, which is the mean of 7, 8, and 9. Values which *follow* tied ranks are assigned the rank they would have received if there were no ties.

3. Adding the rank numbers of n_1 and n_2, we have

$$n_1:\quad 1\;+\;2\;+\;3.5\;+\;5.5\;+\;8\;+\;8\qquad\quad = 28,$$
$$n_2:\quad 3.5\;+\;5.5\;+\;8\;+\;10\;+\;11\;+\;12\;+\;13 = 63.$$

4. T_1, which is the total of the ranks obtained from the set with the *smallest* mean, is 28.

5.
$$U = T_1 - \tfrac{1}{2}n_1(n_1 + 1) = 28 - \tfrac{1}{2}(6)(7)$$
$$= 28 - 21 = 7.$$

6. Turning to Table IX, we find that when $n_1 = 6$ and $n_2 = 7$, $C_{n_1 n_2}$ is 1716. Looking down the U column headed by 7, we find 44 as the number of combinations of ranks that would produce a total of 28 or less. Our probability value is therefore

$$P = \tfrac{44}{1716} = 0.025$$

for a one-tailed test. If a two-tailed test is appropriate, the probability statement would be 0.05.

7. On the basis of either a one- or two-tailed test, we would reject the null hypothesis that no significant difference exists between the rank totals derived from n_1 and n_2.

9.4 RANK CORRELATION

In Chapter 10 we will consider the concept of correlation and the computation of r, which is called the Pearson product moment value for correlation. In doing so, we will assume that the data comprising the X- and Y- distributions are normally distributed.

In cases where it is obvious that such an assumption *cannot* be made, a nonparametric correlation computation called "rank correlation" may be used. This method may also be used in situations where the X-variable is itself based on a ranking system. For example, flower color might be expressed in terms of 1, 2, 3, ... as ranks assigned according to shades from light to dark.

Like most nonparametric techniques, the basic computations connected with rank correlation are simpler than those of its parametric counterpart. The following example will illustrate the procedure.

Example. Ten males were used as subjects in an experiment designed to determine the degree of correlation of age with blood pressure. The following data were obtained:

Subject	Age (X)	Rank	Blood pressure (Y)	Rank	$(X - Y)^2$
1	34	10	120	10	0
2	35	9	122	9	0
3	36	8	128	7	1
4	46	4	180	4	0
5	50	2	190	2	0
6	40	7	140	6	1
7	51	1	185	3	4
8	44	5	175	5	0
9	47	3	200	1	4
10	42	6	126	8	4

$$\Sigma (X - Y)^2 = 14$$

1. As our first step, we assign ranks to the age, or X-values, beginning with 1 for the largest value. We then do the same with the blood pressure, or Y-values.

2. Next, we square the difference between the X and Y ranks associated with each subject. This produces the column headed by $(X - Y)^2$. Summing this column yields 14.

3. We now apply the rank correlation formula,

$$R = 1 - \frac{6 \sum (X - Y)^2}{N(N^2 - 1)}.$$

Substituting, we have

$$R = 1 - \frac{6(14)}{10(99)} = 1 - \frac{84}{990}$$

$$= 1 - 0.08 = 0.92.$$

4. We thus find a rank correlation of 0.92 between the variables X and Y.

9.5 RUNS

The technique of *runs* has useful applications to biological problems. An ecologist may wish to know if annual fluctuations in a population are random from one year to another, or if they appear to follow a pattern, possibly because of environmental influences. Or, it might be desirable to determine whether the number of cases of a certain disease fluctuates randomly from one year to another, or if nonrandom changes in incidence might be found, and thus associated with conditions apparently conducive to increases or decreases in the number of cases.

The technique is extremely simple, as illustrated by the following example.

Example. The numbers of cases of malaria reported from a certain area over a period of successive years were 51, 82, 64, 32, 11, 12, 54, 71, 90, 101, 84, 72, 45, 20, 74, 15. Did the number of cases fluctuate in a random manner or is there some kind of a pattern?

1. First, we establish a reference point from which to work. Usually, the most convenient reference point is the median, which, in this case, is 64.

2. Now we simply assign the letter "a" to those values under 64 and "b" to those above 64. Any value at the median will be discarded and will not be included in the data.

3. Substituting the appropriate letter for each number in the original distribution, we have

$$a, \ b, \ aaaa, \ bbbbb, \ aa, \ b, \ a.$$

Note that each run of *a* or *b* is underlined and that a single *a* or *b* is considered a run.

4. We now need three values: (1) the number of *a*'s, (2) the number of *b*'s, and (3) the total number of runs. Thus

$$a = 8, \qquad b = 7, \qquad \text{runs} = 7.$$

5. Consulting Table X in the appendix, we go across the top row for $a = 8$, and down the left margin for $b = 7$. At the point of intersection of the row and column, we find the numbers 4 and 13. This tells us that if the number of runs is 4 *or less* we can assume that random fluctuation did *not* occur. In other words, the *a*'s and *b*'s are ordered in such a way as to cause us to suspect that some external factor has produced that orderliness. The same would be true if the number of runs found is 13 or more. This would also indicate an orderly alternation of *a*'s and *b*'s and would be inconsistent with randomness.

6. Since our example yielded 7 runs, this number is neither low enough nor high enough to permit a conclusion of nonrandomness. We must therefore assume that the incidence of malaria fluctuated from one year to another in a random manner.

Another application of "runs" is illustrated by the following.

Example. An ecologist counted the number of birds in a specified area by keeping careful track of territories. In successive years he made the observations shown below. Does the size of the population fluctuate randomly from one year to another, or is there a self-limiting mechanism which produces a definite pattern?

Year	1954	1955	1956	1957	1958	1959	1960	1961	1962	1963
Number	13	13	12	10	8	11	9	7	6	5

1. First we determine the median value to be 9.5. Assigning the letter "*a*" to values lower than 9.5 and the letter "*b*" to values larger than 9.5 produces

$$\underline{aaaa} \quad \underline{b} \quad \underline{a} \quad \underline{bbbb}$$
$$a = 5$$
$$b = 5$$
$$\text{runs} = 4$$

2. Consulting Table X, we find the numbers 2 and 10 at the intersection of $a = 5$, and $b = 5$. Since the actual number of runs obtained is 4, this value is neither small enough nor large enough for us to conclude that any kind of pattern other than random fluctuation exists in the annual shifts in the bird population.

9.6 SUMMARY

In this chapter we have seen a few illustrations of distribution-free statistics. Further examples of nonparametric devices may be found among the references listed in the bibliography.

At this point it may be well to reemphasize the dangers of haphazardly substituting nonparametric techniques for the appropriate parametric methods. These devices should be used with proper caution, and the investigator should be careful not to base earth-shaking conclusions on the results derived from such tests. On the other hand, they are admittedly useful for obtaining quick and easy estimates of significance.

PROBLEMS

9.1 Use the sign test to analyze the following set of matched-pair data for significant increase in the values derived from treatment B over those produced by treatment A (see Section 9.2).

Subject	Treatment A	Treatment B
1	46	52
2	41	43
3	37	37
4	32	32
5	28	31
6	43	39
7	42	44
8	51	53
9	28	26
10	27	31

9.2 Analyze the data presented in Problem 6.6 by using the sign test. Determine whether the drug is effective in increasing the hemoglobin level (see Section 9.2).

9.3 Two laboratory methods of determining the level of protein-bound iodine are compared by using 12 female adults. Use the sign test to determine whether the results associated with method B are significantly higher than the values produced by method A (see Section 9.2).

Subject	Method		Subject	Method	
	A	B		A	B
1	4	5	7	9	10
2	6	5	8	3	4
3	3	3	9	4	5
4	5	6	10	4	5
5	7	8	11	5	5
6	8	6	12	4	6

9.4 Two ponds were compared in terms of alkalinity, expressed in milligrams per liter. Five samples were taken from each pond. Use the Wilcoxon two-sample rank test to determine whether a significant difference in alkalinity exists between the ponds (see Section 9.3).

Pond I: 102, 116, 122, 112, 104
Pond II: 108, 117, 115, 120, 105

9.5 Use the Wilcoxon two-sample rank test to determine whether a significant difference exists between the following two sets of data (see Section 9.3).

A: 94, 63, 28, 59, 71, 36, 38
B: 112, 64, 38, 59, 84, 50, 38

9.6 Use the Wilcoxon two-sample rank test to determine whether a significant difference exists between the following two sets of data (see Section 9.3).

A: 82, 86, 30, 21, 38, 29, 29, 19
B: 124, 116, 54, 54, 110, 29, 39, 54

9.7 Apply the rank correlation technique to the following paired data (see Section 9.4).

	X	Y		X	Y
1	21	25	6	63	64
2	21	20	7	84	81
3	42	47	8	84	83
4	42	44	9	105	106
5	63	61	10	105	111

9.8 Apply the rank correlation technique to the following paired data (see Section 9.4).

	X	Y		X	Y
1	24	105	6	33	140
2	36	213	7	38	173
3	48	274	8	27	136
4	34	198	9	31	155
5	28	128			

9.9 The following data represent annual counts of shore birds observed at a specific location on a lake shore during the migratory season. Use the technique of "runs" to determine whether the fluctuation from one year to another is random or whether a pattern is present (see Section 9.5).

Year	1956	1957	1958	1959	1960	1961	1962	1963	1964	1965	1966
Number	489	795	540	680	970	320	830	293	565	460	602

9.10 The following data represent annual catches of fish at a specific location in one of the Great Lakes; the data are expressed in tons. Analyze these data to determine whether the annual fluctuation is random or whether a pattern is evident (see Section 9.5).

Year	1943	1944	1945	1946	1947	1948	1949	1950	1951	1952	1953
Number	56	57	61	59	62	52	56	53	51	49	48

Year	1954	1955	1956	1957	1958	1959	1960	1961	1962	1963	1964
Number	52	50	48	52	51	42	49	53	40	43	42

10
CORRELATION AND REGRESSION

10.1 CORRELATION

It is not unusual to find two or more population variables which show an apparent association. For example, we may find a situation where an increase in variable Y appears to be associated with an increase in variable X, or a decrease in Y seems to be related to a decrease in X. When it can be demonstrated that an association exists between two or more variables, we say they are *correlated*.

This correlation may be positive, as when an increase in Y is associated with an increase in X, or negative, as when a decrease in Y is associated with an increase in X. If only random and haphazard changes in Y are associated with specific changes in X, then there is no association, and therefore no correlation, between the two variables.

A popular misconception related to correlation holds that because variables X and Y are correlated, variable X is therefore the *cause* of variable Y. Now it is true that, given two highly correlated variables, a variation in X *may* produce a variation in Y. Figure 10.1 shows temperature plotted as the X, or independent variable, and gas volume as the Y, or dependent variable. In this case—an application of the familiar Charles's law—a variation in gas volume *is* caused by variation in temperature. Note that all points fall on a straight line, indicating a perfect linear correlation.

Now, consider the high degree of association found between cigarette consumption and lung cancer. Should we automatically conclude that cigarette smoking causes lung cancer? Consider also that a high correlation exists between the incidence of lung cancer and the number of telephone

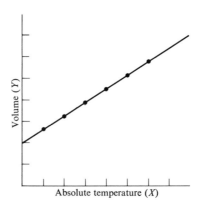

Fig. 10.1 Gas volume plotted against absolute temperature, showing perfect positive correlation.

poles. Should we therefore also conclude that telephone poles cause lung cancer? What about a correlation between lung cancer and the number of automobiles?

As usual, the interpretation of statistics needs to be leavened with common sense and practical biological considerations. A correlation between lung cancer and telephone poles makes no sense in terms of a causal relationship, since there is no biological or medical evidence to support such a contention. A correlation between lung cancer and cigarette smoking, or between lung cancer and automobiles is quite another matter. These can obviously be tied in with the known carcinogens found in cigarettes and automobile exhaust. As far as can be determined, however, one is not exposed to carcinogens by walking in the vicinity of telephone poles!

In brief, *a high correlation between two variables does not necessarily imply causation.* A significant correlation may *suggest* such a possibility to the investigator, but supportive evidence of a biological nature must be found before a conclusion involving causation is warranted.

10.2 THE CORRELATION COEFFICIENT

Correlation is expressed by a coefficient (r) which may range from -1 to $+1$. A coefficient of 1, positive or negative in sign, indicates a perfect correlation between two variables. On the other hand, a coefficient of zero suggests a complete lack of correlation. Varying degrees of correlation are then represented by coefficients ranging from zero to 1 in either direction.

We can plot a series of points representing the magnitudes of each pair of X and Y variables and obtain various patterns, some of which are shown

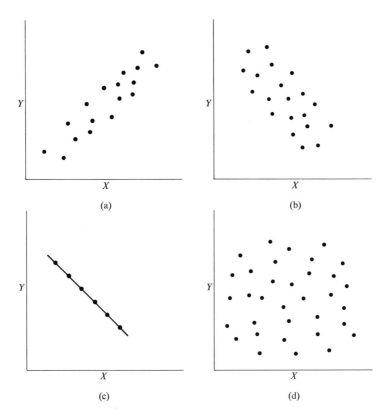

Fig. 10.2 Typical patterns obtained from plotting Y against X.

by Fig. 10.2. Diagram (a) shows a series of points which are not on a straight line. This represents a correlation which is less than perfect, but shows a general trend in a positive direction. If we correlated height and weight in a sample of adult human subjects, we would probably obtain a pattern similar to that shown by (a). A similar pattern of imperfect correlation is shown by (b), but in this case the slope is negative, indicating a negative correlation. A pattern similar to (b) might be obtained by plotting the incidence of dental cavities in children against the level of fluoridation. Diagram (c) shows a perfect negative (-1) correlation, such as might be obtained from plotting acceleration against mass in the application of Newton's second law, $F = ma$. Diagram (d) shows the random scattering of points that might be expected from plotting Y against X when the two variables are not at all associated.

Another common misconception is that the correlation coefficient represents a percent agreement between two variables. Actually, this would be true only if the coefficient were $+1$, -1, or zero! A coefficient of 0.50, however, does not mean that X and Y agree 50% of the time. If percent agreement is plotted against the coefficient r, a pattern similar to that shown in Fig. 10.3 is obtained. It may be seen that percent agreement increases exponentially as r increases.

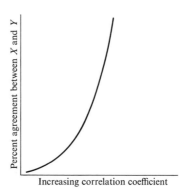

Fig. 10.3 Relation of correlation coefficient to percent agreement between X and Y.

What is a "good" correlation? This obviously depends on what the investigator is doing, or what he hopes to find. If one hopes to show that no association exists between two variables, then a coefficient of zero would be a cause for celebration. If, on the other hand, the investigator hopes to show a strong association, then an r approaching 1 would be considered optimum. As usual, living systems do not usually cooperate by producing nice round figures; variability is the rule rather than the exception. In most cases, therefore, the biologist will probably need to be content with coefficients that are less than perfect.

10.3 COMPUTING THE CORRELATION COEFFICIENT (r)

Consider the following simple example of a bivariate distribution:

Pair	X	Y
1	1	6
2	2	7
3	3	8
4	4	9
5	5	10

It is obvious from a simple inspection of these data that a perfect positive correlation exists between X and Y. Now, if we compute $\bar{X}$ and $\bar{Y}$, and the standard deviations of the X- and Y-distributions, we may use these quantities to compute the Z-value of each variate in the usual manner,

$$Z_X = \frac{X - \bar{X}}{S_X}, \quad \text{and} \quad Z_Y = \frac{Y - \bar{Y}}{S_Y}.$$

This would yield distributions of signed Z-values as follows:

Pair	X	Y	$Z_X Z_Y$
1	$-Z_X \times -Z_Y =$		$+Z_X Z_Y$
2	$-Z_X \times -Z_Y =$		$+Z_X Z_Y$
3	$0 \times 0 =$		0
4	$+Z_X \times +Z_Y =$		$+Z_X Z_Y$
5	$+Z_X \times +Z_Y =$		$+Z_X Z_Y$
	$r = \dfrac{\Sigma Z_X Z_Y}{N} = +1$		

Note that all cross products of Z-values are plus, and if the Y-distribution exactly "fits" the X-distribution, the Z_X- and Z_Y-values will be the same for both members of each pair. Summing the cross products of the Z-values and dividing by N, the number of pairs, yields the correlation coefficient 1. We can see that r is basically the mean of all cross products of Z-values found in the bivariate distribution.

Now consider the following bivariate distribution:

Pair	X	Y
1	1	10
2	2	9
3	3	8
4	4	7
5	5	6

This time we can also see a perfect relationship, but in the opposite direction! In other words, the correlation is negative. Again computing Z-values, we obtain the following distributions.

Pair	X	Y	$Z_X Z_Z$
1	$-Z_X \times +Z_Y =$		$-Z_X Z_Y$
2	$-Z_X \times +Z_Y =$		$-Z_X Z_Y$
3	$0 \times 0 =$		0
4	$+Z_X \times -Z_Y =$		$-Z_X Z_Y$
5	$+Z_X \times -Z_Y =$		$-Z_X Z_Y$
	$r = \dfrac{\sum Z_X Z_Y}{N} = -1$		

Calculating the cross products of Z-values of each pair, we obtain a $Z_X Z_Y$ sum which has a negative sign. Dividing by N, we then obtain -1 as the coefficient. Again, the correlation is perfect, but the Y-distribution is turned end to end before it is superimposed on the X-distribution.

It follows logically that a bivariate distribution in which X- and Y-values do not correlate perfectly will yield $Z_X Z_Y$-values which are signed in a more irregular, haphazard manner. This will yield a mean $Z_X Z_Y$-value ranging downward from $+1$ (or upward from -1), to zero in cases where there is no association at all.

Now, given any significant amount of data, this method of computation would be prohibitively tedious, so we need to develop an easier approach to the calculation of r.

Recalling the formula for computing a Z-value, it may be seen that the cross product, $Z_X Z_Y$, is the same as

$$\frac{X - \bar{X}}{S_X} \times \frac{Y - \bar{Y}}{S_Y},$$

and therefore $\sum Z_X Z_Y$ may be represented by

$$\frac{\sum (X - \bar{X})(Y - \bar{Y})}{N S_X S_Y}.$$

Now, since

$$S_X^2 = \frac{\sum X^2 - (\sum X)^2/N}{N}$$

and

$$S_Y^2 = \frac{\sum Y^2 - (\sum Y)^2/N}{N},$$

some relatively simple algebraic manipulation yields

$$r = \frac{\sum XY - \sum X \sum Y/N}{\sqrt{(\sum X^2 - (\sum X)^2/N)(\sum Y^2 - (\sum Y)^2/N)}},$$

which is a useful computing formula for finding r, the correlation coefficient. To the biologist used to counting the number of legs on a grasshopper, this may be a rather formidable appearing formula, but with a reasonably good desk calculator the values $\sum XY$, $\sum X^2$, $\sum Y^2$, $\sum X$, and $\sum Y$ can be easily obtained with one "run" through a set of bivariate data.

Example. The data below represent observations made on the rate of cricket sounds at different temperatures. Compute the correlation coefficient.

X (°F)	Y (Chirps/15 sec)	X (°F)	Y (Chirps/15 sec)
62	23	55	15
61	21	53	14
60	19	52	12
59	19	50	11
58	19		

1. First, we need to compute the following values:

$$\sum XY = 8811 \qquad \sum X^2 = 29048 \qquad \sum Y^2 = 2739$$

$$\frac{\sum X \sum Y}{N} = 8670 \qquad \frac{(\sum X)^2}{N} = 28900 \qquad \frac{(\sum Y)^2}{N} = 2601$$

$$\sum X = 510$$

$$\sum Y = 153$$

2. The coefficient (r) may now be computed as

$$r = \frac{\sum XY - \sum X \sum Y/N}{\sqrt{(\sum X^2 - (\sum X)^2/N)(\sum Y^2 - (\sum Y)^2/N)}}$$

$$= \frac{8811 - 8670}{\sqrt{(29048 - 28900)(2739 - 2601)}}$$

$$= \frac{141}{\sqrt{20,424}} = \frac{141}{143} = 0.986,$$

which is a very high correlation, and is the basis of the well-known technique of using the calling rate of crickets to estimate temperature!

10.4 TESTING HYPOTHESES ABOUT ρ

Suppose that we draw a sample from a bivariate population and compute r. Suppose further that our sample r turns out to be 0.45. How do we know whether our sample *r* represents a true correlation between the *X* and *Y* variates of the *population,* or if it is only a chance deviation from zero? Actually, if we compute a sample correlation between two variables drawn from almost any source, it would be unusual to obtain a coefficient of *exactly* zero, even if no correlation whatsoever existed between all the *X* and *Y* variates in the population itself. This would be similar to tossing 1000 coins in the air and obtaining exactly 500 heads! This is possible, but not likely!

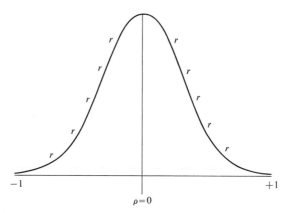

Fig. 10.4 Sampling distribution of *r*, based on population in which *ρ* is zero.

We are therefore back to the familiar problem of determining whether a sample statistic is significant, or if it occurred by chance alone. Figure 10.4 shows a theoretical sampling distribution based on *r*'s associated with an infinitude of samples drawn from a population in which the *parameter* value of the correlation coefficient is zero. In keeping with our established procedure, we let the Greek letter *ρ* (rho) represent the population coefficient. From the sampling distribution, we note that the sample coefficients (*r*) could theoretically range anywhere from −1 to +1, but most of the samples obtained would yield coefficients clustering around the mean of zero. We are therefore saying that, while the probability is admittedly very small, it is nevertheless *possible* to draw a sample from a bivariate population where no correlation whatsoever exists between the variables and, by chance alone, find a perfect correlation between the sample variates. It may also be seen that a sample yielding an *r* of zero is highly improbable, and we are therefore not surprised if a sample drawn from such a population shows a correlation other than zero! The following problem demonstrates a method of determining whether a sample coefficient is significant, or if it is simply a chance deviation from zero.

Statement of the Problem

A sample of $N = 37$ is drawn from a bivariate population. A correlation coefficient is computed and yields $r = 0.25$. Does this indicate a real correlation in the population, or does it result from a chance sampling variation from zero?

The Null Hypothesis

Since we are interested in whether the *population* coefficient differs significantly from zero, we establish the null hypothesis as

$$H_0: \rho = 0.$$

Level of Significance

We set a level of significance of 0.05. Since we are not concerned with a specific direction of difference, we shall use a two-tailed test.

The Sampling Distribution

Figure 10.4 shows a sampling distribution of r's based on a population where $\rho = 0$.

The Standard Error

Now we must, as usual, compute the appropriate standard error, so we may place our statistic on the sampling distribution. The standard error of ρ is computed as

$$S_{rho} = \frac{1}{\sqrt{N-1}} = \frac{1}{\sqrt{36}} = \tfrac{1}{6} = 0.167.$$

The Z-value can now be computed as

$$Z = \frac{0.25 - 0}{0.167} = 1.50.$$

The Decision

Since our Z-value of 1.50 is less than the 1.96 needed to reject a null hypothesis at the 0.05 level, we fail to reject the null hypothesis, $H_0: \rho = 0$. On this basis, we must conclude that our sample data have provided no evidence that a true correlation exists between the variables at the population level.

In cases where the N number (number of pairs) is less than 30, the null hypothesis $H_0: \rho = 0$ should be tested with the t-distribution by use of the formula

$$t = \frac{r - 0}{\sqrt{(1 - r^2)/(N - 2)}}.$$

Significance is determined, as usual, by finding the critical value of t associated with the 0.05 or 0.01 level and $N - 2$ degrees of freedom.

10.5 ESTIMATING ρ

Suppose we find that a particular sample r of 0.45 is significant, and therefore indicates a real correlation between the population X- and Y-variables. At this point it would be an error to assume that the parameter ρ is also 0.45. This would be similar to concluding that μ is, say, 50, because we have drawn a sample yielding an $\bar{X}$ of 50.

As before, it is necessary to estimate the population parameter with confidence limits, using the sample statistics as a basis for the estimation. Before we proceed with this operation, however, it will be necessary to discuss the nature of the distributions that may be obtained relative to ρ.

Looking back at Fig. 10.4, it may be seen that when ρ is zero, the sampling distribution of ρ is symmetrical, since the sample r's distribute normally from -1 to $+1$, with the majority of cases clustering around $\rho = 0$. Suppose, on the other hand, that ρ equals 0.90. From a population such as this, it is apparent that we would obtain a preponderance of samples having high values of r, with fewer samples having low or negative values. This would therefore produce a skewed distribution as shown in Fig. 10.5(a). Another

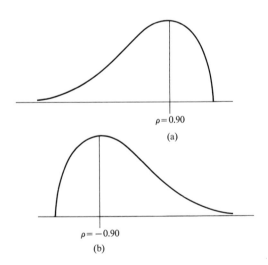

$\rho = 0.90$

(a)

$\rho = -0.90$

(b)

Fig. 10.5 Sampling distributions of r drawn from populations where $\rho = 0.90$ and $\rho = -0.90$.

distribution, based on $\rho = -0.90$, which, as might be expected, is skewed in the other direction is shown in Fig. 10.5(b).

Since we cannot apply normal curve principles to a badly skewed distribution, it is necessary to apply a transformation when working with correlations that are significantly greater or less than zero. The only time this transformation is *not* necessary is when dealing with distributions based on $\rho = 0$, as in Section 10.4. Fortunately, the transformations involving r which normalize distributions of r that would otherwise be skewed have been worked out for us by R. A. Fisher, who applied the formula

$$Z = 1.1513 \left[\log \frac{1 + r}{1 - r} \right]$$

to obtain the so-called r to Z values shown in Table XI. Looking at Table XI, it is evident that the further r is from zero, the more necessary it is to use the r to Z transformation.

Suppose that we demonstrate both the estimation of ρ and the use of the r to Z transformation with the following example.

Example. A sample of 65 pairs of variates was drawn from a population. Computation of the correlation coefficient yielded $r = 0.45$. Estimate the population coefficient ρ from the sample data, using 95% confidence limits.

1. First, we must convert r to Z. Consulting Table XI, we find that a correlation of 0.45 is equivalent to a Z-value of 0.485.

2. Next, we need to compute the standard error of Z. This is given by

$$S_Z = \frac{1}{\sqrt{N - 3}} = \frac{1}{\sqrt{62}} = \frac{1}{7.89} = 0.127.$$

3. Now we can proceed as usual with the estimation by

$$\rho = Z \pm S_Z(1.96) = 0.485 \pm 0.127(1.96)$$
$$= 0.485 \pm 0.249 = 0.236\text{–}0.734.$$

4. Finally, converting back from Z to r, using Table XI, we find that the confidence interval for ρ is

$$0.23\text{–}0.62.$$

5. We may therefore make the statement that, based on our sample data, we estimate that ρ falls between 0.23 and 0.62, and we are confident of being correct in this estimate 95% of the time.

10.6 REGRESSION

The correlation coefficient provides the biologist with an estimation of the *intensity* of the association or relationship between two variables found in a population. While this information is useful, it is usually important to also know something of the *nature* of that relationship. For example, if we know how much of a change in variable Y can be expected as a result of a unit change in variable X, this knowledge can be used to *predict* Y from X.

If the correlation coefficient is $+1$ or -1, and is linear in nature, an examination of the data can usually provide an easy and obvious basis for prediction. However, as indicated previously, we are unlikely to encounter perfect correlations in living systems. We therefore need to develop a way to fit a single line, called a *regression line*, to the more haphazard data we are likely to obtain. Having done this, we will be able to predict Y from X within

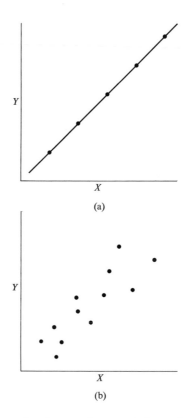

Fig. 10.6 Scatter diagrams showing a perfect correlation and a correlation less than 1.

certain limits. While this prediction will not be 100% precise, it is still useful in many instances.

Figure 10.6(a) illustrates the kind of scatter diagram obtained when the correlation of Y with X is perfect. In this case, all points representing the magnitude of specific X and Y pairs lie on a straight line, and prediction is no problem. Figure 10.6(b) shows a positive, but less than perfect relationship. It is in a situation such as this that we must plot a regression line, or "line of best fit."

Figure 10.7(a) shows a scatter diagram of Y on X consisting of five points. A horizontal line, representing the mean of the Y-values ($\bar{Y}$), is drawn through point P, which represents the point plotted from $\bar{X}$ and $\bar{Y}$, the means of the X and Y distributions. At this time it might be well to point out that the regression line will always pass through the point representing ($\bar{X}$, $\bar{Y}$).

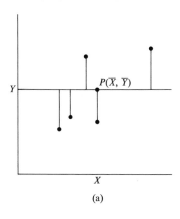

(a)

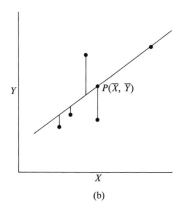

(b)

Fig. 10.7 Placement of regression line so that $\sum (Y_p - Y)^2$ is at a minimum.

Each point outside the line represents a Y-value, and the vertical distances from each Y-value to the line represent deviations of Y from $\bar{Y}$, or $(Y - \bar{Y})$.

Now, suppose that we were able to move the line in Fig. 10.7(a) around the axis formed by point P, until it reaches the position depicted in Fig. 10.7(b). Now it may be seen that the distances representing the deviations of Y from the line are decreased. This new line, called the regression line, represents the Y-values that would then be *predicted* from X. It is apparent that these predicted values, which we will call Y_p, would still deviate in many cases from the *actual* Y-values obtained from the data. However, the regression line has been placed so *the sum of the squared deviations of predicted Y's from actual Y's is at a minimum*. Symbolically, $\sum (Y_p - Y)^2$ is at a minimum. This general method of plotting a "line of best fit" is called the *method of least squares*.

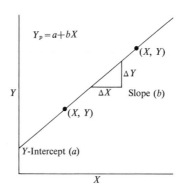

Fig. 10.8 Straight line representing basic linear equation.

Figure 10.8 shows a straight line plotted on a pair of coordinates. Recalling elementary algebra, there are two values that we have to know in order to plot a straight line on a set of coordinates. One of these values is the slope (b) and the other value (a) is the Y-intercept. Knowing these, we can utilize the familiar linear equation,

$$Y_p = a + bX$$

in order to plot the line. In working with regression, however, we will need to use the data from our bivariate distribution in order to obtain a and b. The mathematician has derived the value of b for us by using the methods of differential calculus. Thus the slope of the line may be computed by

$$b_{YX} = \frac{\sum (X - \bar{X})(Y - \bar{Y})}{\sum (X - \bar{X})^2}.$$

A more convenient computation form is

$$b_{YX} = \frac{\sum XY - (\sum X \sum Y/N)}{\sum X^2 - [(\sum X)^2/N]}.$$

The Y-intercept, a, depends on the values $\bar{X}$ and $\bar{Y}$, and is given by

$$a = \bar{Y} - b\bar{X}.$$

This expression may be substituted for a in the basic linear equation as follows:

$$\begin{aligned} Y_p = a + bX &= \bar{Y} - b\bar{X} + bX \\ &= \bar{Y} + bX - b\bar{X} = \bar{Y} + b(X - \bar{X}). \end{aligned}$$

We now have the regression equation in its most useful form as

$$Y_p = \bar{Y} + b(X - \bar{X}),$$

since we can easily compute $\bar{Y}$ and $\bar{X}$, and b can be computed from the formula given previously. Now all we need to do is substitute any appropriate X-value for X, and compute Y_p, or the predicted Y-value. Consider the following example.

Example. Systolic blood pressure measurements were taken on a number of human male subjects of varying ages, resulting in the following paired data. Compute the regression equation so that Y may be predicted from X. Calculate the predicted blood pressure values for ages 35 and 50.

Subject	X (Age in years)	Y (B.P. in mm Hg)
1	19	122
2	25	125
3	30	126
4	42	129
5	46	130
6	52	135
7	57	138
8	62	142
9	70	145

1. First, we need to calculate the following values from the data:

$$\sum X = 403 \qquad\qquad \sum Y = 1192$$
$$\sum X^2 = 20{,}463 \qquad\qquad \bar{Y} = 132.44$$
$$\frac{(\sum X)^2}{N} = 18{,}046 \qquad\qquad \sum XY = 54461$$
$$\bar{X} = 44.78 \qquad\qquad \frac{\sum X \sum Y}{N} = 53375$$

2. Now we may proceed to compute b, the slope of the regression equation, as

$$b = \frac{\sum XY - (\sum X \sum Y/N)}{\sum X^2 - [(\sum X)^2/N]} = \frac{54,461 - 53,375}{20,463 - 18,046}$$
$$= \frac{1086}{2417} = 0.45.$$

3. Now we may make the appropriate substitutions in the regression equation as follows:

$$Y_p = \bar{Y} + b(X - \bar{X})$$
$$= 132.44 + 0.45(X - 44.78).$$

Therefore, for age 35, the predicted blood pressure would be

$$Y_p = 132.44 + 0.45(35 - 44.78) = 132.44 + 0.45(-9.78)$$
$$= 132.44 - 4.40 = 128.04,$$

and for age 50,

$$Y_p = 132.44 + 0.45(50 - 44.78) = 132.44 + 0.45(5.22)$$
$$= 132.44 + 2.35 = 134.79.$$

Figure 10.9 shows a series of nine points representing the magnitudes of the nine X and Y pairs. By plotting two additional points based on the co-ordinates (35, 128.04) and (50, 134.79), and drawing a line through these

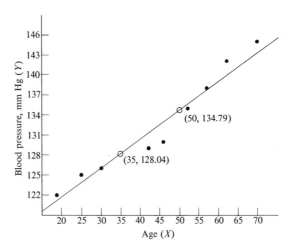

Fig. 10.9 Line of best fit based on Y-values predicted from ages 35 and 50.

points, we obtain the regression line, or "line of best fit." It will be recalled that this regression line contains all the *predicted* *Y*-values. Note that the slope of this line is positive; this is to be expected from the positive value of *b* in the preceding example.

Thus it may be seen that by using the regression equation, we have established the nature of the relationship between age and blood pressure, and we may also use this equation to predict the blood-pressure value associated with any specific age.

10.7 VARIANCE OF THE *Y*-VALUES AROUND THE REGRESSION LINE

It must by now be obvious that when two variables are imperfectly correlated, the regression line is *estimated* from the data, and predicted *Y*-values cannot be considered precise. Also, the lower the correlation, the less precise any estimate of *Y* will be.

We therefore need to provide a means of estimating actual *Y* from Y_p with specified confidence limits. This involves computing the variance of *Y* around the regression line of Y_p's, using the familiar variance relationship

$$S_{YX}^2 = \frac{\sum (Y - Y_p)^2}{N - 2}.$$

Note that in computing S_{YX}^2, two degrees of freedom are lost.

As is often the case, the harmless looking formula above is the most difficult to use in actual practice, particularly when working with large amounts of data. Algebraic manipulation yields a more formidable appearing but more practical formula:

$$S_{YX}^2 = \frac{(\sum Y^2 - (\sum Y)^2/N) - b(\sum XY - \sum X \sum Y/N)}{N - 2}.$$

Taking the square root of S_{YX}^2 yields S_{YX}, the standard deviation of *Y*'s around the regression line. Following the same procedure used in computing the standard error of the mean, the standard error of *Y* becomes

$$S_{\bar{Y}} = \frac{S_{YX}}{\sqrt{N}}.$$

Now we can use the familiar estimation formula

$$Y = Y_p \pm S_{\bar{Y}}(t),$$

where *t* is at the appropriate level (0.05 or 0.01) with $N - 2$ degrees of freedom.

Unfortunately, this procedure is reliable only for estimating Y-values from X when X is in the vicinity of $\bar{X}$. As we go further away from $\bar{X}$ the confidence interval becomes larger, as illustrated by the biconcave dotted line in Fig. 10.10. Therefore, when estimating Y-values from X-values that are some distance from $\bar{X}$, a correction formula should be applied when calculating the standard error. This may be done as follows:

$$S_Y^2(\text{corrected}) = S_{YX}^2\left[\frac{1}{N} + \frac{(X - \bar{X})^2}{\sum (X - \bar{X})^2}\right],$$

where the desired X-value is substituted in the expression, $(X - \bar{X})^2$.

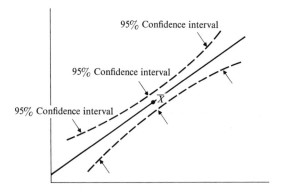

Fig. 10.10 Increasing confidence interval of Y as X deviates further from $\bar{X}$.

Example. Referring to the example involving age vs. blood pressure given in Section 10.6, suppose that we wish to estimate the actual Y from Y_p with 95% confidence limits based on an age of 65.

1. Using the regression equation computed in Section 10.6, we calculate Y_p as follows:

$$Y_p = \bar{Y} + b(X - \bar{X}) = 132.44 + 0.45(65 - 44.78)$$
$$= 132.44 + 0.45(20.22) = 132.44 + 9.10 = 141.54.$$

Thus we would predict from our data that an age of 65 would be associated with a blood pressure of 141.54 mm Hg.

2. Now we need to compute the variance of the actual Y-values around the regression line, or S_{YX}^2. To do this, we need two additional pieces of data, $\sum Y^2$ and $(\sum Y)^2/N$. Calculating these, we obtain

$$\sum Y^2 = 158{,}384, \qquad \frac{(\sum Y)^2}{N} = 157{,}874.$$

Then

$$S_{YX}^2 = \frac{(\sum Y^2 - (\sum Y)^2/N) - b(\sum XY - \sum X \sum Y/N)}{N - 2}$$

$$= \frac{(158,384 - 157,874) - 0.45(54,461 - 53,375)}{7}$$

$$= \frac{510 - 0.45(1086)}{7} = \frac{510 - 488.70}{7} = 3.04.$$

Then

$$S_{YX} = \sqrt{3.04} = 1.74,$$

and

$$S_{\bar{Y}} = \frac{1.74}{\sqrt{9}} = 0.58.$$

If our X-value were near the mean, we could proceed to substitute $S_{\bar{Y}} = 0.58$ in the estimation equation, but since 65 is a considerable distance from $\bar{X}$, we should compute the corrected $S_{\bar{Y}}$ as

$$S_{\bar{Y}}^2(\text{corrected}) = S_{YX}^2 \left[\frac{1}{N} + \frac{(X - \bar{X})^2}{\sum(X - \bar{X})^2} \right]$$

$$= 3.04 \left[\frac{1}{9} + \frac{(65 - 44.78)^2}{2417} \right]$$

$$= 3.04(0.28) = 0.85.$$

Then

$$S_{\bar{Y}} = \sqrt{S_{\bar{Y}}^2} = \sqrt{0.85} = 0.92.$$

Note that the corrected $S_{\bar{Y}}$ is larger than the 0.58 value obtained as the uncorrected $S_{\bar{Y}}$, and will therefore contribute to a larger confidence interval.

3. Looking up the appropriate two-tailed t-value in the 0.05 column with $N - 2$, or 7 degrees of freedom, we obtain $t = 2.36$. Now we may use the estimation equation as follows:

$$Y = Y_p \pm S_{\bar{Y}}(t) = 141.54 \pm 0.92(2.36) = 141.54 \pm 2.17.$$

4. We may therefore state that, given an age of 65, we would estimate with 95% confidence limits that the associated blood pressure value would be in the interval 139.37 to 143.71 mm Hg.

10.8 NONLINEAR RELATIONSHIPS

In this chapter we have assumed that the relationships involving correlation and regression were linear. In other words, a scatter diagram resulting from

Y plotted against *X* would be a straight line, or at least a roughly approximate straight line. This assumption is necessary if we are to be justified in applying the regression equation, which is itself a form of the basic linear equation, $Y = a + bX$.

In practice, biological data do not always take a linear form. The general pattern of population growth, for example, is represented by a curve similar to Fig. 10.11. Note that as time increases arithmetically, the population *N*

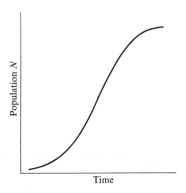

Fig. 10.11 General pattern of population growth.

increases geometrically until limiting factors such as food, oxygen, etc., begin to slow it down. This type of curve is rather common in biological work, and since we cannot apply the regression equation to a curve that is not linear, we need to apply a transformation that will literally straighten it out.

This is easily accomplished by substituting the appropriate logarithm value for each value of the data showing nonlinear change. The following example will demonstrate the use of this transformation procedure.

Example. The following data were obtained from periodic observations made on the growth of a population of yeast cells; the counts were taken every two hours.

Hours	Number of cells
2	19
4	37
6	72
8	142
10	295
12	584
14	995

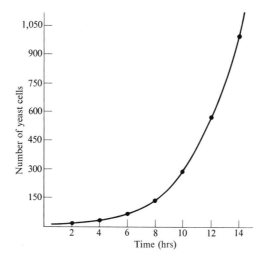

Fig. 10.12 Nonlinear curve resulting from number of yeast cells plotted against time.

1. Figure 10.12 shows the nonlinear curve which results when the cell number is plotted against time. Note that cell number increases exponentially while time increases arithmetically.

2. In order to "straighten out" the curve, we will substitute the common logarithm value for each cell count, yielding

Count	Log
19	1.2788
37	1.5682
72	1.8573
142	2.1523
295	2.4698
584	2.7664
995	2.9978

3. Figure 10.13 shows the curve resulting from plotting the log values of the cell counts against time. This new curve is linear in nature, permitting the application of the principles of linear regression considered in previous sections.

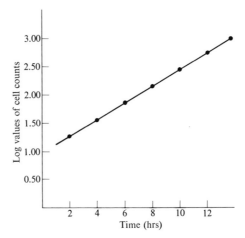

Fig. 10.13 Log values of yeast cell counts plotted against time.

10.9 SUMMARY

In this chapter we have seen two general ways to handle the data showing a linear relationship. First, we can measure the relative *intensity* of a relationship existing between two variables by computing a correlation coefficient. Second, we can establish a regression line which will allow us to *predict* the value of a Y-variable associated with a specific X-value. As usual, since we are rarely sure of anything, it is necessary to qualify this prediction by the use of confidence limits.

PROBLEMS

10.1 The X-variable in the data below represents the size of stomata in ferns, and the Y-variable represents the size of the spores produced by the same plant. Analyze these data for correlation between the sizes of stomata and spores. Data are expressed in millimicrons (see Section 10.3).

Plant	Stomata (X)	Spores (Y)
1	31	36
2	34	31
3	35	32
4	38	33
5	41	36
6	48	51
7	52	46
8	58	41

10.2 Given the following bivariate distribution, determine the correlation coefficient (see Section 10.3).

Number	X	Y
1	11	10
2	34	53
3	28	48
4	36	46
5	40	40
6	16	21
7	12	20
8	24	38
9	49	30
10	38	47

10.3 Given the following bivariate distribution, determine the coefficient of correlation between X and Y (see Section 10.3).

Number	X	Y
1	50	20
2	54	19
3	36	23
4	63	18
5	53	20
6	49	21
7	52	18
8	58	17
9	46	16
10	45	25

10.4 Referring to the correlation coefficient computed in Problem 2, test the hypothesis, H_0: $\rho = 0$ (see Section 10.4).

10.5 Referring to the correlation coefficient computed in Problem 3, test the hypothesis, H_0: $\rho = 0$ (see Section 10.4).

10.6 A bivariate distribution of $N = 52$ yields a correlation coefficient of 0.36. Estimate ρ with 95% confidence (see Section 10.5).

10.7 A sample correlation coefficient of 0.80 is computed from a sample of $N = 60$. Estimate ρ with 99% confidence (see Section 10.7).

10.8 A sample of 12 leaves is collected and the length and width of each leaf are measured. Use the data given below, where the measurements are in millimeters:
   a) Compute the correlation coefficient.
   b) Compute the regression line of Y on X.
   c) Compute the 95% confidence limits for the Y-value associated with $\bar{X}$.
(See Sections 10.6 and 10.7.)

Leaf	Width (X)	Length (Y)
1	35	55
2	21	44
3	25	46
4	35	60
5	26	55
6	40	57
7	35	64
8	40	68
9	25	51
10	42	61
11	23	46
12	25	44

10.9 A sample of 12 adult males provided the following bivariate data consisting of height and weight measurements.
   a) Compute the correlation coefficient.
   b) Compute the regression line of Y on X.
   c) Compute the 95% confidence limits for the weight value associated with a height of 63 in., using the corrected value for $S_{\bar{Y}}$.
(See Sections 10.6 and 10.7.)

Subject	Height (X)	Weight (Y)
1	62	112
2	63	144
3	64	130
4	65	160
5	66	143
6	67	128
7	68	138
8	69	176
9	70	150
10	71	185
11	72	170
12	73	168

11
ANALYSIS OF COVARIANCE

11.1 INTRODUCTION

In Chapter 8 we applied the analysis of variance to multiple group designs, and Chapter 10 included the concept of regression analysis. In this chapter, we will show an analysis of data by a technique which combines analysis of variance with the principles of regression analysis. This is called *analysis of covariance*, and it is a powerful statistical tool for attacking problems found in many areas of biological research.

Let us begin by posing a very simple problem. Suppose that we wish to compare two methods of teaching statistics in terms of performance on an examination. Two classes, randomly selected, will be taught by methods *A* and *B*, respectively. At the end of the course, we will compare the final examination scores achieved by the class taught by method *A* with those achieved by the class taught by method *B*. The results could then be analyzed by the usual method, either with a *t*-test or with analysis of variance.

Now, any conclusions drawn from this analysis will necessarily assume that the two groups were pretty much alike to begin with, at least as far as knowledge of statistics is concerned! In other words, if the results are to be considered valid, the students in each of the two classes must start the course with similar backgrounds. To carry this concept to the ultimate, what conclusions could be drawn if the "method *A*" group were composed of statisticians and the "method *B*" group contained only students who had never heard of the word?

Consider the following hypothetical sets of scores obtained on the examination:

Group A		Group B	
Student	Score	Student	Score
1	70	1	92
2	72	2	84
3	68	3	80
4	81	4	95
5	78	5	90

No statistical analysis is needed to see that group B obviously fared much better on the examination, and it would seem that method B has a great deal going for it!

But now, suppose that we had given the same examination as a pretest when the course was just beginning, and further suppose the results listed in Table 11.1.

Table 11.1

Student	Group A		Student	Group B	
	Pretest (X_A)	Post-test (Y_A)		Pretest (X_B)	Post-test (Y_B)
1	45	70	1	60	92
2	40	72	2	61	84
3	38	68	3	58	80
4	54	81	4	73	95
5	42	78	5	71	90

From this somewhat extreme example, it is now clear that comparing group A with group B is like putting the author in the ring with the heavyweight champion of the world! It is therefore apparent that no conclusion can be drawn concerning the comparative efficiency of the two methods of teaching statistics.

This same concept can easily be applied to such variables as blood pressure, cholesterol content, plot production, and a host of situations found in biological experimentation. If, for example, we wish to compare fertilizers by comparing the yields of treated plots, it is apparent that the differential effects of *previous* fertilizer treatments must be considered. In general, we could more accurately evaluate treatment effects of various kinds if we could take into consideration the value of the variable found in each subject *before* the treatment is applied. This would be especially useful when working with biological data, where values are often questionable.

The analysis of covariance makes use of ancillary information in the form of pretreatment data in order to compensate for the effects of prior treatment or the pretreatment condition. This pretreatment measurement is usually called the concomitant variable, or control variable. It may be seen that such control variables are essentially *predictors* of post-treatment measurements.

11.2 RATIONALE UNDERLYING ANALYSIS OF COVARIANCE

Suppose that we wish to compare the effects of two different diets on the weights of mice. We shall use five mice/diet, keeping the number small so the arithmetic will be less tedious.

We could, of course, simply randomize the assignment of the 10 mice to the diets, and statistically compare their weights after a specific time period, using the unmatched *t*-test or analysis of variance. Suppose that we were to do this, and further suppose that we obtain the following set of post-treatment weights in grams:

Diet *A*	Diet *B*
80	54
51	78
78	59
81	61
72	78

Now, it would be useful to know what each of these subjects weighed before the diet treatment, since the final weight of each mouse will quite obviously be affected in part by what the mouse weighed in the first place! Suppose that we had kept just such a record, and we can now add this pre-treatment weight to the data. Our complete set of data would then appear as follows, where the *X*'s are the pretreatment weights, or concomitant variable, and the *Y*'s are the post-treatment weights.

Diet A		Diet B	
X_A	Y_A	X_B	Y_B
60	80	42	54
38	51	52	78
54	78	45	59
55	81	43	61
50	72	50	78
$\bar{X}_A = 51.40$	$\bar{Y}_A = 72.40$	$\bar{X}_B = 46.40$	$\bar{Y}_B = 66.00$

It is fairly obvious that a correlation exists between pretreatment weights (X) and post-treatment weights (Y). This is confirmed by the scatter diagram shown in Fig. 11.1.

It is therefore apparent that the postdiet weights are influenced by initial weights as well as by diet effects. It is further apparent that a more accurate comparison might be made if we were to adjust the postdiet weights according to the prediet values. In other words, we could adjust the Y-values on the basis of the initial advantage or disadvantage possessed by the individual animal.

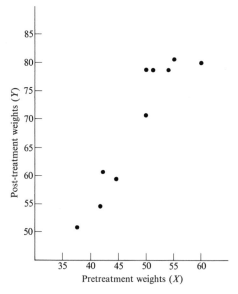

Fig. 11.1 Scatter diagram showing correlation between pre- and post-treatment weights.

This could be done by con puting a regression coefficient which is based on the relationship between the X's and Y's in the total distribution. Computing this regression coefficient by the method described in Chapter 10, we obtain $b = 1.61$. Now, computing the mean of all 10 X-values yields 48.90. We may now determine the initial advantage or disadvantage in each case by multiplying the regression coefficient, 1.61, by the difference between each prediet weight and the mean of all prediet weights, 48.90. Where the initial weight is *above* the mean, we will subtract the initial advantage from the associated postdiet weight. Where the initial weight is *less* than the mean of all initial weights, we will add the initial disadvantage to the associated postdiet value. In this way we may *adjust* the Y-values for initial weights; in other words, we tend to negate pretreatment advantages or disadvantages that might be present.

The results of this adjusting procedure are listed in Table 11.2.

Table 11.2

Diet A X_A	Y_A	Y_A adj.
$60 - 48.90 \times 1.61 = 17.87$	80	62.13
$38 - 48.90 \times 1.61 = 17.55$	51	68.55
$54 - 48.90 \times 1.61 = 8.21$	78	69.79
$55 - 48.90 \times 1.61 = 9.82$	81	71.18
$50 - 48.90 \times 1.61 = 1.77$	72	70.23

Diet B X_B	Y_B	Y_B adj.
$42 - 48.90 \times 1.61 = 11.11$	54	65.11
$52 - 48.90 \times 1.61 = 4.99$	78	73.01
$45 - 48.90 \times 1.61 = 6.28$	59	65.28
$43 - 48.90 \times 1.61 = 9.50$	61	70.50
$50 - 48.90 \times 1.61 = 1.77$	78	76.23

We could now perform analysis of variance on the *adjusted* Y-values, and the resulting F-value could be assumed free from bias due to initial weights.

As is so often the case in statistics, this "simple" approach is obviously tedious, even with the unrealistically small amount of data used in the illustration. As usual, we will look for a method that will accomplish the same end result, but with less time and effort.

This time, we shall begin by plotting a regression line based on the same bivariate data shown in the preceding illustration. A review of Chapter 10 shows that we can predict the Y-value (Y_p) that will be associated with a specific X-value by using the regression equation,

$$Y_p = \bar{Y} + b(X - \bar{X}).$$

Figure 11.2 shows a regression line formed by the Y_p-values which were predicted from the weights taken before the treatment. The Y-values, or *actual* post-treatment weights, are also shown, together with the distance of each actual Y-value from its associated Y_p, or *predicted* value. The distances between the Y and Y_p-values are often called the *residuals*.

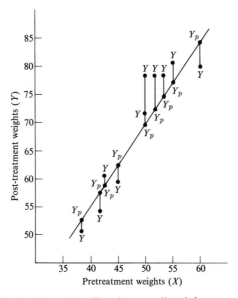

Fig. 11.2 Regression line formed by Y_p-values predicted from pretreatment weights.

Now we come to the essential rationale underlying the technique of covariance. The total variability in Y consists of two elements: (1) the variability in Y due to the variability in X, and (2) the variability in Y that is due to the components involving treatment and experimental error. It may be seen that if we can remove that variability in Y due to the variability in X, we could then analyze the resulting data in terms of treatment and error. This data would be uncontaminated, as it were, by the influence of the pretreatment values.

Now, expressing this idea in the form of an equation, we have

$$\sum (Y - \bar{Y})^2 = \sum (Y_p - \bar{Y})^2 + \sum (Y - Y_p)^2,$$

which, symbolically, states that the total variability in Y is equal to the variability in Y predicted from the variability in X, plus the variability in Y that is *not* predicted from X. Since it is this latter variability which is of interest, we shall rearrange the equation so that we have

$$\sum (Y - Y_p)^2 = \sum (Y - \bar{Y})^2 - \sum (Y_p - \bar{Y})^2.$$

Since the expression $\sum (Y_p - \bar{Y})^2$ represents the variability in Y due to pretreatment, or X-values, and since it may be predicted from those X-values, we simply need to assess this predicted variability and remove it from the total variability in Y. To do this, we need to recall that the regression coefficient is computed as

$$b = \frac{\sum (X - \bar{X})(Y - \bar{Y})}{\sum (X - \bar{X})^2}$$

or, in deviation form,

$$b = \frac{\sum xy}{\sum x^2}.$$

Now, since

$$(Y_p - \bar{Y}) = b(X - \bar{X}),$$

a little algebraic monkey business leads to the following equation:

$$\sum (Y - Y_p)^2 = \sum (Y - \bar{Y})^2 - b \sum xy,$$

where the expression $b \sum xy$ has been substituted as an identity to $\sum (Y_p - \bar{Y})^2$.

This is the critical equation of covariance, and is used to compute the variability in Y due to X, so that it may be removed from the total variability in Y. This leaves $\sum (Y - Y_p)^2$, which is the variability in Y due to the influence of treatment and error.

It will be recalled that in performing the analysis of variance, we separated the variability of Y into two components: (1) the variability due to treatment effect, and (2) the variability due to experimental error, or sampling error. Our next step in covariance, then, is to partition the remaining variability in Y into two similar components. The significance of the treatment effect can then be assessed in the usual manner by the F-ratio.

11.3 SINGLE CLASSIFICATION ANALYSIS OF COVARIANCE

In the preceding section, we discussed the theoretical basis underlying covariance. Now we will get down to practical matters involving the application of this technique. As an illustration, we will work through a single classification analysis in a step-by-step fashion, using an extension of the mouse diet problem.

Example. An experiment using two randomly assigned groups of mice was performed to determine the comparative effects of diet A and diet B. The pretreatment weights were recorded and the final weights were determined after a specified treatment time, resulting in the data listed in Table 11.3.

Table 11.3

	Diet A			Diet B	
	Prediet	Postdiet		Prediet	Postdiet
Animal	X_A	Y_A	Animal	X_B	Y_B
1	60	80	1	58	81
2	55	81	2	46	58
3	54	78	3	50	75
4	50	72	4	39	60
5	38	51	5	41	59
6	42	54	6	45	60
7	50	78	7	42	58
8	45	59	8	55	72
9	43	61	9	52	75
10	52	78	10	45	57
	$\bar{X}_A = 48.90$	$\bar{Y}_A = 69.20$		$\bar{X}_B = 47.30$	$\bar{Y}_B = 65.50$

1. The first step in the analysis involves the computation of several "pieces" of data. This may appear somewhat tedious at first, but with a desk calculator it may be done rather quickly. The data needed, with their numerical values, are:

$$\sum XY = 65{,}943 \qquad \sum X = 962 \qquad \sum Y = 1347$$
$$\sum X^2 = 47{,}052 \qquad \sum X_A = 489 \qquad \sum Y_A = 692$$
$$\sum Y^2 = 92{,}769 \qquad \sum X_B = 473 \qquad \sum Y_B = 655$$
$$N = 20 \qquad k_A = 10 \qquad k_B = 10$$

Note that the absence of a subscript indicates the sum of *all* X's, Y's, or XY cross products. The subscript is used to indicate the specific treatment with which the value is concerned. For example, the sum of all X's involved with diet A is symbolized by $\sum X_A$.

2. Next, we partition the total S.S. of X-values into S.S. for diet and S.S. for within, or error:

$$\text{S.S.}_{\text{total}} = \Sigma X^2 - \frac{(\Sigma X)^2}{N} = 47{,}052 - \frac{(962)^2}{20}$$

$$= 47{,}052 - 46{,}272 = 780,$$

$$\text{S.S.}_{\text{diet}} = \frac{(\Sigma X_A)^2}{k_A} + \frac{(\Sigma X_B)^2}{k_B} - \frac{(\Sigma X)^2}{N}$$

$$= \frac{(489)^2}{10} + \frac{(473)^2}{10} - \frac{(962)^2}{20}$$

$$= 46{,}285 - 46{,}272 = 13,$$

$$\text{S.S.}_{\text{within}} = \text{S.S.}_{\text{total}} - \text{S.S.}_{\text{diet}} = 780 - 13 = 767.$$

3. Next, we partition the total S.S. for the Y-variable into S.S. for diet and S.S. for within:

$$\text{S.S.}_{\text{total}} = \Sigma Y^2 - \frac{(\Sigma Y)^2}{N} = 92{,}769 - \frac{(1347)^2}{20}$$

$$= 92{,}769 - 90{,}720 = 2049,$$

$$\text{S.S.}_{\text{diet}} = \frac{(\Sigma Y_A)^2}{k_A} + \frac{(\Sigma Y_B)^2}{k_B} - \frac{(\Sigma Y)^2}{N}$$

$$= \frac{(692)^2}{10} + \frac{(655)^2}{10} - \frac{(1347)^2}{20}$$

$$= 90{,}789 - 90{,}720 = 69,$$

$$\text{S.S.}_{\text{within}} = \text{S.S.}_{\text{total}} - \text{S.S.}_{\text{diet}} = 2049 - 69 = 1980.$$

4. Now we partition the S.S. for cross products (XY) into S.S. for diet and S.S. for within:

$$\text{S.S.}_{\text{total}} = \Sigma XY - \frac{\Sigma X \Sigma Y}{N}$$

$$= 65{,}943 - \frac{(962)(1347)}{20} = 1152,$$

$$\text{S.S.}_{\text{diet}} = \frac{(\Sigma X_A)(\Sigma Y_A)}{k_A} + \frac{(\Sigma X_B)(\Sigma Y_B)}{k_B} - \frac{\Sigma X \Sigma Y}{N}$$

$$= \frac{(489)(692)}{10} + \frac{(473)(655)}{10} - \frac{(962)(1347)}{20} = 30,$$

$$\text{S.S.}_{\text{within}} = \text{S.S.}_{\text{total}} - \text{S.S.}_{\text{diet}} = 1152 - 30 = 1122.$$

5. Now we set up a table containing the computed S.S. as follows:

Source	S.S.(X)	S.S.(Y)	S.S.(XY)
Total	780	2049	1152
Diet	13	69	30
Within	767	1980	1122

6. Next, we add the within S.S. in each case to the diet S.S. This yields "within plus diet" values:

$$\begin{array}{ccc} \text{S.S.}(X) & \text{S.S.}(Y) & \text{S.S.}(XY) \\ 780 & 2049 & 1152 \end{array}$$

7. Now we compute the regression coefficient for the "within plus diet" values. This is done by the use of the formula

$$b = \frac{\sum xy}{\sum x^2},$$

where "$\sum xy$" is another way of expressing S.S.(XY), and "$\sum x^2$" is another symbol for S.S.(X). Thus

$$b = \frac{1152}{780} = 1.48.$$

8. Now we apply the basic covariance equation. This allows the removal of the variability in Y that is due to, and predicted from, the variability in X. Thus

$$\begin{aligned} \sum (Y - Y_p)^2 &= \sum (Y - \bar{Y})^2 - b\sum xy \\ &= 2049 - (1.48)(1152) \\ &= 2049 - 1705 = 344. \end{aligned}$$

9. Next, we perform the same operation for the "within" sum of squares in order to assess the experimental error when the variability due to X is removed. Thus

$$b = \frac{\sum xy}{\sum x^2} = \frac{1122}{767} = 1.46$$

and

$$\begin{aligned} \sum (Y - Y_p)^2 &= \sum (Y - \bar{Y})^2 - b\sum xy \\ &= 1980 - (1.46)(1122) \\ &= 1980 - 1638 = 342. \end{aligned}$$

10. To determine degrees of freedom associated with each source, we begin by subtracting one from the total, leaving 19. Now we subtract one degree of freedom associated with the control variable (X) and one degree of freedom associated with the main effect from 19. This yields 17 as the degrees of freedom associated with the within, or error effect. Thus we have

Source	D.F.	S.S.	M.S.
Diet	1	2	2.00
Within	17	342	20.12
Within + diet		344	

Note that the S.S. due to diet alone has been found by subtracting the residual S.S. for "within" from the S.S. for "within plus diet."

11. Computing the F-value in the usual way, we have

$$F = \frac{\text{M.S.(diet)}}{\text{M.S.(within)}} = \frac{2.00}{20.12} = 0.099,$$

and since the obtained F is below unity, we automatically assume a lack of significance. Therefore, we must conclude that our experimental and statistical evidence does not support a contention that diet A and diet B produce significantly different effects in terms of final weights.

11.4 COVARIANCE APPLIED TO A FACTORIAL DESIGN

In the previous section, analysis of covariance was applied to a single factor design. In this section the covariance technique will be applied to a more complicated situation involving a factorial design. The principles related to factorial designs that were discussed in Chapter 8 also apply here, and the similarity of the computational procedure to that of analysis of variance should again be noted.

Example. An investigator wishes to test three special diets in terms of their differential effects on reducing cholesterol content. In addition, he wishes to test the effect of a drug on cholesterol content, and finally, he is interested in the presence of possible interaction effects between the diet and the drug. He therefore designs a factorial experiment, where the three diets are the levels of one factor, and the drug and a placebo are the levels of the other factor. Thirty adult males are randomly assigned in groups of five to each

Table 11.4

	Diet A		Diet B		Diet C			
	X_{AP}	Y_{AP}	X_{BP}	Y_{BP}	X_{CP}	Y_{CP}		
Placebo	180	145	190	150	190	150		
	195	150	185	155	180	140		
	205	160	200	150	190	160		
	200	155	190	150	185	150		
	195	150	185	140	185	150		
	$\bar{X}_{AP} = 195.00$ $\bar{Y}_{AP} = 152.00$		$\bar{X}_{BP} = 190.00$ $\bar{Y}_{BP} = 149.00$		$\bar{X}_{CP} = 186.00$ $\bar{Y}_{CP} = 150.00$		$\bar{X}_P = 190.33$ $\bar{Y}_P = 150.33$	
	X_{AD}	Y_{AD}	X_{BD}	Y_{BD}	X_{CD}	Y_{CD}		
Drug	195	145	200	160	185	145		
	210	155	195	150	195	155		
	195	140	190	140	205	160		
	200	160	195	150	175	140		
	180	140	190	155	185	140		
	$\bar{X}_{AD} = 197.60$ $\bar{Y}_{AD} = 148.00$		$\bar{X}_{BD} = 194.00$ $\bar{Y}_{BD} = 151.00$		$\bar{X}_{CD} = 189.00$ $\bar{Y}_{CD} = 148.00$		$\bar{X}_D = 193.53$ $\bar{Y}_D = 149.67$	
	$\bar{X}_A = 196.80$ $\bar{Y}_A = 150.00$		$\bar{X}_B = 192.00$ $\bar{Y}_B = 150.00$		$\bar{X}_C = 187.50$ $\bar{Y}_C = 149.00$			

of the combinations of factors. Subjects were chosen from a limited age range to minimize the effect of age on cholesterol content. The cholesterol content of all subjects was measured before and after treatment, and Table 11.4 shows the general design along with the raw data, where cholesterol content is measured in grams/100 ml serum. Note that the subscripts are descriptive in terms of the factor or combination of factors involved.

1. Before starting the actual computations, we shall first code the raw data by subtracting 140 from each value. This makes the work easier, even when using a calculator. Remember, subtracting a constant from each member of a distribution in no way changes the variance of that distribution; therefore we can base our computations on the coded data listed in Table 11.5.

2. Again, we need to begin by computing several "pieces" of data, as follows:

$$
\begin{array}{lll}
\sum XY = 16{,}100 & \sum X = 1558 & \sum Y = 290 \\
\sum X^2 = 82{,}804 & \sum X_A = 563 & \sum Y_A = 100 \\
\sum Y^2 = 4200 & \sum X_B = 520 & \sum Y_B = 100 \\
N = 30 & \sum X_C = 475 & \sum Y_C = 90 \\
& \sum X_D = 803 & \sum Y_D = 135 \\
& \sum X_P = 755 & \sum Y_P = 155 \\
& \sum X_{AP} = 275 & \sum Y_{AP} = 60 \\
& \sum X_{BP} = 250 & \sum Y_{BP} = 45 \\
& \sum X_{CP} = 230 & \sum Y_{CP} = 50 \\
& \sum X_{AD} = 288 & \sum Y_{AD} = 40 \\
& \sum X_{BD} = 270 & \sum Y_{BD} = 55 \\
& \sum X_{CD} = 245 & \sum Y_{CD} = 40 \\
\end{array}
$$

Again, it should be noted that no subscript indicates that *all* X or Y variables are involved.

3. Next, we partition the S.S. for the X-variable into the S.S. for diet, the S.S. for drug, the S.S. for interaction, and the S.S. for within, or error. Thus

$$
\text{S.S.}_{\text{total}} = \sum X^2 - \frac{(\sum X)^2}{N} = 82{,}804 - \frac{(1558)^2}{30}
$$

$$
= 82{,}804 - 80{,}912 = 1892,
$$

$$
\text{S.S.}_{\text{diet}} = \frac{(\sum X_A)^2}{k_A} + \frac{(\sum X_B)^2}{k_B} + \frac{(\sum X_C)^2}{k_C} - \frac{(\sum X)^2}{N}
$$

$$
= \frac{(563)^2}{10} + \frac{(520)^2}{10} + \frac{(475)^2}{10} - \frac{(1558)^2}{30}
$$

$$
= 81{,}299 - 80{,}912 = 387,
$$

$$S.S._{\text{drug}} = \frac{(\sum X_D)^2}{k_D} + \frac{(\sum X_P)^2}{k_P} - \frac{(\sum X)^2}{N}$$

$$= \frac{(803)^2}{15} + \frac{(755)^2}{15} - \frac{(1558)^2}{30}$$

$$= 80{,}989 - 80{,}912 = 77,$$

$$S.S._{\text{interaction}} = \frac{(\sum X_{AP})^2}{k_{AP}} + \frac{(\sum X_{BP})^2}{k_{BP}} + \frac{(\sum X_{CP})^2}{k_{CP}}$$

$$+ \frac{(\sum X_{AD})^2}{k_{AD}} + \frac{(\sum X_{BD})^2}{k_{BD}} + \frac{(\sum X_{CD})^2}{k_{CD}}$$

$$- \frac{(\sum X)^2}{N} - (S.S._{\text{drug}} + S.S._{\text{diet}})$$

$$= \frac{(275)^2}{5} + \frac{(250)^2}{5} - \frac{(230)^2}{5} + \frac{(288)^2}{5}$$

$$+ \frac{(270)^2}{5} + \frac{(245)^2}{5} - \frac{(1558)^2}{30} - (77 + 387)$$

$$= 81{,}379 - 80{,}912 - (77 + 387) = 3,$$

$$S.S._{\text{within}} = S.S._{\text{total}} - (S.S._{\text{drug}} + S.S._{\text{diet}} + S.S._{\text{interaction}})$$

$$= 1892 - (77 + 387 + 3) = 1425.$$

Table 11.5

Diet A		Diet B		Diet C	
X_{AP}	Y_{AP}	X_{BP}	Y_{BP}	X_{CP}	Y_{CP}
40	5	50	10	50	10
55	10	45	15	40	0
65	20	60	10	50	20
60	15	50	10	45	10
55	10	45	0	45	10
X_{AD}	Y_{AD}	X_{BD}	Y_{BD}	X_{CD}	Y_{CD}
55	5	60	20	45	5
70	15	55	10	55	15
55	0	50	0	65	20
60	20	55	10	35	0
48	0	50	15	45	0

4. Next, we partition the S.S. for the Y-variable into the S.S. for diet, the S.S. for drug, the S.S. for interaction, and the S.S. for within, or error. Thus

$$S.S._{total} = \sum Y^2 - \frac{(\sum Y)^2}{N} = 4200 - \frac{(290)^2}{30}$$

$$= 4200 - 2804 = 1396,$$

$$S.S._{diet} = \frac{(\sum Y_A)^2}{k_A} + \frac{(\sum Y_B)^2}{k_B} + \frac{(\sum Y_C)^2}{k_C} - \frac{(\sum Y)^2}{N}$$

$$= \frac{(100)^2}{10} + \frac{(100)^2}{10} + \frac{(90)^2}{10} - \frac{(290)^2}{30}$$

$$= 2810 - 2804 = 6,$$

$$S.S._{drug} = \frac{(\sum Y_D)^2}{k_D} + \frac{(\sum Y_P)^2}{k_P} - \frac{(\sum Y)^2}{N}$$

$$= \frac{(135)^2}{15} + \frac{(155)^2}{15} - \frac{(290)^2}{30}$$

$$= 2817 - 2804 = 13,$$

$$S.S._{interaction} = \frac{(\sum Y_{AP})^2}{k_{AP}} + \frac{(\sum Y_{BP})^2}{k_{BP}} + \frac{(\sum Y_{CP})^2}{k_{CP}}$$

$$+ \frac{(\sum Y_{AD})^2}{k_{AD}} + \frac{(\sum Y_{BD})^2}{k_{BD}} + \frac{(\sum Y_{CD})^2}{k_{CD}}$$

$$- \frac{(\sum Y)^2}{N} - (S.S._{drug} + S.S._{diet})$$

$$= \frac{(60)^2}{5} + \frac{(45)^2}{5} + \frac{(50)^2}{5} + \frac{(40)^2}{5}$$

$$+ \frac{(55)^2}{5} + \frac{(40)^2}{5} - 2804 - (6 + 13)$$

$$= 2870 - 2804 - (6 + 13) = 47,$$

$$S.S._{within} = S.S._{total} - (S.S._{drug} + S.S._{diet} + S.S._{interaction})$$

$$= 1396 - (6 + 13 + 47) = 1330.$$

5. Finally, we partition the S.S. for the cross products (XY) into the S.S. for diet, the S.S. for drug, the S.S. for interaction, and the S.S. for within, or error. Thus

$$S.S._{total} = \sum XY - \frac{\sum X \sum Y}{N} = 16,100 - \frac{(1558)(290)}{30}$$

$$= 16,100 - 15,061 = 1039,$$

$$\text{S.S.}_{\text{diet}} = \frac{\Sigma X_A \Sigma Y_A}{k_A} + \frac{\Sigma X_B \Sigma Y_B}{k_B} + \frac{\Sigma X_C \Sigma Y_C}{k_C} - \frac{\Sigma X \Sigma Y}{N}$$

$$= \frac{(563)(100)}{10} + \frac{(520)(100)}{10} + \frac{(475)(90)}{10} - \frac{(1558)(290)}{30}$$

$$= 5630 + 5200 + 4266 - 15{,}061$$

$$= 15{,}096 - 15{,}061 = 35,$$

$$\text{S.S.}_{\text{drug}} = \frac{\Sigma X_D \Sigma Y_D}{k_D} + \frac{\Sigma X_P \Sigma Y_P}{k_P} - \frac{\Sigma X \Sigma Y}{N}$$

$$= \frac{(803)(135)}{15} + \frac{(755)(155)}{15} - \frac{(1558)(290)}{30}$$

$$= 7227 + 7802 - 15{,}061$$

$$= 15{,}029 - 15{,}061 = -32,$$

$$\text{S.S.}_{\text{interaction}} = \frac{\Sigma X_{AP} \Sigma Y_{AP}}{k_{AP}} + \frac{\Sigma X_{BP} \Sigma Y_{BP}}{k_{BP}} + \frac{\Sigma X_{CP} \Sigma Y_{CP}}{k_{CP}}$$

$$+ \frac{\Sigma X_{AD} \Sigma Y_{AD}}{k_{AD}} + \frac{\Sigma X_{BD} \Sigma Y_{BD}}{k_{BD}}$$

$$+ \frac{\Sigma X_{CD} \Sigma Y_{CD}}{k_{CD}} - \frac{\Sigma X \Sigma Y}{N}$$

$$- (\text{S.S.}_{\text{diet}} + \text{S.S.}_{\text{drug}})$$

$$= \frac{(275)(60)}{5} + \frac{(250)(45)}{5} + \frac{(230)(50)}{5}$$

$$+ \frac{(288)(40)}{5} + \frac{(270)(55)}{5} + \frac{(245)(40)}{5}$$

$$- \frac{(1558)(290)}{30} - (35 - 32)$$

$$= 15{,}084 - 15{,}061 - (35 - 32) = 20,$$

$$\text{S.S.}_{\text{within}} = \text{S.S.}_{\text{total}} - (\text{S.S.}_{\text{diet}} + \text{S.S.}_{\text{drug}} + \text{S.S.}_{\text{interaction}})$$

$$= 1039 - (35 - 32 + 20) = 1016.$$

6. As before, we now set up a table containing the computed S.S.:

Source	S.S.(X)	S.S.(Y)	S.S.(XY)
Total	1892	1396	1039
Diet	387	6	35
Drug	77	13	-32
Interaction	3	47	20
Within	1425	1330	1016

7. Next, we add the within S.S. in each case to the appropriate source, yielding the "within plus effect" values:

Source	S.S.(X)	S.S.(Y)	S.S.(XY)
Diet	1812	1336	1051
Drug	1502	1343	984
Interaction	1428	1377	1036

8. Next, referring to the "within plus" values, we compute the S.S. for residuals in the case of each effect. In other words, we remove from the variability in Y that component of variability that is due to and predicted from X. Thus

Diet

$$b = \frac{\sum xy}{\sum x^2} = \frac{1051}{1812} = 0.580,$$

$$\sum (Y - Y_p)^2 = \sum (Y - \bar{Y})^2 - b \sum xy = 1336 - (0.580)(1051)$$
$$= 1336 - 610 = 726.$$

Drug

$$b = \frac{\sum xy}{\sum x^2} = \frac{984}{1502} = 0.655,$$

$$\sum (Y - Y_p)^2 = \sum (Y - \bar{Y})^2 - b \sum xy = 1343 - (0.655)(984)$$
$$= 1343 - 645 = 698.$$

Interaction

$$b = \frac{\sum xy}{\sum x^2} = \frac{1036}{1428} = 0.725,$$

$$\sum (Y - Y_p)^2 = \sum (Y - \bar{Y})^2 - b \sum xy = 1377 - (0.725)(1036)$$
$$= 1377 - 751 = 626.$$

9. Computing the S.S. for residuals for the "within," or error component, we have

$$b = \frac{\sum xy}{\sum x^2} = \frac{1016}{1425} = 0.712,$$

$$\sum (Y - Y_p)^2 = \sum (Y - \bar{Y})^2 - b \sum xy = 1330 - (0.712)(1016)$$
$$= 1330 - 723 = 607.$$

10. Now we are ready to compute the mean squares in order to perform the appropriate F-tests. To obtain the degrees of freedom in each case, we begin by subtracting one from the total, or, $30 - 1$, leaving 29. Since there are three diets, two degrees of freedom are associated with the diet effect. Since there are two drugs, one degree of freedom is associated with the drug effect. Multiplying 2 times 1 yields two degrees of freedom associated with interaction between the diet and the drug. Subtracting 2, 1, and 2 from 29 leaves 24. Then we subtract one degree of freedom associated with the control variable from 24, and we have 23 degrees of freedom associated with the within, or error component.

11. The analysis of variance table therefore appears as follows, where the residual sum of squares for within has been subtracted from the residual sum of squares for each "within plus effect" found in step 8.

	D.F.	S.S.	M.S.
Diet	2	119	59.50
Drug	1	91	91.00
Interaction	2	19	9.50
Within	23	607	26.39

12. Computing the F-values, we have

$$F_{2,23}(\text{diet}) = \frac{\text{M.S.(diet)}}{\text{M.S.(within)}} = \frac{59.50}{26.39} = 2.25,$$

$$F_{1,23}(\text{drug}) = \frac{\text{M.S.(drug)}}{\text{M.S.(within)}} = \frac{91.00}{26.39} = 3.45,$$

$$F_{2,23}(\text{interaction}) = \frac{\text{M.S.(interaction)}}{\text{M.S.(within)}} = \frac{9.50}{26.39} = 0.36.$$

13. Consulting Table VII, we find that none of the F-values are significant at the 0.05 level. We must therefore conclude that no significant difference exists among diets A, B, and C, in terms of effect on cholesterol content. Similarly, we must conclude that the drug did not significantly lower the cholesterol content of the drug group below that of the placebo group. Finally, we have found no evidence of interaction between the diet and the drug.

11.5 SUMMARY

It may be seen from the foregoing material that covariance is a very useful and powerful statistical tool. It should also be noted that while the computations are admittedly somewhat lengthy, they are not as difficult as they first appear, providing the procedure is worked through in a step-by-step fashion.

The basic similarity to analysis of variance should be noted. In fact, the assumptions underlying the analysis of variance also apply to covariance. Treatment effects, for example, should be constant and additive, and the experimenter would do well to check the variances for homogeneity before proceeding with the analysis.

In addition, when designing experiments to which covariance is to be applied, *it is very important to make certain that the control variable used is not in any way affected by the treatment.* This would quite obviously destroy any effectiveness of the control variable in terms of the theory underlying analysis of covariance.

Further uses of covariance will be found in books listed in the bibliography.

PROBLEMS

11.1 An experiment to compare two drugs, A and B, in terms of their effectiveness in lowering systolic blood pressure, yielded the following data.

A		B	
X_A (Predrug)	Y_A (Postdrug)	X_B (Predrug)	Y_B (Postdrug)
160	151	150	127
145	138	146	133
149	139	150	132
170	168	180	165
150	147	170	154
175	170	165	150
190	182	172	162
160	162	155	150
180	170	160	142
172	161	165	147

Twenty subjects were randomly assigned to two groups of 10 each. The blood pressures of both groups were measured both prior to and following drug administration. Analyze the data for significant difference between the drugs (see Section 11.3).

11.2 Analyze the following data for significant differences among Treatments I, II, and III (see Section 11.3).

Treatment I		Treatment II		Treatment III	
X_1	Y_1	X_2	Y_2	X_3	Y_3
80	96	61	40	73	39
64	76	59	79	44	22
57	63	60	61	48	32
51	76	53	47	51	57
57	88	56	69	43	28
		50	49	50	47
		45	40	41	13
				51	56
				62	22

11.3 A sample was randomly drawn from each of two ethnic groups in order to determine whether a significant difference in cholesterol content existed between the groups. All subjects were males, and the factor of age was used as a concomitant variable on which to base an adjustment of Y. Analyze the following data for significant difference between the two groups in terms of cholesterol content (see Section 11.3).

Group I		Group II	
Age (X_1)	Cholesterol (Y_1)	Age (X_2)	Cholesterol (Y_2)
45	175	20	130
52	220	44	175
37	180	32	176
68	240	76	240
55	254	50	222
34	196	42	220
72	340	46	190
43	112	59	240
60	175	61	340
40	188	24	181

11.4 An experiment was performed to compare the effects of two factors and to determine the degree of interaction. One factor consisted of Treatments A and B, and the other factor was sex. Measurements were taken before and after treatment and there were five replications per combination of factors. Analyze the following data for significance involving (1) treatment, (2) sex, and (3) interaction between the treatment and sex (see Section 11.4).

| Treatment A | | | | Treatment B | | | |
| Males | | Females | | Males | | Females | |
X_A	Y_A	X_A	Y_A	X_B	Y_B	X_B	Y_B
12	40	11	60	18	54	25	64
15	53	20	75	18	55	14	61
26	63	6	58	14	66	5	53
28	58	25	63	16	54	15	60
12	54	8	54	6	49	20	55

Appendix A
BIBLIOGRAPHY

The following books are suggested for additional reading. The list is divided into two parts: (1) those recommended for collateral reading with the present text, and (2) those recommended for further exploration of statistical and experimental procedures.

Recommended for collateral reading:

Alder, H. L., and Roessler, E. B., *Introduction to Probability and Statistics*. San Francisco: W. H. Freeman, 1964. While not designed primarily for biologists, this volume presents a lucid exposition of the basic concepts in statistics, with some well-done proofs for the more mathematically inclined. It contains a plentiful supply of problems.

Bancroft, H., *Introduction to Biostatistics*. New York: Harper and Row, 1965. Of special interest to those interested primarily in applications of statistics to medicine, this text is written especially for those who wish to avoid a rigorous mathematical treatment.

Bishop, O. N., *Statistics for Biology*. Boston: Houghton-Mifflin, 1966. This paperback presents very practical suggestions on handling experimental data. Mathematical treatment is minimized. The use of transformations is emphasized.

Franzblau, A. N., *A Primer of Statistics for Non-Statisticians*. New York: Harcourt, Brace, and World, 1958. This small, very well written book was written primarily for the statistics consumer, and provides easy reading for the student who is approaching the basic concepts for the first time.

Huff, D., *How to Lie With Statistics*. New York: W. W. Norton, 1954. This is a delightful and useful little book which describes some of the less creditable ways by which statistics are used—and misused. Written in an informal and entertaining style, it is a fascinating exposé of statistical chicanery.

Moroney, M. J., *Facts from Figures*. Baltimore: Penguin Books, 1956. A skillfully written paperback which is entertaining as well as informative. Its applications are general and cover a wide range of topics. Excellent for collateral reading.

Recommended for further reading:

Bliss, C. I., *Statistics in Biology*, Vol. I. New York: McGraw-Hill, 1967. A very comprehensive book, covering a wide variety of statistical techniques and applications to biological research. It is recommended as further reading beyond the level and scope of this text. Also, it contains many examples of data along with methods of handling special cases.

Goldstein, A., *Biostatistics, an Introductory Text*. New York: The Macmillan Co., 1964. This book is very readable, with excellent examples. It contains a good discussion of elementary principles of experimental design, and carries regression analysis into an excellent presentation of bio-assay methods.

Lewis, A. E., *Biostatistics*. New York: Reinhold, 1966. In addition to commonly used statistical methods, this volume also presents material on quality control and elements of sequential analysis.

Li, C. C., *Introduction to Experimental Statistics*. New York: McGraw-Hill, 1964. This book presents a wide range of experimental designs. Although it is above the level of this text, the first part offers an especially useful review of basic mathematics principles.

Simpson, G. G., A. Roe, and R. Lewontin, *Quantitative Zoology*. New York: Harcourt-Brace, 1960. Of special interest to zoologists, this text includes an excellent treatment of measurement associated with zoological data. It also treats graphic methods of presenting zoological data.

Wadley, F. M., *Experimental Statistics in Entomology*. Washington, D.C.: Graduate School Press, U.S. Department of Agriculture, 1967. This book presents experimental designs and statistical methods with special emphasis on problems of interest to the experimental entomologist. The emphasis is on practical applications.

Appendix B
SOLUTIONS TO EVEN-NUMBERED PROBLEMS

Chapter 1

1.2 (1)

X	x	x^2
6	-3	9
12	3	9
11	2	4
7	-2	4
8	-1	1
10	1	1
6	-3	9
12	3	9
9	0	0

$$\sum X = 81 \qquad\qquad \sum x^2 = 46$$
$$N = 9$$
$$\bar{X} = 9$$

(2)

$$S^2 = \frac{\sum x^2}{N} \qquad\qquad S = \sqrt{S^2}$$

$$= \tfrac{46}{9} \qquad\qquad\qquad = \sqrt{5.11}$$

$$= 5.11 \qquad\qquad\qquad = 2.26$$

1.4 (1)   Code by subtracting 66:

X	X_c	x_c	x_c^2
63	-3	-4	16
68	2	1	1
62	-4	-5	25
66	0	-1	1
68	2	1	1
67	1	0	0
63	-3	-4	16
70	4	3	9
69	3	2	4
73	7	6	36
68	2	1	1
67	1	0	0
	$\sum X_c = 12$		$\sum x_c^2 = 110$
	$N = 12$		

(2) $\bar{X}_c = \dfrac{\sum X_c}{N}$ $S^2 = \dfrac{\sum x_c^2}{N}$ $S = \sqrt{S^2}$

$= \frac{12}{12}$ $= \frac{110}{12}$ $= \sqrt{9.17}$

$= 1$ $= 9.17$ $= 3.03$

(3) $\bar{X} = 1 + 66$

$= 67$

1.6 (1)

	f	x_c	fx_c	x_c^2	fx_c^2
70–79	4	3	12	9	36
60–69	7	2	14	4	28
50–59	12	1	12	1	12
40–49	9	0	0	0	0
30–39	5	-1	-5	1	5
20–29	3	-2	-6	4	12

(2) $\sum fx_c = 27$ $N = 40$

$\sum fx_c^2 = 93$

$A \quad = 44.50$

(3) $\bar{X} = A + i\left(\dfrac{\sum fx_c}{N}\right) = 44.50 + 10(\frac{27}{40})$

$= 44.50 + 10(0.675) = 44.50 + 6.75 = 51.25$

(4) $\qquad S^2 = i^2\left[\dfrac{fx_c^2}{N} - \left(\dfrac{fx_c}{N}\right)^2\right]$

$\qquad = 100[\frac{93}{40} - (\frac{27}{40})^2]$

$\qquad = 100(2.33 - 0.456) = 100(1.87) = 187$

(5) $\qquad\qquad S = 13.67$

1.8

a. (1)

Class interval	f	x_c	fx_c	x_c^2	fx_c^2
81–83	2	4	8	16	32
78–80	3	3	9	9	27
75–77	5	2	10	4	20
72–74	8	1	8	1	8
69–71	12	0	0	0	0
66–68	8	−1	−8	1	8
63–65	6	−2	−12	4	24
60–62	4	−3	−12	9	36
57–59	2	−4	−8	16	32

$$\Sigma fx_c = -5 \qquad N = 50$$
$$\Sigma fx_c^2 = 187 \qquad i = 3$$
$$A = 70$$

(2) $\qquad \bar{X} = A + i\left(\dfrac{\Sigma fx_c}{N}\right) = 70 + 3\left(\dfrac{-5}{50}\right)$

$\qquad = 70 - 3(0.10) = 69.70$

(3) $\qquad S^2 = i^2\left[\dfrac{\Sigma fx_c^2}{N} - \left(\dfrac{\Sigma fx_c}{N}\right)^2\right]$

$\qquad = 9\left[\dfrac{187}{50} - \left(\dfrac{-5}{50}\right)^2\right]$

$\qquad = 9(3.64) = 32.76$

(4) $\qquad S = \sqrt{S^2} = \sqrt{32.76} = 5.72$

b. (1) $\qquad$ Compute: $\Sigma X^2 = 244{,}206$

$\qquad\qquad\qquad \Sigma X = 3482$

$\qquad\qquad\qquad N = 50$

(2) $\qquad S^2 = \dfrac{\Sigma X^2 - \dfrac{\Sigma X^2}{N}}{N}$

$\qquad = \dfrac{244{,}206 - \dfrac{(3482)^2}{50}}{50} = 34.40$

(3) $$S = \sqrt{S^2} = \sqrt{34.40} = 5.87$$

(4) $$\bar{X} = \frac{\Sigma X}{N} = \frac{3482}{50} = 69.64$$

Chapter 2

2.2

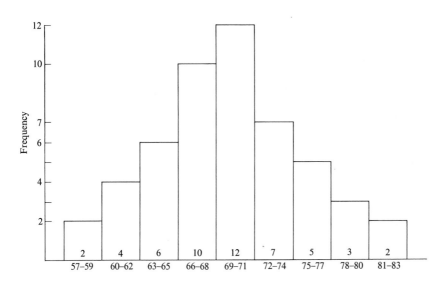

2.4

a. 43.32% of the curve is found between $\bar{X}$ and a standard score of 1.50. Subtracting 43.32% from 50.00% yields 6.68%.

b. Adding 50.00% to 43.32% yields 93.32%.

c. Subtracting 48.78% from 50.00% yields 1.22%.

d. Subtracting 47.50% from 50.00% yields 2.50%.

2.6

a. 19.15% of the curve is found between $\bar{X}$ and a standard score of 0.50. Adding 19.15% and 19.15% yields 38.30%.

b. Subtracting 39.44% from 43.32% yields 3.88%.

c. Subtracting 24.22% from 36.43% yields 12.21%.

d. Subtracting 41.92% from 45.05% yields 3.13%.

Chapter 3

3.2 $\frac{1}{6} \times \frac{1}{6} \times \frac{5}{6} = \frac{5}{216}$

3.4 (1) Both persons were produced from
$$Pp \times Pp$$
$$PP, Pp, Pp, pp$$

(2) Since they are both normal, the probability that each is a carrier (Pp) is $\frac{2}{3}$.

(3) $\frac{2}{3}Pp \times \frac{2}{3}Pp = \frac{4}{9}$

(4) If they are carriers, the probability they will have a PKU child (pp) is $\frac{1}{4}$.

(5) Therefore $\frac{4}{9} \times \frac{1}{4} = \frac{4}{36}$, or $\frac{1}{9}$.

3.6 (1) Since his mother was normal, the man's genotype must be Bb.

(2) Since the wife is normal, her genotype must be bb.

(3) Therefore $Bb \times bb$ yields Bb, Bb, bb, bb.

(4) The probability that any child produced will have brachydactyly is therefore $\frac{1}{2}$.

(5) The probability of all three children being brachydactylous is
$$\frac{1}{2} \times \frac{1}{2} \times \frac{1}{2} = \frac{1}{8}.$$

3.8

a. $\frac{2}{5} \times \frac{2}{5} = \frac{4}{25}$

b. $\frac{2}{5} \times \frac{1}{4} = \frac{2}{20}$, or $\frac{1}{10}$

3.10 (1) Zero heads $= (\frac{1}{2})^6 = \frac{1}{64}$

(2) One head $= (6!/1!\,5!)\frac{1}{2} \times (\frac{1}{2})^5 = \frac{6}{64}$

(3) Two heads $= (6!/2!\,4!)\,(\frac{1}{2})^2 \times (\frac{1}{2})^4 = \frac{15}{64}$

(4) At most two heads $= \frac{1}{64} + \frac{6}{64} + \frac{15}{64} = \frac{22}{64}$, or $\frac{11}{32}$

3.12 (1) $AaBb \times AaBb$ produces one out of 16 offspring with genotype $aabb$.

(2) Two $aabb = (3!/2!\,1!)(\frac{1}{16})^2(\frac{15}{16}) = \frac{45}{4096}$

(3) Three $aabb = (\frac{1}{16})^3 = \frac{1}{4096}$

(4) At least two $aabb = \frac{45}{4096} + \frac{1}{4096} = \frac{46}{4096}$, or $\frac{23}{2048}$

3.14 (1) $\bar{X} = np = \frac{1}{4}(100) = 25$

(2) $S = \sqrt{npq} = \sqrt{\frac{1}{4} \times \frac{3}{4} \times 100} = 4.33$

(3) $Z = \dfrac{45.5 - 25}{4.33} = 2.42$

(4) $Z(2.42) = 0.4922$

(5) $0.5000 + 0.4922 = 0.9922$

Chapter 4

4.2

a. $S^2 = \dfrac{\sum X^2 - (\sum X)^2/N}{N-1} = \dfrac{415{,}679 - 408{,}375}{14} = 521.71$

b. $S = \sqrt{S^2} = \sqrt{521.71} = 22.84$

4.4 $S_{\bar{X}} = S/\sqrt{N} = 14/\sqrt{49} = \frac{14}{7} = 2$

4.6

a. $\Sigma X = 2232$

$\bar{X} = \Sigma X/N = \frac{2232}{36} = 62$

b.   (1) $S^2 = \dfrac{\Sigma X^2 - (\Sigma X)^2/N}{N - 1}$

$= \dfrac{149{,}122 - (2232)^2/36}{35} = \dfrac{10{,}738}{35} = 306.80$

(2) $S = \sqrt{S^2} = \sqrt{306.80} = 17.52$

c. $S_{\bar{X}} = \dfrac{S}{\sqrt{N}} = \dfrac{17.52}{\sqrt{36}} = 2.92$

d. $\mu = \bar{X} \pm S_{\bar{X}}(1.96) = 62 \pm 2.92(1.96) = 62 \pm 5.72 = 56.28\text{--}67.72$

4.8   (1) $S_{\bar{X}} = \dfrac{S}{\sqrt{N}} = \dfrac{12}{\sqrt{36}} = 2$

(2) $\mu = \bar{X} \pm S_{\bar{X}}(2.58) = 82.50 \pm 2(2.58) = 82.50 \pm 5.16 = 77.34\text{--}87.66$

4.10   (1) $\sigma_{\bar{X}}(1.96) = 1.96$

$\sigma_{\bar{X}} = 1$

(2) $\sigma_{\bar{X}} = \sigma/\sqrt{N}$ $1 = 13/\sqrt{N}$

$\sqrt{N} = 13$ $N = 169$

4.12   (1) $S_{\bar{X}}(1.96) = 6.80$

$S_{\bar{X}} = 3.47$

(2) $S_{\bar{X}} = S/\sqrt{N}$ $3.47 = S/8$ $S = 27.26$

Chapter 5

5.2   (1) $P(vv) = \frac{1}{2};$ $P(Vv) = \frac{1}{2}$

(2) $\bar{X} = np = 20 \times \frac{1}{2} = 10$

(3) $S = \sqrt{npq} = \sqrt{\frac{1}{2} \times \frac{1}{2} \times 20} = \sqrt{5} = 2.23$

(4) $Z = \dfrac{11.5 - 10}{2.23} = 0.67$

(5) The probability of obtaining 12 or more vestigial-winged flies out of 20 is 0.25. The statistical evidence points to validity of the genetic model.

5.4 (1)
$$H_0: \mu - \bar{X} = 0$$

(2)
$$S_{\bar{X}} = \frac{S}{\sqrt{N}} = \frac{4}{\sqrt{40}} = 0.632$$

(3)
$$Z = \frac{\mu - \bar{X}}{S_{\bar{X}}} = \frac{20 - 18.50}{0.632} = 2.37$$

(4) Reject the null hypothesis beyond the 0.05 level, but not at the 0.01 level, using a one-tailed test.

5.6 (1)
$$H_0: \mu_1 - \mu_2 = 0$$

(2) $S_{\bar{X}_1 - \bar{X}_2} = \sqrt{S_1^2/N_1 + S_2^2/N_2} = \sqrt{\frac{225}{42} + \frac{169}{56}} = \sqrt{8.38} = 2.89$

(3)
$$Z = \frac{\bar{X}_1 - \bar{X}_2}{S_{\bar{X}_1 - \bar{X}_2}} = \frac{78 - 74}{2.89} = 1.38$$

(4) Fail to reject null hypothesis at the 0.05 level, using a two-tailed test.

5.8 (1)
$$H_0: \mu_P - \mu_D = 0$$

(2)
$$S_{\bar{X}_P - \bar{X}_D} = \sqrt{\frac{S_P^2}{N_P} + \frac{S_D^2}{N_D}} = \sqrt{\frac{12.96}{64} + \frac{10.24}{64}}$$
$$= \sqrt{0.362} = 0.602$$

(3)
$$Z = \frac{\bar{X}_P - \bar{X}_D}{S_{\bar{X}_P - \bar{X}_D}} = \frac{7.45 - 6.30}{0.602} = 1.91$$

(4) Reject the null hypothesis beyond the 0.05 level, but not at the 0.01 level, using a one-tailed test.

Chapter 6

6.2 (1)
$$S_{\bar{X}} = \frac{S}{\sqrt{N}} = \frac{5}{\sqrt{14}} = \frac{5}{3.74} = 1.34$$

(2) $\mu = \bar{X} \pm S_{\bar{X}}(t_{0.01}) = 50 \pm 1.34(3.01) = 50 \pm 4.03 = 45.97\text{–}54.03$

6.4 (1)
$$\sum x_E^2 = 20.80$$
$$\sum x_C^2 = 15.18$$

(2)
$$S_p^2 = \frac{\sum x_E^2 + \sum x_C^2}{N_1 + N_2 - 2} = \frac{20.80 + 15.18}{20} = 1.80$$

(3)
$$S_{\bar{X}_E - \bar{X}_C} = \sqrt{\frac{S_p^2}{N_E} + \frac{S_p^2}{N_C}} = \sqrt{\frac{1.80}{12} + \frac{1.80}{10}}$$
$$= \sqrt{0.33} = 0.575$$

(4) $$t = \frac{\bar{X}_E - \bar{X}_C}{S_{\bar{X}_E - \bar{X}_C}} = \frac{5.2 - 4.2}{0.575} = 1.74$$

(5) With 20 degrees of freedom, t is not significant at the 0.05 level, assuming a two-tailed test.

6.6 (1)

	D	$(\bar{D} - D)$	$(\bar{D} - D)^2$
1.	+2	0	0
2.	+2	0	0
3.	+2	0	0
4.	+2	0	0
5.	+1	−1	1
6.	+3	1	1
7.	0	−2	4
8.	+4	2	4
	$\bar{D} = 2$		$10 = \Sigma (\bar{D} - D)^2$

(2) $$S_D = \sqrt{\frac{\Sigma (D - D)^2}{N - 1}} = \sqrt{\frac{10}{7}} = 1.20$$

(3) $$S_{\bar{D}} = \frac{S_D}{\sqrt{N}} = \frac{1.20}{\sqrt{8}} = 0.425$$

(4) $$t = \frac{\bar{D} - 0}{S_D} = \frac{2}{0.425} = 4.71$$

(5) Assuming a one-tailed test, t is significant beyond the 0.01 level.

6.8 (1) $$\Sigma x_1^2 = 478$$
$$\Sigma x_2^2 = 438$$

(2) $$S_p^2 = \frac{478 + 438}{18} = 50.89$$

(3) $$S_{\bar{X}_1 - \bar{X}_2} = \sqrt{\frac{50.89}{10} + \frac{50.89}{10}} = 3.19$$

(4) $$t = \frac{\bar{X}_1 - \bar{X}_2}{S_{\bar{X}_1 - \bar{X}_2}} = \frac{29.00 - 32.50}{3.19} = -1.10$$

(5) Assuming a two-tailed test, t is not significant at the 0.05 level, with 18 degrees of freedom.

6.10 (1)

	D	$D - \bar{D}$	$(D - \bar{D})^2$
1.	$+1$	0.25	0.063
2.	0	-0.75	0.563
3.	$+2$	1.25	1.563
4.	$+3$	2.25	5.063
5.	$+1$	0.25	0.063
6.	-2	-2.75	7.563
7.	$+2$	1.25	1.563
8.	-1	-1.75	3.063
	$\bar{D} = 0.75$		$19.504 = \sum (D - \bar{D})^2$

(2)
$$S_D = \sqrt{\frac{19.504}{7}} = 1.67$$

(3)
$$S_{\bar{D}} = \frac{1.67}{\sqrt{8}} = 0.592$$

(4)
$$t = \frac{0.75}{0.592} = 1.27$$

(5) With 7 degrees of freedom, t is not significant at the 0.05 level, assuming a two-tailed test.

Chapter 7

7.2 (1)

	Red	Grey
Observed	16	8
Expected	18	6

(2)
$$\chi^2 = \frac{(2 - 0.5)^2}{18} + \frac{(2 - 0.5)^2}{6}$$
$$= 0.125 + 0.375 = 0.500$$

(3) χ^2 is not significant; therefore there is no reason to assume that observed frequencies do not fit the 3:1 genetic model.

7.4 (1) Compute the expected frequencies, yielding:

		Species B		
		Present	Absent	
Species A	Present	40/37.74	35/37.19	75
	Absent	28/30.19	32/29.75	60
		68	67	135

(2) $\quad \chi^2 = \dfrac{(2.26 - 0.5)^2}{37.74} + \dfrac{(2.19 - 0.5)^2}{37.19} + \dfrac{(2.19 - 0.5)^2}{30.19} + \dfrac{(2.25 - 0.5)^2}{29.75}$

$\qquad = 0.082 + 0.076 + 0.094 + 0.102$

$\qquad = 0.354$

(3) χ^2 is not significant; the species therefore appear to be associated.

7.6 (1) Compute expected frequencies, yielding:

	AB	A	O	B	Totals
Group I	25/20.48	215/216.06	200/201.73	60/61.44	500
Group II	15/19.48	207/205.51	194/191.88	60/58.44	476
	40	422	394	120	976

(2) $\quad \chi^2 = \dfrac{(4.52)^2}{20.48} + \dfrac{(1.06)^2}{216.06} + \dfrac{(1.73)^2}{201.73} + \dfrac{(1.44)^2}{61.44} + \dfrac{(4.48)^2}{19.48} + \dfrac{(1.49)^2}{205.51}$

$\qquad\qquad + \dfrac{(2.12)^2}{191.88} + \dfrac{(1.56)^2}{58.44}$

$\qquad = 0.997 + 0.005 + 0.014 + 0.033 + 1.030 + 0.010 + 0.023 + 0.041$

$\qquad = 2.153$

(3) Chi-square value is not significant; therefore the differences in frequencies between the two groups are due to chance.

7.8 (1) Compute expected frequencies, yielding:

	Male	Female	
Black	26/20.65	15/20.29	41
Brown	17/20.65	24/20.29	41
White	15/16.59	18/16.30	33
	58	57	115

(2) $\quad \chi^2 = \dfrac{(5.35)^2}{20.65} + \dfrac{(5.29)^2}{20.29} + \dfrac{(3.65)^2}{20.65} + \dfrac{(3.71)^2}{20.29} + \dfrac{(1.59)^2}{16.59} + \dfrac{(1.70)^2}{16.30}$

$\qquad = 1.39 + 1.38 + 0.65 + 0.68 + 0.15 + 0.18$

$\qquad = 4.43$

(3) Chi square is not significant; there is no statistical evidence that an association exists between sex and color.

7.10 (1) Compute expected frequencies, yielding:

	Reaction	No reaction	
Men	15/28.44	1485/1470.87	1500
Women	40/24.10	1360/1371.29	1400
	55	2845	2900

(2) $\chi^2 = \dfrac{(13.44 - 0.5)^2}{28.44} + \dfrac{(15.90 - 0.5)^2}{24.10} + \dfrac{(14.13 - 0.5)^2}{1470.87} + \dfrac{(11.29 - 0.5)^2}{1371.29}$

$= 5.89 + 9.84 + 0.13 + 0.09$

$= 15.95$

(3) Chi square is significant beyond the 0.01 level. There is an apparent association between sex and reacting to the drug.

7.12 (1) Probability of drawing a white marble is $\frac{1}{10}$.

(2) $\lambda = np = \frac{1}{10}(10) = 1$

(3) When λ is 1, $e^{-\lambda}$ is 0.368.

(4) $P(\text{exactly two}) = \dfrac{e^{-\lambda}\lambda^2}{2!} = \dfrac{(0.368)(1)}{2} = 0.184$

7.14 (1)

$$98 \times 0 = 0$$
$$52 \times 1 = 52$$
$$28 \times 2 = 56$$
$$22 \times 3 = 66$$
$$\overline{174} \text{ Crickets}$$

(2)

$$\tfrac{174}{200} = 0.87 \text{ Crickets/quadrat}$$
$$\lambda = 0.87$$

(3) When λ is 0.87, $e^{-\lambda}$ is 0.419.

(4)

$$P(0) = e^{-\lambda} = 0.419$$
$$P(1) = e^{-\lambda}\lambda = 0.365$$
$$P(2) = \dfrac{e^{-\lambda}\lambda^2}{2!} = 0.158$$
$$P(3) = \dfrac{e^{-\lambda}\lambda^3}{3!} = 0.046$$

(5) The expected quadrat frequencies, assuming random distribution, are:

$$200 \times 0.419 = 83.8$$
$$200 \times 0.365 = 73.0$$
$$200 \times 0.158 = 31.6$$
$$200 \times 0.046 = 9.2$$

(6)

	0	1	2	3
Observed	98	52	28	22
Expected	83.8	73.0	31.6	9.2

$$\chi^2 = \frac{(14.2)^2}{83.8} + \frac{(21)^2}{73} + \frac{(3.6)^2}{31.6} + \frac{(12.8)^2}{9.2}$$
$$= 2.41 + 6.04 + 0.41 + 17.81$$
$$= 26.67$$

(7) Chi square, with 3 degrees of freedom, is significant beyond the 0.01 level. The assumption can therefore be made that the crickets are not randomly distributed.

7.16 (1) $$C = 256$$

(2) $$\lambda = C \pm \sqrt{C}(1.96) = 256 \pm \sqrt{256}(1.96)$$
$$= 256 \pm 31.36 = 224.64\text{--}287.36 \text{ cells/ml}$$

Chapter 8

8.2 (1)

$$\sum X^2 = 1{,}636{,}350 \qquad \sum X_A = 2052$$
$$\sum X = 6192 \qquad \sum X_B = 2103$$
$$\sum X_C = 2037$$

(2) $$\text{S.S.}_{\text{total}} = 1{,}636{,}350 - \frac{(6192)^2}{24} = 39{,}214$$

(3) $$\text{S.S.}_{\text{location}} = \frac{(2052)^2 + (2103)^2 + (2037)^2}{8} - \frac{(6192)^2}{24} = 299$$

(4) $$\text{S.S.}_{\text{error}} = 39{,}214 - 299 = 38{,}915$$

(5)

Source	D.F.	S.S.	M.S.
Location	2	299	149.50
Error	22	38,915	1768.86
Total	23	39,214	

(6) $$F_{2,22} = 0.084 \text{ (not significant)}$$

8.4 (1) Perform arc sine transformation by use of Table VIII:

A	B
18.4	22.8
22.8	26.6
20.3	23.6
26.6	30.0
22.0	26.6

(2) $\qquad \sum X^2 = 5854.0 \qquad\qquad \sum X_A = 110.1$

$\qquad\qquad \sum X = 239.7 \qquad\qquad \sum X_B = 129.6$

(3) $\qquad\qquad \text{S.S.}_{\text{total}} = 5854 - \dfrac{(239.7)^2}{10} = 108.4$

(4) $\qquad \text{S.S.}_{\text{bait}} = \dfrac{(110.1)^2 + (129.6)^2}{5} - \dfrac{(239.7)^2}{10} = 38.0$

(5) $\qquad\qquad \text{S.S.}_{\text{error}} = 108.4 - 38.0 = 70.4$

(6)

Source	D.F.	S.S.	M.S.
Bait	1	38.0	38.0
Error	8	70.4	8.8
Total	9	108.4	

(7) $\qquad\qquad F_{1,8} = \dfrac{38}{8.8} = 4.32 \text{ (not significant)}$

8.6 (1) Obtain block and treatment totals:

	A	B	C	D	E	F	Treatments
Method 1	14	12	16	15	10	11	78
Method 2	18	16	17	19	12	13	95
Method 3	15	14	12	14	12	9	76
Blocks	47	42	45	48	34	33	249

(2) $\qquad\qquad\qquad \sum X^2 = 3571$

$\qquad\qquad\qquad \sum X = 249$

(3) $$\text{S.S.}_{\text{total}} = 3571 - \frac{(249)^2}{18} = 130$$

(4) $$\text{S.S.}_{\text{blocks}} = \frac{(47)^2 + (42)^2 + (45)^2 + (48)^2 + (34)^2 + (33)^2}{3} - \frac{(249)^2}{18}$$
$$= 75$$

(5) $$\text{S.S.}_{\text{method}} = \frac{(78)^2 + (95)^2 + (76)^2}{6} - \frac{(249)^2}{18} = 40$$

(6) $$\text{S.S.}_{\text{error}} = 130 - (75 + 40) = 15$$

(7)

Source	D.F.	S.S.	M.S.
Blocks	5	75	
Method	2	40	20
Error	10	15	1.5
Total	17	130	

(8) $$F_{2,10} = \frac{20}{1.5} = 13.33 \text{ (significant beyond the 0.01 level)}$$

8.8 (1)

$\sum X^2 = 240{,}331$	$\sum X_B = 1132$
$\sum X = 2189$	$\sum X_{IA} = 509$
$\sum X_I = 1070$	$\sum X_{IB} = 561$
$\sum X_{II} = 1119$	$\sum X_{IIA} = 548$
$\sum X_A = 1057$	$\sum X_{IIB} = 571$

(2) $$\text{S.S.}_{\text{total}} = 240{,}331 - \frac{(2189)^2}{20} = 745$$

(3) $$\text{S.S.}_{\text{location}} = \frac{(1070)^2 + (1119)^2}{10} - \frac{(2189)^2}{20} = 120$$

(4) $$\text{S.S.}_{\text{time}} = \frac{(1057)^2 + (1132)^2}{10} - \frac{(2189)^2}{20} = 281$$

(5) $$\text{S.S.}_{\text{interaction}} = \frac{(509)^2 + (548)^2 + (561)^2 + (571)^2}{5} - \frac{(2189)^2}{20}$$
$$= 443 - (120 + 281) = 42$$

(6) $$\text{S.S.}_{\text{error}} = 745 - (120 + 281 + 42) = 302$$

(7)

Source	D.F.	S.S.	M.S.
Location	1	120	120.00
Time	1	281	281.00
Interaction	1	42	42.00
Error	16	302	18.88
Total	19		

(8) $F_{1,16}(\text{location}) = \dfrac{120.00}{18.88} = 6.36$ (significant beyond 0.05 level)

$F_{1,16}(\text{time}) = \dfrac{281.00}{18.88} = 14.88$ (significant beyond 0.01 level)

$F_{1,16}(\text{interaction}) = \dfrac{42.00}{18.88} = 2.22$ (not significant)

8.10 (1) $\sum X^2 = 139{,}307$ $\sum X_1 = 725$ $\sum X_C = 884$ $\sum X_{B2} = 252$
        $\sum X = 2445$ $\sum X_2 = 805$ $\sum X_{A1} = 236$ $\sum X_{B3} = 290$
        $N = 45$ $\sum X_3 = 915$ $\sum X_{A2} = 257$ $\sum X_{C1} = 263$
                   $\sum X_A = 793$ $\sum X_{A3} = 300$ $\sum X_{C2} = 296$
                   $\sum X_B = 768$ $\sum X_{B1} = 226$ $\sum X_{C3} = 325$

(2) $\text{S.S.}_{\text{total}} = 139{,}307 - \dfrac{(2445)^2}{45} = 6462$

(3) $\text{S.S.}_{\text{insecticide}} = \dfrac{(725)^2 + (805)^2 + (915)^2}{15} - \dfrac{(2445)^2}{45} = 1213$

(4) $\text{S.S.}_{\text{strain}} = \dfrac{(793)^2 + (768)^2 + (884)^2}{15} - \dfrac{(2445)^2}{45} = 497$

(5) $\text{S.S.}_{\text{interaction}} = \dfrac{(236)^2}{5} + \dfrac{(257)^2}{5} + \dfrac{(300)^2}{5} + \dfrac{(226)^2}{5} + \dfrac{(252)^2}{5}$

$$+ \dfrac{(290)^2}{5} + \dfrac{(263)^2}{5} + \dfrac{(296)^2}{5} + \dfrac{(325)^2}{5}$$

$$- \dfrac{(2445)^2}{45} - (1213 + 497) = 12$$

(6) $\text{S.S.}_{\text{error}} = 6462 - (1213 + 497 + 12) = 4740$

(7)

Source	D.F.	S.S	M.S.
Insecticide	2	1213	606.50
Strain	2	497	248.50
Interaction	4	12	3.00
Error	36	4740	131.67
Total	44	6462	

(8) $F_{2,36}(\text{insecticide}) = \dfrac{606.50}{131.67} = 4.61$ (significant beyond 0.05 level)

$F_{2,36}(\text{strain}) = \dfrac{248.50}{131.67} = 1.89$ (not significant)

$F_{4,36}(\text{interaction}) = \dfrac{3.00}{131.67} = 0.02$ (not significant)

Chapter 9

9.2 (1)

		Sign
10	12	+
9	11	+
11	13	+
12	14	+
8	9	+
7	10	+
12	12	0
10	14	+
		$N = 7$

(2) $\bar{X} = np = \tfrac{1}{2}(7) = 3.50$

(3) $S = \sqrt{npq} = \sqrt{(\tfrac{1}{2})(\tfrac{1}{2})(7)} = 1.32$

(4) $Z = \dfrac{6.50 - 3.50}{1.32} = 2.27$ (significant beyond 0.05 level)

9.4 (1)

102	104	105	108	112	115	116	117	120	122
1	2	3	4	5	6	7	8	9	10

(2) $n_1: 1 + 2 + 5 + 7 + 10 = 25$
$n_2: 3 + 4 + 6 + 8 + 9 = 30$

(3) $U = T_1 - \tfrac{1}{2}n_1(n_1 + 1) = 25 - \tfrac{1}{2}(5)(6) = 10$

(4) $P = \tfrac{87}{252} = 0.35$ (not significant)

9.6 (1)

19	21	29	29	29	30	38	39	54	54	54	82	86	110	116	124
1	2	4	4	4	6	7	8	10	10	10	12	13	14	15	16

(2) $n_1: 1 + 2 + 4 + 4 + 6 + 7 + 12 + 13 = 49$
$n_2: 4 + 8 + 10 + 10 + 10 + 14 + 15 + 16 = 87$

(3) $U = 49 - \tfrac{1}{2}(8)(9) = 49 - 36 = 13$

(4) $P = \dfrac{321}{12{,}870} = 0.024$ (significant beyond 0.05 level)

9.8   (1)

X	Rank	Y	Rank	$(X - Y)^2$
24	9	105	9	0
36	3	213	2	1
48	1	274	1	0
34	4	198	3	1
28	7	128	8	1
33	5	140	6	1
38	2	173	4	4
27	8	136	7	1
31	6	155	5	1

$$\sum (X - Y)^2 = 10$$

(2) $R = 1 - \dfrac{6 \sum (X - Y)^2}{N(N^2 - 1)} = 1 - \dfrac{6(10)}{9(64)} = 0.896$

9.10 (1)

56	57	61	59	62	52	56	53	51	49	48	52	50
a	a	a	a	a	a	a	a	a	b	b	a	Median

48	52	51	42	49	53	40	43	42
b	a	a	b	b	b	b	b	b

(2)   6 runs   12 a's   9 b's

(3) Six runs or less indicates a nonrandom fluctuation; therefore a pattern exists.

Chapter 10

10.2 (1) $\sum X = 288$ $\sum Y = 353$

$\sum X^2 = 9778$ $\sum Y^2 = 14{,}323$

$\sum XY = 11{,}256$

(2) $r = \dfrac{11{,}256 - (288)(353)/10}{\sqrt{[9778 - (288)^2/10][14{,}323 - (353)^2/10]}} = 0.66$

10.4 (1) $r = 0.66$

$N = 10$

(2) $t = \dfrac{0.66}{\sqrt{[1 - (0.66)^2/10 - 2]}} = 2.50$ (significant beyond 0.05 level)

10.6 (1) $r = 0.36$

$N = 52$

(2) Converting r to Z yields $Z = 0.377$.

(3) $$S_z = \frac{1}{\sqrt{49}} = 0.142$$

(4) $\rho = 0.377 \pm 0.142(1.96) = 0.099–0.655$

(5) $\rho = 0.09–0.57$

10.8

a.   (1) $\sum X = 376$ $\sum Y = 651$
                         $\sum X^2 = 12{,}160$ $\sum Y^2 = 36{,}045$
                         $\bar{X} = 31.00$ $\bar{Y} = 54.25$
                              $\sum XY = 20{,}764$

(2) $$r = \frac{20{,}764 - (372)(651)/12}{\sqrt{[12{,}160 - (372)^2/12][36{,}045 - (651)^2/12]}} = 0.86$$

b.   (1) $$b = \frac{20{,}764 - (372)(651)/12}{12{,}160 - (372)^2/12} = 0.93$$

(2) Selecting X values, 25, 35, and 40,
   $Y_p = \bar{Y} + b(X - \bar{X}) = 54.25 + 0.93(25 - 31) = 48.67$
   $Y_p = 54.25 + 0.93(35 - 31) = 57.97$
   $Y_p = 54.25 + 0.93(40 - 31) = 62.62$

(3) Plot a straight line connecting the coordinates, (25, 48.67), (35, 57.97), and (40, 62.62).

c.   (1) $$S_{YX}^2 = \frac{36{,}045 - (651)^2/12 - 0.93[20{,}764 - (372)(651)/12]}{12 - 2}$$
             $$= 18.60$$

(2) $S_{YX} = \sqrt{18.60} = 4.32$

(3) $$S_{\bar{Y}} = \frac{4.32}{\sqrt{12}} = \frac{4.32}{3.46} = 1.25$$

(4) Since $\bar{Y}$ (54.25) would be predicted from $\bar{X}$,

(5) $Y = Y_p \pm S_{\bar{Y}}(t_{0.05}$, with 10 d.f.)
                 $= 54.25 \pm 1.25(2.23)$
                 $= 51.80–56.70$

Chapter 11

11.2 (1) $\sum X^2 = 65{,}641$ $\sum X = 1157$ $k_1 = 5$
                 $\sum Y^2 = 68{,}074$ $\sum Y = 1100$ $k_2 = 7$
                 $\sum X_1 = 310$ $\sum Y_1 = 399$ $k_3 = 9$
                 $\sum X_2 = 384$ $\sum Y_2 = 385$
                 $\sum X_3 = 463$ $\sum Y_3 = 316$
                         $\sum XY = 63{,}034$
                         $N = 21$

(2) $\quad$ S.S.$(X)_{total} = 65,641 - \dfrac{(1157)^2}{21} = 1896$

$$\text{S.S.}(X)_{treatment} = \dfrac{(310)^2}{5} + \dfrac{(384)^2}{7} + \dfrac{(463)^2}{9} - \dfrac{(1157)^2}{21} = 359$$

$$\text{S.S.}(X)_{within} = 1896 - 359 = 1537$$

(3) $\quad$ S.S.$(Y)_{total} = 68,074 - \dfrac{(1100)^2}{21} = 10,455$

$$\text{S.S.}(Y)_{treatment} = \dfrac{(399)^2}{5} + \dfrac{(385)^2}{7} + \dfrac{(316)^2}{9} - \dfrac{(1100)^2}{21} = 6491$$

$$\text{S.S.}(Y)_{within} = 10,455 - 6491 = 3964$$

(4) $\quad$ S.S.$(XY)_{total} = 63,034 - \dfrac{(1157)(1100)}{21} = 2429$

$$\text{S.S.}(XY)_{treatment} = \dfrac{(310)(399)}{5} + \dfrac{(384)(385)}{7} + \dfrac{(463)(316)}{9} - \dfrac{(1157)(1100)}{21}$$
$$= 1509$$
$$\text{S.S.}(XY)_{within} = 2429 - 1509 = 920$$

(5)

	S.S.(X)	S.S.(Y)	S.S.(XY)
Total	1896	10,455	2429
Diet	359	6491	1509
Within	1537	3964	920

(6) Diet plus within:

S.S.(X)	S.S.(Y)	S.S.(XY)
1896	10,455	2429

(7) Within alone:

S.S.(X)	S.S.(Y)	S.S.(XY)
1537	3964	920

(8) Residuals for treatment:

$$b = \dfrac{2429}{1896} = 1.28$$

$$\sum (Y - Y_p)^2 = 10,455 - 1.28(2429) = 7346$$

(9) Residuals for within:

$$b = \frac{920}{1537} = 0.60$$

$$\sum (Y - Y_p)^2 = 3964 - 0.60(920) = 3412$$

(10)

Source	S.S.	D.F.	M.S.
Total	7346		
Treatment	3934	2	1967.00
Within	3412	16	213.25

(11)
$$F_{2,16} = \frac{1967.00}{213.25} = 9.22$$

11.4 (1)

$$\sum X^2 = 5826 \qquad \sum X = 314$$
$$\sum Y^2 = 66{,}997 \qquad \sum Y = 1149$$
$$\sum X_A = 163 \qquad \sum Y_A = 578$$
$$\sum X_B = 151 \qquad \sum Y_B = 571$$
$$\sum X_M = 165 \qquad \sum Y_M = 546$$
$$\sum X_F = 149 \qquad \sum Y_F = 603$$
$$\sum X_{AM} = 93 \qquad \sum Y_{AM} = 268$$
$$\sum X_{AF} = 70 \qquad \sum Y_{AF} = 310$$
$$\sum X_{BM} = 72 \qquad \sum Y_{BM} = 278$$
$$\sum X_{BF} = 79 \qquad \sum Y_{BF} = 293$$
$$\sum XY = 18{,}463$$

(2)
$$\text{S.S.}(X)_{\text{total}} = 5826 - \frac{(314)^2}{20} = 896$$

$$\text{S.S.}(X)_{\text{treatment}} = \frac{(163)^2 + (151)^2}{10} - \frac{(314)^2}{20} = 7$$

$$\text{S.S.}(X)_{\text{sex}} = \frac{(165)^2 + (149)^2}{10} - \frac{(314)^2}{20} = 13$$

$$\text{S.S.}(X)_{\text{interaction}} = \frac{(93)^2 + (70)^2 + (72)^2 + (79)^2}{5} - \frac{(314)^2}{20}$$

$$= 65 - (7 + 13) = 45$$

$$\text{S.S.}(X)_{\text{within}} = 896 - (7 + 13 + 45) = 831$$

(3) $\text{S.S.}(Y)_{\text{total}} = 66{,}997 - \dfrac{(1149)^2}{20} = 987$

$\text{S.S.}(Y)_{\text{treatment}} = \dfrac{(578)^2 + (571)^2}{10} - \dfrac{(1149)^2}{20} = 3$

$\text{S.S.}(Y)_{\text{sex}} = \dfrac{(546)^2 + (603)^2}{10} - \dfrac{(1149)^2}{20} = 163$

$\text{S.S.}(Y)_{\text{interaction}} = \dfrac{(268)^2 + (310)^2 + (278)^2 + (293)^2}{5} - \dfrac{(1149)^2}{20}$

$= 201 - (3 + 163) = 35$

$\text{S.S.}(Y)_{\text{within}} = 987 - (3 + 163 + 35) = 786$

(4) $\text{S.S.}(XY)_{\text{total}} = 18{,}463 - \dfrac{(314)(1149)}{20} = 424$

$\text{S.S.}(XY)_{\text{treatment}} = \dfrac{(163)(578) + (151)(571)}{10} - \dfrac{(314)(1149)}{20} = 5$

$\text{S.S.}(XY)_{\text{sex}} = \dfrac{(165)(546) + (149)(603)}{10} - \dfrac{(314)(1149)}{20} = -45$

$\text{S.S.}(XY)_{\text{interaction}} = \dfrac{(93)(268) + (70)(310) + (72)(278) + (79)(293)}{5}$

$- \dfrac{(314)(1149)}{20} = -82 - (5 - 45) = -42$

$\text{S.S.}(XY)_{\text{within}} = 424 - (5 - 87) = 506$

(5)

	S.S.(X)	S.S.(Y)	S.S.(XY)
Total	896	987	424
Treatment	7	3	5
Sex	13	163	-45
Interaction	45	35	-42
Within	831	786	506

(6) Within plus:

	S.S.(X)	S.S.(Y)	S.S.(XY)
Treatment	838	789	511
Sex	844	949	561
Interaction	876	821	464

(7) Within alone:

S.S.(X)	S.S.(Y)	S.S.(XY)
831	786	506

(8) Residuals for treatment:
$$b = \tfrac{511}{838} = 0.61$$
$$\Sigma (Y - Y_p)^2 = 789 - 0.61(511) = 477$$

(9) Residuals for sex:
$$b = \tfrac{461}{949} = 0.49$$
$$\Sigma (Y - Y_p)^2 = 949 - 0.49(461) = 723$$

(10) Residuals for interaction:
$$b = \tfrac{464}{876} = 0.53$$
$$\Sigma (Y - Y_p)^2 = 821 - 0.53(464) = 575$$

(11) Residuals for within:
$$b = \tfrac{506}{831} = 0.61$$
$$\Sigma (Y - Y_p)^2 = 786 - 0.61(506) = 477$$

(12)

Source	S.S	D.F.	M.S.
Within plus treatment	477		
Treatment	0	1	0
Within	477	15	31.80

$$F_{1,15} = \frac{0}{31.80} = 0$$

(not significant)

(13)

Source	S.S.	D.F.	M.S.
Within plus sex	723		
Sex	246	1	246.00
Within	477	15	31.80

$$F_{1,15} = \frac{246.00}{31.80}$$
$$= 7.74$$

(14)

Source	S.S.	D.F.	M.S.
Within plus interaction	575		
Interaction	98	1	98.00
Within	477	15	31.80

$$F_{1,15} = \frac{98.00}{31.80}$$

$$= 3.08$$

Appendix C
TABLES

Table I POWERS AND ROOTS

No.	Sq.	Sq. Root	Cube	Cube Root	No.	Sq.	Sq. Root	Cube	Cube Root
1	1	1.000	1	1.000	51	2,601	7.141	132,651	3.708
2	4	1.414	8	1.260	52	2,704	7.211	140,608	3.733
3	9	1.732	27	1.442	53	2,809	7.280	148,877	3.756
4	16	2.000	64	1.587	54	2,916	7.348	157,464	3.780
5	25	2.236	125	1.710	55	3,025	7.416	166,375	3.803
6	36	2.449	216	1.817	56	3,136	7.483	175,616	3.826
7	49	2.646	343	1.913	57	3,249	7.550	185,193	3.849
8	64	2.828	512	2.000	58	3,364	7.616	195,112	3.871
9	81	3.000	729	2.080	59	3,481	7.681	205,379	3.893
10	100	3.162	1,000	2.154	60	3,600	7.746	216,000	3.915
11	121	3.317	1,331	2.224	61	3,721	7.810	226,981	3.936
12	144	3.464	1,728	2.289	62	3,844	7.874	238,328	3.958
13	169	3.606	2,197	2.351	63	3,969	7.937	250,047	3.979
14	196	3.742	2,744	2.410	64	4,096	8.000	262,144	4.000
15	225	3.873	3,375	2.466	65	4,225	8.062	274,625	4.021
16	256	4.000	4,096	2.520	66	4,356	8.124	287,496	4.041
17	289	4.123	4,913	2.571	67	4,489	8.185	300,763	4.062
18	324	4.243	5,832	2.621	68	4,624	8.246	314,432	4.082
19	361	4.359	6,859	2.668	69	4,761	8.307	328,509	4.102
20	400	4.472	8,000	2.714	70	4,900	8.367	343,000	4.121
21	441	4.583	9,261	2.759	71	5,041	8.426	357,911	4.141
22	484	4.690	10,648	2.802	72	5,184	8.485	373,248	4.160
23	529	4.796	12,167	2.844	73	5,329	8.544	389,017	4.179
24	576	4.899	13,824	2.884	74	5,476	8.602	405,224	4.198
25	625	5.000	15,625	2.924	75	5,625	8.660	421,875	4.217
26	676	5.099	17,576	2.962	76	5,776	8.718	438,976	4.236
27	729	5.196	19,683	3.000	77	5,929	8.775	456,533	4.254
28	784	5.292	21,952	3.037	78	6,084	8.832	474,552	4.273
29	841	5.385	24,389	3.072	79	6,241	8.888	493,039	4.291
30	900	5.477	27,000	3.107	80	6,400	8.944	512,000	4.309
31	961	5.568	29,791	3.141	81	6,561	9.000	531,441	4.327
32	1,024	5.657	32,768	3.175	82	6,724	9.055	551,368	4.344
33	1,089	5.745	35,937	3.208	83	6,889	9.110	571,787	4.362
34	1,156	5.831	39,304	3.240	84	7,056	9.165	592,704	4.380
35	1,225	5.916	42,875	3.271	85	7,225	9.220	614,125	4.397
36	1,296	6.000	46,656	3.302	86	7,396	9.274	636,056	4.414
37	1,369	6.083	50,653	3.332	87	7,569	9.327	658,503	4.431
38	1,444	6.164	54,872	3.362	88	7,744	9.381	681,472	4.448
39	1,521	6.245	59,319	3.391	89	7,921	9.434	704,969	4.465
40	1,600	6.325	64,000	3.420	90	8,100	9.487	729,000	4.481
41	1,681	6.403	68,921	3.448	91	8,281	9.539	753,571	4.498
42	1,764	6.481	74,088	3.476	92	8,464	9.592	778,688	4.514
43	1,849	6.557	79,507	3.503	93	8,649	9.644	804,357	4.531
44	1,936	6.633	85,184	3.530	94	8,836	9.695	830,584	4.547
45	2,025	6.708	91,125	3.557	95	9,025	9.747	857,375	4.563
46	2,116	6.782	97,336	3.583	96	9,216	9.798	884,736	4.579
47	2,209	6.856	103,823	3.609	97	9,409	9.849	912,673	4.595
48	2,304	6.928	110,592	3.634	98	9,604	9.899	941,192	4.610
49	2,401	7.000	117,649	3.659	99	9,801	9.950	970,299	4.626
50	2,500	7.071	125,000	3.684	100	10,000	10.000	1,000,000	4.642

Table II RANDOM NUMBERS

09	18	82	00	97	32	82	53	95	27	04	22	08	63	04	83	38	98	73	74
90	04	58	54	97	51	98	15	06	54	94	93	88	19	97	91	87	07	61	50
73	18	95	02	07	47	67	72	62	69	62	29	06	44	64	27	12	46	70	18
75	76	87	64	90	20	97	18	17	49	90	42	91	22	72	95	37	50	58	71
54	01	64	40	56	66	28	13	10	03	00	68	22	73	98	20	71	45	32	95
08	35	86	99	10	78	54	24	27	85	13	66	15	88	73	04	61	89	75	53
28	30	60	32	64	81	33	31	05	91	40	51	00	78	93	32	60	46	04	75
53	84	08	62	33	81	59	41	36	28	51	21	59	02	90	28	46	66	87	95
91	75	75	37	41	61	61	36	22	69	50	26	39	02	12	55	78	17	65	14
89	41	59	26	94	00	39	75	83	91	12	60	71	76	46	48	94	97	23	06
77	51	30	38	20	86	83	42	99	01	68	41	48	27	74	51	90	81	39	80
19	50	23	71	74	69	97	92	02	88	55	21	02	97	73	74	28	77	52	51
21	81	85	93	13	93	27	88	17	57	05	68	67	31	56	07	08	28	50	46
51	47	46	64	99	68	10	72	36	21	94	04	99	13	45	42	83	60	91	91
99	55	96	83	31	62	53	52	41	70	69	77	71	28	30	74	81	97	81	42
33	71	34	80	07	93	58	47	28	69	51	92	66	47	21	58	30	32	98	22
85	27	48	68	93	11	30	32	92	70	28	83	43	41	37	73	51	59	04	00
84	13	38	96	40	44	03	55	21	66	73	85	27	00	91	61	22	26	05	61
56	73	21	62	34	17	39	59	61	31	10	12	39	16	22	85	49	65	75	60
65	13	85	68	06	87	64	88	52	61	34	31	36	58	61	45	87	52	10	69
38	00	10	21	76	81	71	91	17	11	71	60	29	29	37	74	21	40	96	49
37	40	29	63	97	01	30	47	75	86	56	27	11	00	86	47	32	59	26	05
97	12	54	03	48	87	08	33	14	17	21	81	53	92	50	75	23	20	20	47
21	82	64	11	34	47	14	33	40	72	64	63	88	59	02	49	13	64	64	41
73	13	54	27	42	95	71	90	90	35	85	79	47	42	96	08	78	98	81	56

Table II *(continued)*

43	50	34	50	18	81	47	66	11	76	07	05	74	43	86	03	73	32	12	31	56	99	90	67	83
58	47	73	78	96	94	16	53	55	14	12	39	88	07	78	20	19	98	64	78	05	40	17	56	67
42	51	71	40	63	15	92	62	50	22	54	14	75	63	02	45	21	20	49	49	40	63	05	18	30
65	75	87	55	21	97	45	37	82	11	03	43	27	85	54	37	20	01	50	52	29	98	62	41	08
64	01	72	06	57	09	61	46	26	87	73	47	43	53	30	17	59	83	09	98	95	66	80	55	95
63	35	14	21	05	87	69	54	03	87	14	33	96	68	79	42	09	66	87	37	50	82	18	83	69
61	10	03	96	89	64	61	76	18	99	97	67	48	63	87	32	32	70	49	25	96	56	46	96	50
09	49	49	05	25	05	99	00	47	55	06	46	22	10	28	04	87	49	24	74	43	20	06	18	20
82	70	30	71	85	78	84	67	30	10	49	72	43	41	47	99	66	01	23	44	92	31	85	78	90
59	25	22	17	25	46	59	47	94	08	29	47	24	57	24	45	76	39	81	76	14	70	90	24	40
77	15	21	67	43	80	18	60	07	71	77	43	35	05	87	78	86	14	82	03	94	19	60	61	89
82	40	92	18	33	26	08	72	03	57	89	52	43	11	90	26	80	46	05	77	79	31	86	68	82
44	07	05	04	80	35	77	25	59	18	18	61	52	16	91	14	39	39	70	29	41	85	45	48	00
44	57	16	58	47	04	54	73	99	84	30	06	52	39	62	30	00	45	83	36	55	67	11	79	67
32	88	95	80	60	95	45	31	86	35	85	54	98	90	26	37	92	16	99	07	49	49	64	41	90
74	22	73	02	00	92	30	89	03	75	84	38	92	04	26	24	84	94	86	91	49	59	60	13	04
68	82	78	21	56	27	10	75	74	89	35	43	62	20	73	28	14	15	39	80	51	75	03	31	05
54	88	08	81	40	74	49	55	03	58	74	51	73	56	75	14	97	65	21	12	88	93	57	39	68
01	10	88	74	94	06	24	94	17	34	76	02	21	87	12	31	73	62	69	07	46	55	61	27	39
94	74	62	11	17	66	54	30	69	08	27	13	80	10	54	60	49	78	66	44	41	94	41	50	41

07	63	87	79	29	03	06	11	80	72	96	20	74	41	56	23	82	19	95	38
60	52	88	34	41	07	95	41	98	14	59	17	52	06	95	05	53	35	21	39
83	59	63	56	55	06	95	89	29	83	05	12	80	97	19	77	43	35	37	83
10	85	06	27	46	99	59	91	05	07	13	49	90	63	19	53	07	57	18	39
39	82	09	89	52	43	62	26	31	47	64	42	18	08	14	43	80	00	93	51
59	58	00	64	78	75	56	97	88	00	88	83	55	44	86	23	76	80	61	56
38	50	80	73	41	23	79	34	87	63	90	82	29	70	22	17	71	90	42	07
30	69	27	06	68	94	68	81	61	27	56	19	68	00	91	82	06	76	34	00
65	44	39	56	59	18	28	82	74	37	49	63	22	40	41	08	33	76	56	76
27	26	75	02	64	13	19	27	22	94	07	47	74	46	06	17	98	54	89	11
91	30	70	69	91	19	07	22	42	10	36	69	95	37	28	28	82	53	57	93
68	43	49	46	88	84	47	31	36	22	62	12	69	84	08	12	84	38	25	90
48	90	81	58	77	54	74	52	45	91	35	70	00	47	54	83	82	45	26	92
06	91	34	51	97	42	67	27	86	01	11	88	30	95	28	63	01	19	89	01
10	45	51	60	19	14	21	03	37	12	91	34	23	78	21	88	32	58	08	51
12	88	39	73	43	65	02	76	11	84	04	28	50	13	92	17	97	41	50	77
21	77	83	09	76	38	80	73	69	61	31	64	94	20	96	63	28	10	20	23
19	52	35	95	15	65	12	25	96	59	86	28	36	82	58	69	57	21	37	98
67	24	55	26	70	35	58	31	65	63	79	24	68	66	86	76	46	33	42	22
60	58	44	73	77	07	50	03	79	92	45	13	42	65	29	26	76	08	36	37
53	85	34	13	77	36	06	69	48	50	58	83	87	38	59	49	36	47	33	31
24	63	73	87	36	74	38	48	93	42	52	62	30	79	92	12	36	91	86	01
83	08	01	24	51	38	99	22	28	15	07	75	95	17	77	97	37	72	75	85
16	44	42	43	34	36	15	19	90	73	27	49	37	09	39	85	13	03	25	52
60	79	01	81	57	57	17	86	57	62	11	16	17	85	76	45	81	95	29	79

From W. J. Dixon and F. J. Massey, *Introduction to Statistical Analysis*, 2nd edition. New York: McGraw-Hill, 1957. Reprinted by permission of McGraw-Hill and the Rand Corporation.

Table III CRITICAL VALUES OF *t*

For any given df, the table shows the values of t corresponding to various levels of probability. Obtained t is significant at a given level if it is equal to or <u>greater than</u> the value shown in the table.

df	Level of significance for one-tailed test					
	.10	.05	.025	.01	.005	.0005
	Level of significance for two-tailed test					
	.20	.10	.05	.02	.01	.001
1	3.078	6.314	12.706	31.821	63.657	636.619
2	1.886	2.920	4.303	6.965	9.925	31.598
3	1.638	2.353	3.182	4.541	5.841	12.941
4	1.533	2.132	2.776	3.747	4.604	8.610
5	1.476	2.015	2.571	3.365	4.032	6.859
6	1.440	1.943	2.447	3.143	3.707	5.959
7	1.415	1.895	2.365	2.998	3.499	5.405
8	1.397	1.860	2.306	2.896	3.355	5.041
9	1.383	1.833	2.262	2.821	3.250	4.781
10	1.372	1.812	2.228	2.764	3.169	4.587
11	1.363	1.796	2.201	2.718	3.106	4.437
12	1.356	1.782	2.179	2.681	3.055	4.318
13	1.350	1.771	2.160	2.650	3.012	4.221
14	1.345	1.761	2.145	2.624	2.977	4.140
15	1.341	1.753	2.131	2.602	2.947	4.073
16	1.337	1.746	2.120	2.583	2.921	4.015
17	1.333	1.740	2.110	2.567	2.898	3.965
18	1.330	1.734	2.101	2.552	2.878	3.922
19	1.328	1.729	2.093	2.539	2.861	3.883
20	1.325	1.725	2.086	2.528	2.845	3.850
21	1.323	1.721	2.080	2.518	2.831	3.819
22	1.321	1.717	2.074	2.508	2.819	3.792
23	1.319	1.714	2.069	2.500	2.807	3.767
24	1.318	1.711	2.064	2.492	2.797	3.745
25	1.316	1.708	2.060	2.485	2.787	3.725
26	1.315	1.706	2.056	2.479	2.779	3.707
27	1.314	1.703	2.052	2.473	2.771	3.690
28	1.313	1.701	2.048	2.467	2.763	3.674
29	1.311	1.699	2.045	2.462	2.756	3.659
30	1.310	1.697	2.042	2.457	2.750	3.646
40	1.303	1.684	2.021	2.423	2.704	3.551
60	1.296	1.671	2.000	2.390	2.660	3.460
120	1.289	1.658	1.980	2.358	2.617	3.373
∞	1.282	1.645	1.960	2.326	2.576	3.291

From R. A. Fisher and F. Yates, *Statistical Tables for Biological, Agricultural and Medical Research.* Edinburgh: Oliver and Boyd, Ltd., 1948. Reprinted by permission of the authors and publisher.

Table IV NORMAL CURVE AREAS

Z	.00	.01	.02	.03	.04	.05	.06	.07	.08	.09
0.0	.0000	.0040	.0080	.0120	.0160	.0199	.0239	.0279	.0319	.0359
0.1	.0398	.0438	.0478	.0517	.0557	.0596	.0636	.0675	.0714	.0753
0.2	.0793	.0832	.0871	.0910	.0948	.0987	.1026	.1064	.1103	.1141
0.3	.1179	.1217	.1255	.1293	.1331	.1368	.1406	.1443	.1480	.1517
0.4	.1554	.1591	.1628	.1664	.1700	.1736	.1772	.1808	.1844	.1879
0.5	.1915	.1950	.1985	.2019	.2054	.2088	.2123	.2157	.2190	.2224
0.6	.2257	.2291	.2324	.2357	.2389	.2422	.2454	.2486	.2517	.2549
0.7	.2580	.2611	.2642	.2673	.2704	.2734	.2764	.2794	.2823	.2852
0.8	.2881	.2910	.2939	.2967	.2995	.3023	.3051	.3078	.3106	.3133
0.9	.3159	.3186	.3212	.3238	.3264	.3289	.3315	.3340	.3365	.3389
1.0	.3413	.3438	.3461	.3485	.3508	.3531	.3554	.3577	.3599	.3621
1.1	.3643	.3665	.3686	.3708	.3729	.3749	.3770	.3790	.3810	.3830
1.2	.3849	.3869	.3888	.3907	.3925	.3944	.3962	.3980	.3997	.4015
1.3	.4032	.4049	.4066	.4082	.4099	.4115	.4131	.4147	.4162	.4177
1.4	.4192	.4207	.4222	.4236	.4251	.4265	.4279	.4292	.4306	.4319
1.5	.4332	.4345	.4357	.4370	.4382	.4394	.4406	.4418	.4429	.4441
1.6	.4452	.4463	.4474	.4484	.4495	.4505	.4515	.4525	.4535	.4545
1.7	.4554	.4564	.4573	.4582	.4591	.4599	.4608	.4616	.4625	.4633
1.8	.4641	.4649	.4656	.4664	.4671	.4678	.4686	.4693	.4699	.4706
1.9	.4713	.4719	.4726	.4732	.4738	.4744	.4750	.4756	.4761	.4767
2.0	.4772	.4778	.4783	.4788	.4793	.4798	.4803	.4808	.4812	.4817
2.1	.4821	.4826	.4830	.4834	.4838	.4842	.4846	.4850	.4854	.4857
2.2	.4861	.4864	.4868	.4871	.4875	.4878	.4881	.4884	.4887	.4890
2.3	.4893	.4896	.4898	.4901	.4904	.4906	.4909	.4911	.4913	.4916
2.4	.4918	.4920	.4922	.4925	.4927	.4929	.4931	.4932	.4934	.4936
2.5	.4938	.4940	.4941	.4943	.4945	.4946	.4948	.4949	.4951	.4952
2.6	.4953	.4955	.4956	.4957	.4959	.4960	.4961	.4962	.4963	.4964
2.7	.4965	.4966	.4967	.4968	.4969	.4970	.4971	.4972	.4973	.4974
2.8	.4974	.4975	.4976	.4977	.4977	.4978	.4979	.4979	.4980	.4981
2.9	.4981	.4982	.4982	.4983	.4984	.4984	.4985	.4985	.4986	.4986
3.0	.4987	.4987	.4987	.4988	.4988	.4989	.4989	.4989	.4990	.4990
3.1	.49903									
3.2	.49931									
3.3	.49952									
3.4	.49966									
3.5	.49977									
3.6	.49984									
3.7	.49989									
3.8	.49993									
3.9	.49995									
4.0	.50000									

Table V   CHI SQUARE

Column headings indicate probability of chance

deviation between O and E.

P D.F.	0.25	0.10	0.05	0.025	0.01	0.005
1.	1.323	2.706	3.841	5.024	6.635	7.879
2.	2.773	4.605	5.991	7.378	9.210	10.597
3.	4.108	6.251	7.815	9.348	11.345	12.838
4.	5.385	7.779	9.488	11.143	13.277	14.860
5.	6.626	9.236	11.071	12.833	15.086	16.750
6.	7.841	10.645	12.592	14.449	16.812	18.548
7.	9.037	12.017	14.067	16.013	18.475	20.278
8.	10.219	13.362	15.507	17.535	20.090	21.955
9.	11.389	14.684	16.919	19.023	21.666	23.589
10.	12.549	15.987	18.307	20.483	23.209	25.188
11.	13.701	17.275	19.675	21.920	24.725	26.757
12.	14.845	18.549	21.026	23.337	26.217	28.299
13.	15.984	19.812	22.362	24.736	27.688	29.819
14.	17.117	21.064	23.685	26.119	29.141	31.319
15.	18.245	22.307	24.996	27.488	30.578	32.801

Adapted from table of χ^2 appearing in *Handbook of Statistical Tables* by D. B. Owen, Addison-Wesley, 1962, p. 50. Reprinted by permission of the U.S. Atomic Energy Commission.

Table VI VALUES OF THE EXPONENTIAL FUNCTION $e^{-\lambda}$

λ	0.00	0.01	0.02	0.03	0.04	0.05	0.06	0.07	0.08	0.09
0.00	1.000	0.990	0.980	0.970	0.961	0.951	0.942	0.932	0.923	0.914
0.10	0.905	0.896	0.887	0.878	0.869	0.861	0.852	0.844	0.835	0.827
0.20	0.819	0.811	0.803	0.795	0.787	0.779	0.771	0.763	0.756	0.748
0.30	0.741	0.733	0.726	0.719	0.712	0.705	0.698	0.691	0.684	0.677
0.40	0.670	0.664	0.657	0.651	0.644	0.638	0.631	0.625	0.619	0.613
0.50	0.607	0.600	0.595	0.589	0.583	0.577	0.571	0.566	0.560	0.554
0.60	0.549	0.543	0.538	0.533	0.527	0.522	0.517	0.512	0.507	0.502
0.70	0.497	0.492	0.487	0.482	0.477	0.472	0.468	0.463	0.458	0.454
0.80	0.449	0.445	0.440	0.436	0.432	0.427	0.423	0.419	0.415	0.411
0.90	0.407	0.403	0.399	0.395	0.391	0.387	0.383	0.379	0.375	0.372
1.00	0.368	0.364	0.361	0.357	0.353	0.350	0.346	0.343	0.340	0.336
1.10	0.333	0.330	0.326	0.323	0.320	0.317	0.313	0.310	0.307	0.304
1.20	0.301	0.298	0.295	0.292	0.289	0.287	0.284	0.281	0.278	0.275
1.30	0.273	0.270	0.267	0.264	0.262	0.259	0.257	0.254	0.252	0.249
1.40	0.247	0.244	0.242	0.239	0.237	0.235	0.232	0.230	0.228	0.225
1.50	0.223	0.221	0.219	0.217	0.214	0.212	0.210	0.208	0.206	0.204
1.60	0.202	0.200	0.198	0.196	0.194	0.192	0.190	0.188	0.186	0.185
1.70	0.183	0.181	0.179	0.177	0.176	0.174	0.172	0.170	0.169	0.167
1.80	0.165	0.164	0.162	0.160	0.159	0.157	0.156	0.154	0.153	0.151
1.90	0.150	0.148	0.147	0.145	0.144	0.142	0.141	0.139	0.138	0.137
2.00	0.135	0.134	0.133	0.131	0.130	0.129	0.127	0.126	0.125	0.124
2.10	0.122	0.121	0.120	0.119	0.118	0.116	0.115	0.114	0.113	0.112
2.20	0.111	0.110	0.109	0.108	0.106	0.105	0.104	0.103	0.102	0.101
2.30	0.100	0.0992	0.0983	0.0973	0.0963	0.0953	0.0944	0.0935	0.0926	0.0916
2.40	0.0907	0.0898	0.0889	0.0880	0.0872	0.0863	0.0854	0.0846	0.0837	0.0829
2.50	0.0821	0.0813	0.0805	0.0797	0.0789	0.0781	0.0773	0.0765	0.0758	0.0750
2.60	0.0743	0.0735	0.0728	0.0721	0.0714	0.0707	0.0699	0.0693	0.0686	0.0679
2.70	0.0672	0.0665	0.0659	0.0652	0.0646	0.0639	0.0633	0.0627	0.0620	0.0614
2.80	0.0608	0.0602	0.0596	0.0590	0.0584	0.0578	0.0573	0.0567	0.0561	0.0556
2.90	0.0550	0.0545	0.0539	0.0534	0.0529	0.0523	0.0518	0.0513	0.0508	0.0503

From Avram Goldstein, *Biostatistics.* New York: Macmillan, 1964. Reprinted by permission.

Table VII CRITICAL VALUES OF F

The obtained F is significant at a given level if it is equal to or greater than the value shown in the table.
0.05 (light row) and 0.01 (dark row) points for the distribution of F

Degrees of freedom for greater mean square

df	1	2	3	4	5	6	7	8	9	10	11	12	14	16	20	24	30	40	50	75	100	200	500	∞
1	161 / 4052	200 / 4999	216 / 5403	225 / 5625	230 / 5764	234 / 5859	237 / 5928	239 / 5981	241 / 6022	242 / 6056	243 / 6082	244 / 6106	245 / 6142	246 / 6169	248 / 6208	249 / 6234	250 / 6258	251 / 6286	252 / 6302	253 / 6323	253 / 6334	254 / 6352	254 / 6361	254 / 6366
2	18.51 / 98.49	19.00 / 99.01	19.16 / 99.17	19.25 / 99.25	19.30 / 99.30	19.33 / 99.33	19.36 / 99.34	19.37 / 99.36	19.38 / 99.38	19.39 / 99.40	19.40 / 99.41	19.41 / 99.42	19.42 / 99.43	19.43 / 99.44	19.44 / 99.45	19.45 / 99.46	19.46 / 99.47	19.47 / 99.48	19.47 / 99.48	19.48 / 99.49	19.49 / 99.49	19.49 / 99.49	19.50 / 99.50	19.50 / 99.50
3	10.13 / 34.12	9.55 / 30.81	9.28 / 29.46	9.12 / 28.71	9.01 / 28.24	8.94 / 27.91	8.88 / 27.67	8.84 / 27.49	8.81 / 27.34	8.78 / 27.23	8.76 / 27.13	8.74 / 27.05	8.71 / 26.92	8.69 / 26.83	8.66 / 26.69	8.64 / 26.60	8.62 / 26.50	8.60 / 26.41	8.58 / 26.30	8.57 / 26.27	8.56 / 26.23	8.54 / 26.18	8.54 / 26.14	8.53 / 26.12
4	7.71 / 21.20	6.94 / 18.00	6.59 / 16.69	6.39 / 15.98	6.26 / 15.52	6.16 / 15.21	6.09 / 14.98	6.04 / 14.80	6.00 / 14.66	5.96 / 14.54	5.93 / 14.45	5.91 / 14.37	5.87 / 14.24	5.84 / 14.15	5.80 / 14.02	5.77 / 13.93	5.74 / 13.83	5.71 / 13.74	5.70 / 13.69	5.68 / 13.61	5.66 / 13.57	5.65 / 13.52	5.64 / 13.48	5.63 / 13.46
5	6.61 / 16.26	5.79 / 13.27	5.41 / 12.06	5.19 / 11.39	5.05 / 10.97	4.95 / 10.67	4.88 / 10.45	4.82 / 10.27	4.78 / 10.15	4.74 / 10.05	4.70 / 9.96	4.68 / 9.89	4.64 / 9.77	4.60 / 9.68	4.56 / 9.55	4.53 / 9.47	4.50 / 9.38	4.46 / 9.29	4.44 / 9.24	4.42 / 9.17	4.40 / 9.13	4.38 / 9.07	4.37 / 9.04	4.36 / 9.02
6	5.99 / 13.74	5.14 / 10.92	4.76 / 9.78	4.53 / 9.15	4.39 / 8.75	4.28 / 8.47	4.21 / 8.26	4.15 / 8.10	4.10 / 7.98	4.06 / 7.87	4.03 / 7.79	4.00 / 7.72	3.96 / 7.60	3.92 / 7.52	3.87 / 7.39	3.84 / 7.31	3.81 / 7.23	3.77 / 7.14	3.75 / 7.09	3.72 / 7.02	3.71 / 6.99	3.69 / 6.94	3.68 / 6.90	3.67 / 6.88
7	5.59 / 12.25	4.74 / 9.55	4.35 / 8.45	4.12 / 7.85	3.97 / 7.46	3.87 / 7.19	3.79 / 7.00	3.73 / 6.84	3.68 / 6.71	3.63 / 6.62	3.60 / 6.54	3.57 / 6.47	3.52 / 6.35	3.49 / 6.27	3.44 / 6.15	3.41 / 6.07	3.38 / 5.98	3.34 / 5.90	3.32 / 5.85	3.29 / 5.78	3.28 / 5.75	3.25 / 5.70	3.24 / 5.67	3.23 / 5.65
8	5.32 / 11.26	4.46 / 8.65	4.07 / 7.59	3.84 / 7.01	3.69 / 6.63	3.58 / 6.37	3.50 / 6.19	3.44 / 6.03	3.39 / 5.91	3.34 / 5.82	3.31 / 5.74	3.28 / 5.67	3.23 / 5.56	3.20 / 5.48	3.15 / 5.36	3.12 / 5.28	3.08 / 5.20	3.05 / 5.11	3.03 / 5.06	3.00 / 5.00	2.98 / 4.96	2.96 / 4.91	2.94 / 4.88	2.93 / 4.86
9	5.12 / 10.56	4.26 / 8.02	3.86 / 6.99	3.63 / 6.42	3.48 / 6.06	3.37 / 5.80	3.29 / 5.62	3.23 / 5.47	3.18 / 5.35	3.13 / 5.26	3.10 / 5.18	3.07 / 5.11	3.02 / 5.00	2.98 / 4.92	2.93 / 4.80	2.90 / 4.73	2.86 / 4.64	2.82 / 4.56	2.80 / 4.51	2.77 / 4.45	2.76 / 4.41	2.73 / 4.36	2.72 / 4.33	2.71 / 4.31
10	4.96 / 10.04	4.10 / 7.56	3.71 / 6.55	3.48 / 5.99	3.33 / 5.64	3.22 / 5.39	3.14 / 5.21	3.07 / 5.06	3.02 / 4.95	2.97 / 4.85	2.94 / 4.78	2.91 / 4.71	2.86 / 4.60	2.82 / 4.52	2.77 / 4.41	2.74 / 4.33	2.70 / 4.25	2.67 / 4.17	2.64 / 4.12	2.61 / 4.05	2.59 / 4.01	2.56 / 3.96	2.55 / 3.93	2.54 / 3.91
11	4.84 / 9.65	3.98 / 7.20	3.59 / 6.22	3.36 / 5.67	3.20 / 5.32	3.09 / 5.07	3.01 / 4.88	2.95 / 4.74	2.90 / 4.63	2.86 / 4.54	2.82 / 4.46	2.79 / 4.40	2.74 / 4.29	2.70 / 4.21	2.65 / 4.10	2.61 / 4.02	2.57 / 3.94	2.53 / 3.86	2.50 / 3.80	2.47 / 3.74	2.45 / 3.70	2.42 / 3.66	2.41 / 3.62	2.40 / 3.60
12	4.75 / 9.33	3.88 / 6.93	3.49 / 5.95	3.26 / 5.41	3.11 / 5.06	3.00 / 4.82	2.92 / 4.65	2.85 / 4.50	2.80 / 4.39	2.76 / 4.30	2.72 / 4.22	2.69 / 4.16	2.64 / 4.05	2.60 / 3.98	2.54 / 3.86	2.50 / 3.78	2.46 / 3.70	2.42 / 3.61	2.40 / 3.56	2.36 / 3.49	2.35 / 3.46	2.32 / 3.41	2.31 / 3.38	2.30 / 3.36
13	4.67 / 9.07	3.80 / 6.70	3.41 / 5.74	3.18 / 5.20	3.02 / 4.86	2.92 / 4.62	2.84 / 4.44	2.77 / 4.30	2.72 / 4.19	2.67 / 4.10	2.63 / 4.02	2.60 / 3.96	2.55 / 3.85	2.51 / 3.78	2.46 / 3.67	2.42 / 3.59	2.38 / 3.51	2.34 / 3.42	2.32 / 3.37	2.28 / 3.30	2.26 / 3.27	2.24 / 3.21	2.22 / 3.18	2.21 / 3.16
14	4.60 / 8.86	3.74 / 6.51	3.34 / 5.56	3.11 / 5.03	2.96 / 4.69	2.85 / 4.46	2.77 / 4.28	2.70 / 4.14	2.65 / 4.03	2.60 / 3.94	2.56 / 3.86	2.53 / 3.80	2.48 / 3.70	2.44 / 3.62	2.39 / 3.51	2.35 / 3.43	2.31 / 3.34	2.27 / 3.26	2.24 / 3.21	2.21 / 3.14	2.19 / 3.11	2.16 / 3.06	2.14 / 3.02	2.13 / 3.00
15	4.54 / 8.68	3.68 / 6.36	3.29 / 5.42	3.06 / 4.89	2.90 / 4.56	2.79 / 4.32	2.70 / 4.14	2.64 / 4.00	2.59 / 3.89	2.55 / 3.80	2.51 / 3.73	2.48 / 3.67	2.43 / 3.56	2.39 / 3.48	2.33 / 3.36	2.29 / 3.29	2.25 / 3.20	2.21 / 3.12	2.18 / 3.07	2.15 / 3.00	2.12 / 2.97	2.10 / 2.92	2.08 / 2.89	2.07 / 2.87

Degrees of freedom for lesser mean square

0.05 (light row) and 0.01 (dark row) points for the distribution of F

Cells show 0.05 point / 0.01 point.

df (lesser)	1	2	3	4	5	6	7	8	9	10	11	12	14	16	20	24	30	40	50	75	100	200	500	∞
16	4.49 / 8.53	3.63 / 6.23	3.24 / 5.29	3.01 / 4.77	2.85 / 4.44	2.74 / 4.20	2.66 / 4.03	2.59 / 3.89	2.54 / 3.78	2.49 / 3.69	2.45 / 3.61	2.42 / 3.55	2.37 / 3.45	2.33 / 3.37	2.28 / 3.25	2.24 / 3.18	2.20 / 3.10	2.16 / 3.01	2.13 / 2.96	2.09 / 2.89	2.07 / 2.86	2.04 / 2.80	2.02 / 2.77	2.01 / 2.75
17	4.45 / 8.40	3.59 / 6.11	3.20 / 5.18	2.96 / 4.67	2.81 / 4.34	2.70 / 4.10	2.62 / 3.93	2.55 / 3.79	2.50 / 3.68	2.45 / 3.59	2.41 / 3.52	2.38 / 3.45	2.33 / 3.35	2.29 / 3.27	2.23 / 3.16	2.19 / 3.08	2.15 / 3.00	2.11 / 2.92	2.08 / 2.86	2.04 / 2.79	2.02 / 2.76	1.99 / 2.70	1.97 / 2.67	1.96 / 2.65
18	4.41 / 8.28	3.55 / 6.01	3.16 / 5.09	2.93 / 4.58	2.77 / 4.25	2.66 / 4.01	2.58 / 3.85	2.51 / 3.71	2.46 / 3.60	2.41 / 3.51	2.37 / 3.44	2.34 / 3.37	2.29 / 3.27	2.25 / 3.19	2.19 / 3.07	2.15 / 3.00	2.11 / 2.91	2.07 / 2.83	2.04 / 2.78	2.00 / 2.71	1.98 / 2.68	1.95 / 2.62	1.93 / 2.59	1.92 / 2.57
19	4.38 / 8.18	3.52 / 5.93	3.13 / 5.01	2.90 / 4.50	2.74 / 4.17	2.63 / 3.94	2.55 / 3.77	2.48 / 3.63	2.43 / 3.52	2.38 / 3.43	2.34 / 3.36	2.31 / 3.30	2.26 / 3.19	2.21 / 3.12	2.15 / 3.00	2.11 / 2.92	2.07 / 2.84	2.02 / 2.76	2.00 / 2.70	1.96 / 2.63	1.94 / 2.60	1.91 / 2.54	1.90 / 2.51	1.88 / 2.49
20	4.35 / 8.10	3.49 / 5.85	3.10 / 4.94	2.87 / 4.43	2.71 / 4.10	2.60 / 3.87	2.52 / 3.71	2.45 / 3.56	2.40 / 3.45	2.35 / 3.37	2.31 / 3.30	2.28 / 3.23	2.23 / 3.13	2.18 / 3.05	2.12 / 2.94	2.08 / 2.86	2.04 / 2.77	1.99 / 2.69	1.96 / 2.63	1.92 / 2.56	1.90 / 2.53	1.87 / 2.47	1.85 / 2.44	1.84 / 2.42
21	4.32 / 8.02	3.47 / 5.78	3.07 / 4.87	2.84 / 4.37	2.68 / 4.04	2.57 / 3.81	2.49 / 3.65	2.42 / 3.51	2.37 / 3.40	2.32 / 3.31	2.28 / 3.24	2.25 / 3.17	2.20 / 3.07	2.15 / 2.99	2.09 / 2.88	2.05 / 2.80	2.00 / 2.72	1.96 / 2.63	1.93 / 2.58	1.89 / 2.51	1.87 / 2.47	1.84 / 2.42	1.82 / 2.38	1.81 / 2.36
22	4.30 / 7.94	3.44 / 5.72	3.05 / 4.82	2.82 / 4.31	2.66 / 3.99	2.55 / 3.76	2.47 / 3.59	2.40 / 3.45	2.35 / 3.35	2.30 / 3.26	2.26 / 3.18	2.23 / 3.12	2.18 / 3.02	2.13 / 2.94	2.07 / 2.83	2.03 / 2.75	1.98 / 2.67	1.93 / 2.58	1.91 / 2.53	1.87 / 2.46	1.84 / 2.42	1.81 / 2.37	1.80 / 2.33	1.78 / 2.31
23	4.28 / 7.88	3.42 / 5.66	3.03 / 4.76	2.80 / 4.26	2.64 / 3.94	2.53 / 3.71	2.45 / 3.54	2.38 / 3.41	2.32 / 3.30	2.28 / 3.21	2.24 / 3.14	2.20 / 3.07	2.14 / 2.97	2.10 / 2.89	2.04 / 2.78	2.00 / 2.70	1.96 / 2.62	1.91 / 2.53	1.88 / 2.48	1.84 / 2.41	1.82 / 2.37	1.79 / 2.32	1.77 / 2.28	1.76 / 2.26
24	4.26 / 7.82	3.40 / 5.61	3.01 / 4.72	2.78 / 4.22	2.62 / 3.90	2.51 / 3.67	2.43 / 3.50	2.36 / 3.36	2.30 / 3.25	2.26 / 3.17	2.22 / 3.09	2.18 / 3.03	2.13 / 2.93	2.09 / 2.85	2.02 / 2.74	1.98 / 2.66	1.94 / 2.58	1.89 / 2.49	1.86 / 2.44	1.82 / 2.36	1.80 / 2.33	1.76 / 2.27	1.74 / 2.23	1.73 / 2.21
25	4.24 / 7.77	3.38 / 5.57	2.99 / 4.68	2.76 / 4.18	2.60 / 3.86	2.49 / 3.63	2.41 / 3.46	2.34 / 3.32	2.28 / 3.21	2.24 / 3.13	2.20 / 3.05	2.16 / 2.99	2.11 / 2.89	2.06 / 2.81	2.00 / 2.70	1.96 / 2.62	1.92 / 2.54	1.87 / 2.45	1.84 / 2.40	1.80 / 2.32	1.77 / 2.29	1.74 / 2.23	1.72 / 2.19	1.71 / 2.17
26	4.22 / 7.72	3.37 / 5.53	2.98 / 4.64	2.74 / 4.14	2.59 / 3.82	2.47 / 3.59	2.39 / 3.42	2.32 / 3.29	2.27 / 3.17	2.22 / 3.09	2.18 / 3.02	2.15 / 2.96	2.10 / 2.86	2.05 / 2.77	1.99 / 2.66	1.95 / 2.58	1.90 / 2.50	1.85 / 2.41	1.82 / 2.36	1.78 / 2.28	1.76 / 2.25	1.72 / 2.19	1.70 / 2.15	1.69 / 2.13
27	4.21 / 7.68	3.35 / 5.49	2.96 / 4.60	2.73 / 4.11	2.57 / 3.79	2.46 / 3.56	2.37 / 3.39	2.30 / 3.26	2.25 / 3.14	2.20 / 3.06	2.16 / 2.98	2.13 / 2.93	2.08 / 2.83	2.03 / 2.74	1.97 / 2.63	1.93 / 2.55	1.88 / 2.47	1.84 / 2.38	1.80 / 2.33	1.76 / 2.28	1.74 / 2.21	1.71 / 2.16	1.68 / 2.12	1.67 / 2.10
28	4.20 / 7.64	3.34 / 5.45	2.95 / 4.57	2.71 / 4.07	2.56 / 3.76	2.44 / 3.53	2.36 / 3.36	2.29 / 3.23	2.24 / 3.11	2.19 / 3.03	2.15 / 2.95	2.12 / 2.90	2.06 / 2.80	2.02 / 2.71	1.96 / 2.60	1.91 / 2.52	1.87 / 2.44	1.81 / 2.35	1.78 / 2.30	1.75 / 2.22	1.72 / 2.18	1.69 / 2.13	1.67 / 2.09	1.65 / 2.06
29	4.18 / 7.60	3.33 / 5.42	2.93 / 4.54	2.70 / 4.04	2.54 / 3.73	2.43 / 3.50	2.35 / 3.32	2.28 / 3.20	2.22 / 3.08	2.18 / 3.00	2.14 / 2.92	2.10 / 2.87	2.05 / 2.77	2.00 / 2.68	1.94 / 2.57	1.90 / 2.49	1.85 / 2.41	1.80 / 2.32	1.77 / 2.27	1.73 / 2.19	1.71 / 2.15	1.68 / 2.10	1.65 / 2.06	1.64 / 2.03
30	4.17 / 7.56	3.32 / 5.39	2.92 / 4.51	2.69 / 4.02	2.53 / 3.70	2.42 / 3.47	2.34 / 3.30	2.27 / 3.17	2.21 / 3.06	2.16 / 2.98	2.12 / 2.90	2.09 / 2.84	2.04 / 2.74	1.99 / 2.66	1.93 / 2.55	1.89 / 2.47	1.84 / 2.38	1.79 / 2.29	1.76 / 2.24	1.72 / 2.16	1.69 / 2.13	1.66 / 2.07	1.64 / 2.03	1.62 / 2.01

Degrees of freedom for greater mean square (column headings)

Degrees of freedom for lesser mean square (row headings)

(continued)

Table VII (continued)

0.05 (light row) and 0.01 (dark row) points for the distribution of F

Degrees of freedom for greater mean square

Values given as (0.05 light) / (0.01 dark).

df lesser	1	2	3	4	5	6	7	8	9	10	11	12	14	16	20	24	30	40	50	75	100	200	500	∞
32	4.15/7.50	3.30/5.34	2.90/4.46	2.67/3.97	2.51/3.66	2.40/3.42	2.32/3.25	2.25/3.12	2.19/3.01	2.14/2.94	2.10/2.86	2.07/2.80	2.02/2.70	1.97/2.62	1.91/2.51	1.86/2.42	1.82/2.34	1.76/2.25	1.74/2.20	1.69/2.12	1.67/2.08	1.64/2.02	1.61/1.98	1.59/1.96
34	4.13/7.44	3.28/5.29	2.88/4.42	2.65/3.93	2.49/3.61	2.38/3.38	2.30/3.21	2.23/3.08	2.17/2.97	2.12/2.89	2.08/2.82	2.05/2.76	2.00/2.66	1.95/2.58	1.89/2.47	1.84/2.38	1.80/2.30	1.74/2.21	1.71/2.15	1.67/2.08	1.64/2.04	1.61/1.98	1.59/1.94	1.57/1.91
36	4.11/7.39	3.26/5.25	2.86/4.38	2.63/3.89	2.48/3.58	2.36/3.35	2.28/3.18	2.21/3.04	2.15/2.94	2.10/2.86	2.06/2.78	2.03/2.72	1.98/2.62	1.93/2.54	1.87/2.43	1.82/2.35	1.78/2.26	1.72/2.17	1.69/2.12	1.65/2.04	1.62/2.00	1.59/1.94	1.56/1.90	1.55/1.87
38	4.10/7.35	3.25/5.21	2.85/4.34	2.62/3.86	2.46/3.54	2.35/3.32	2.26/3.15	2.19/3.02	2.14/2.91	2.09/2.82	2.05/2.75	2.02/2.69	1.96/2.59	1.92/2.51	1.85/2.40	1.80/2.32	1.76/2.22	1.71/2.14	1.67/2.08	1.63/2.00	1.60/1.97	1.57/1.90	1.54/1.86	1.53/1.84
40	4.08/7.31	3.23/5.18	2.84/4.31	2.61/3.83	2.45/3.51	2.34/3.29	2.25/3.12	2.18/2.99	2.12/2.88	2.07/2.80	2.04/2.73	2.00/2.66	1.95/2.56	1.90/2.49	1.84/2.37	1.79/2.29	1.74/2.20	1.69/2.11	1.66/2.05	1.61/1.97	1.59/1.94	1.55/1.88	1.53/1.84	1.51/1.81
42	4.07/7.27	3.22/5.15	2.83/4.29	2.59/3.80	2.44/3.49	2.32/3.26	2.24/3.10	2.17/2.96	2.11/2.86	2.06/2.77	2.02/2.70	1.99/2.64	1.94/2.54	1.89/2.46	1.82/2.35	1.78/2.26	1.73/2.17	1.68/2.08	1.64/2.02	1.60/1.94	1.57/1.91	1.54/1.85	1.51/1.80	1.49/1.78
44	4.06/7.24	3.21/5.12	2.82/4.26	2.58/3.78	2.43/3.46	2.31/3.24	2.23/3.07	2.16/2.94	2.10/2.84	2.05/2.75	2.01/2.68	1.98/2.62	1.92/2.52	1.88/2.44	1.81/2.32	1.76/2.24	1.72/2.15	1.66/2.06	1.63/2.00	1.58/1.92	1.56/1.88	1.52/1.82	1.50/1.78	1.48/1.75
46	4.05/7.21	3.20/5.10	2.81/4.24	2.57/3.76	2.42/3.44	2.30/3.22	2.22/3.05	2.14/2.92	2.09/2.82	2.04/2.73	2.00/2.66	1.97/2.60	1.91/2.50	1.87/2.42	1.80/2.30	1.75/2.22	1.71/2.13	1.65/2.04	1.62/1.98	1.57/1.90	1.54/1.86	1.51/1.80	1.48/1.76	1.46/1.72
48	4.04/7.19	3.19/5.08	2.80/4.22	2.56/3.74	2.41/3.42	2.30/3.20	2.21/3.04	2.14/2.90	2.08/2.80	2.03/2.71	1.99/2.64	1.96/2.58	1.90/2.48	1.86/2.40	1.79/2.28	1.74/2.20	1.70/2.11	1.64/2.02	1.61/1.96	1.56/1.88	1.53/1.84	1.50/1.78	1.47/1.73	1.45/1.70
50	4.03/7.17	3.18/5.06	2.79/4.20	2.56/3.72	2.40/3.41	2.29/3.18	2.20/3.02	2.13/2.88	2.07/2.78	2.02/2.70	1.98/2.62	1.95/2.56	1.90/2.46	1.85/2.39	1.78/2.26	1.74/2.18	1.69/2.10	1.63/2.00	1.60/1.94	1.55/1.86	1.52/1.82	1.48/1.76	1.46/1.71	1.44/1.68
55	4.02/7.12	3.17/5.01	2.78/4.16	2.54/3.68	2.38/3.37	2.27/3.15	2.18/2.98	2.11/2.85	2.05/2.75	2.00/2.66	1.97/2.59	1.93/2.53	1.88/2.43	1.83/2.35	1.76/2.23	1.72/2.15	1.67/2.06	1.61/1.96	1.58/1.90	1.52/1.82	1.50/1.78	1.46/1.71	1.43/1.66	1.41/1.64
60	4.00/7.08	3.15/4.98	2.76/4.13	2.52/3.65	2.37/3.34	2.25/3.12	2.17/2.95	2.10/2.82	2.04/2.72	1.99/2.63	1.95/2.56	1.92/2.50	1.86/2.40	1.81/2.32	1.75/2.20	1.70/2.12	1.65/2.03	1.59/1.93	1.56/1.87	1.50/1.79	1.48/1.74	1.44/1.68	1.41/1.63	1.39/1.60
65	3.99/7.04	3.14/4.95	2.75/4.10	2.51/3.62	2.36/3.31	2.24/3.09	2.15/2.93	2.08/2.79	2.02/2.70	1.98/2.61	1.94/2.54	1.90/2.47	1.85/2.37	1.80/2.30	1.73/2.18	1.68/2.09	1.63/2.00	1.57/1.90	1.54/1.84	1.49/1.76	1.46/1.71	1.42/1.64	1.39/1.60	1.37/1.56
70	3.98/7.01	3.13/4.92	2.74/4.08	2.50/3.60	2.35/3.29	2.23/3.07	2.14/2.91	2.07/2.77	2.01/2.67	1.97/2.59	1.93/2.51	1.89/2.45	1.84/2.35	1.79/2.28	1.72/2.15	1.67/2.07	1.62/1.98	1.56/1.88	1.53/1.82	1.47/1.74	1.45/1.69	1.40/1.62	1.37/1.56	1.35/1.53
80	3.96/6.96	3.11/4.88	2.72/4.04	2.48/3.56	2.33/3.25	2.21/3.04	2.12/2.87	2.05/2.74	1.99/2.64	1.95/2.55	1.91/2.48	1.88/2.41	1.82/2.32	1.77/2.24	1.70/2.11	1.65/2.03	1.60/1.94	1.54/1.84	1.51/1.78	1.45/1.70	1.42/1.65	1.38/1.57	1.35/1.52	1.32/1.49

Degrees of freedom for lesser mean square

0.05 (light row) and 0.01 (dark row) points for the distribution of F

Degrees of freedom for greater mean square

Degrees of freedom for lesser mean square	1	2	3	4	5	6	7	8	9	10	11	12	14	16	20	24	30	40	50	75	100	200	500	∞
100	3.94	3.09	2.70	2.46	2.30	2.19	2.10	2.03	1.97	1.92	1.88	1.85	1.79	1.75	1.68	1.63	1.57	1.51	1.48	1.42	1.39	1.34	1.30	1.28
	6.90	4.82	3.98	3.51	3.20	2.99	2.82	2.69	2.59	2.51	2.43	2.36	2.26	2.19	2.06	1.98	1.89	1.79	1.73	1.64	1.59	1.51	1.46	1.43
125	3.92	3.07	2.68	2.44	2.29	2.17	2.08	2.01	1.95	1.90	1.86	1.83	1.77	1.72	1.65	1.60	1.55	1.49	1.45	1.39	1.36	1.31	1.27	1.25
	6.84	4.78	3.94	3.47	3.17	2.95	2.79	2.65	2.56	2.47	2.40	2.33	2.23	2.15	2.03	1.94	1.85	1.75	1.68	1.59	1.54	1.46	1.40	1.37
150	3.91	3.06	2.67	2.43	2.27	2.16	2.07	2.00	1.94	1.89	1.85	1.82	1.76	1.71	1.64	1.59	1.54	1.47	1.44	1.37	1.34	1.29	1.25	1.22
	6.81	4.75	3.91	3.44	3.13	2.92	2.76	2.62	2.53	2.44	2.37	2.30	2.20	2.12	2.00	1.91	1.83	1.72	1.66	1.56	1.51	1.43	1.37	1.33
200	3.89	3.04	2.65	2.41	2.26	2.14	2.05	1.98	1.92	1.87	1.83	1.80	1.74	1.69	1.62	1.57	1.52	1.45	1.42	1.35	1.32	1.26	1.22	1.19
	6.76	4.71	3.88	3.41	3.11	2.90	2.73	2.60	2.50	2.41	2.34	2.28	2.17	2.09	1.97	1.88	1.79	1.69	1.62	1.53	1.48	1.39	1.33	1.28
400	3.86	3.02	2.62	2.39	2.23	2.12	2.03	1.96	1.90	1.85	1.81	1.78	1.72	1.67	1.60	1.54	1.49	1.42	1.38	1.32	1.28	1.22	1.16	1.13
	6.70	4.66	3.83	3.36	3.06	2.85	2.69	2.55	2.46	2.37	2.29	2.23	2.12	2.04	1.92	1.84	1.74	1.64	1.57	1.47	1.42	1.32	1.24	1.19
1000	3.85	3.00	2.61	2.38	2.22	2.10	2.02	1.95	1.89	1.84	1.80	1.76	1.70	1.65	1.58	1.53	1.47	1.41	1.36	1.30	1.26	1.19	1.13	1.08
	6.66	4.62	3.80	3.34	3.04	2.82	2.66	2.53	2.43	2.34	2.26	2.20	2.09	2.01	1.89	1.81	1.71	1.61	1.54	1.44	1.38	1.28	1.19	1.11
∞	3.84	2.99	2.60	2.37	2.21	2.09	2.01	1.94	1.88	1.83	1.79	1.75	1.69	1.64	1.57	1.52	1.46	1.40	1.35	1.28	1.24	1.17	1.11	1.00
	6.64	4.60	3.78	3.32	3.02	2.80	2.64	2.51	2.41	2.32	2.24	2.18	2.07	1.99	1.87	1.79	1.69	1.59	1.52	1.41	1.36	1.25	1.15	1.00

From G. W. Snedecor, *Statistical Methods*, 5th edition. Copyright © 1956 by the Iowa State University Press, Ames, Iowa. Reprinted by permission of the publisher.

Table VIII TRANSFORMATION OF PERCENTAGE TO ARCSIN $\sqrt{\text{PERCENTAGE}}$

The numbers in this table are the angles (in degrees) corresponding to given percentages under the transformation arcsin $\sqrt{\text{percentage}}$.

%	0	1	2	3	4	5	6	7	8	9
0.0	0	0.57	0.81	0.99	1.15	1.28	1.40	1.52	1.62	1.72
0.1	1.81	1.90	1.99	2.07	2.14	2.22	2.29	2.36	2.43	2.50
0.2	2.56	2.63	2.69	2.75	2.81	2.87	2.92	2.98	3.03	3.09
0.3	3.14	3.19	3.24	3.29	3.34	3.39	3.44	3.49	3.53	3.58
0.4	3.63	3.67	3.72	3.76	3.80	3.85	3.89	3.93	3.97	4.01
0.5	4.05	4.09	4.13	4.17	4.21	4.25	4.29	4.33	4.37	4.40
0.6	4.44	4.48	4.52	4.55	4.59	4.62	4.66	4.69	4.73	4.76
0.7	4.80	4.83	4.87	4.90	4.93	4.97	5.00	5.03	5.07	5.10
0.8	5.13	5.16	5.20	5.23	5.26	5.29	5.32	5.35	5.38	5.41
0.9	5.44	5.47	5.50	5.53	5.56	5.59	5.62	5.65	5.68	5.71
1	5.74	6.02	6.29	6.55	6.80	7.04	7.27	7.49	7.71	7.92
2	8.13	8.33	8.53	8.72	8.91	9.10	9.28	9.46	9.63	9.81
3	9.98	10.14	10.31	10.47	10.63	10.78	10.94	11.09	11.24	11.39
4	11.54	11.68	11.83	11.97	12.11	12.25	12.39	12.52	12.66	12.79
5	12.92	13.05	13.18	13.31	13.44	13.56	13.69	13.81	13.94	14.06
6	14.18	14.30	14.42	14.54	14.65	14.77	14.89	15.00	15.12	15.23
7	15.34	15.45	15.56	15.68	15.79	15.89	16.00	16.11	16.22	16.32
8	16.43	16.54	16.64	16.74	16.85	16.95	17.05	17.16	17.26	17.36
9	17.46	17.56	17.66	17.76	17.85	17.95	18.05	18.15	18.24	18.34
10	18.44	18.53	18.63	18.72	18.81	18.91	19.00	19.09	19.19	19.28
11	19.37	19.46	19.55	19.64	19.73	19.82	19.91	20.00	20.09	20.18
12	20.27	20.36	20.44	20.53	20.62	20.70	20.79	20.88	20.96	21.05
13	21.13	21.22	21.30	21.39	21.47	21.56	21.64	21.72	21.81	21.89
14	21.97	22.06	22.14	22.22	22.30	22.38	22.46	22.55	22.63	22.71
15	22.79	22.87	22.95	23.03	23.11	23.19	23.26	23.34	23.42	23.50
16	23.58	23.66	23.73	23.81	23.89	23.97	24.04	24.12	24.20	24.27
17	24.35	24.43	24.50	24.58	24.65	24.73	24.80	24.88	24.95	25.03
18	25.10	25.18	25.25	25.33	25.40	25.48	25.55	25.62	25.70	25.77
19	25.84	25.92	25.99	26.06	26.13	26.21	26.28	26.35	26.42	26.49
20	26.56	26.64	26.71	26.78	26.85	26.92	26.99	27.06	27.13	27.20
21	27.28	27.35	27.42	27.49	27.56	27.63	27.69	27.76	27.83	27.90
22	27.97	28.04	28.11	28.18	28.25	28.32	28.38	28.45	28.52	28.59
23	28.66	28.73	28.79	28.86	28.93	29.00	29.06	29.13	29.20	29.27
24	29.33	29.40	29.47	29.53	29.60	29.67	29.73	29.80	29.87	29.93
25	30.00	30.07	30.13	30.20	30.26	30.33	30.40	30.46	30.53	30.59
26	30.66	30.72	30.79	30.85	30.92	30.98	31.05	31.11	31.18	31.24
27	31.31	31.37	31.44	31.50	31.56	31.63	31.69	31.76	31.82	31.88
28	31.95	32.01	32.08	32.14	32.20	32.27	32.33	32.39	32.46	32.52
29	32.58	32.65	32.71	32.77	32.83	32.90	32.96	33.02	33.09	33.15
30	33.21	33.27	33.34	33.40	33.46	33.52	33.58	33.65	33.71	33.77

Table VIII *(continued)*

%	0	1	2	3	4	5	6	7	8	9
31	33.83	33.89	33.96	34.02	34.08	34.14	34.20	34.27	34.33	34.39
32	34.45	34.51	34.57	34.63	34.70	34.76	34.82	34.88	34.94	35.00
33	35.06	35.12	35.18	35.24	35.30	35.37	35.43	35.49	35.55	35.61
34	35.67	35.73	35.79	35.85	35.91	35.97	36.03	36.09	36.15	36.21
35	36.27	36.33	36.39	36.45	36.51	36.57	36.63	36.69	36.75	36.81
36	36.87	36.93	36.99	37.05	37.11	37.17	37.23	37.29	37.35	37.41
37	37.47	37.52	37.58	37.64	37.70	37.76	37.82	37.88	37.94	38.00
38	38.06	38.12	38.17	38.23	38.29	38.35	38.41	38.47	38.53	38.59
39	38.65	38.70	38.76	38.82	38.88	38.94	39.00	39.06	39.11	39.17
40	39.23	39.29	39.35	39.41	39.47	39.52	39.58	39.64	39.70	39.76
41	39.82	39.87	39.93	39.99	40.05	40.11	40.16	40.22	40.28	40.34
42	40.40	40.46	40.51	40.57	40.63	40.69	40.74	40.80	40.86	40.92
43	40.98	41.03	41.09	41.15	41.21	41.27	41.32	41.38	41.44	41.50
44	41.55	41.61	41.67	41.73	41.78	41.84	41.90	41.96	42.02	42.07
45	42.13	42.19	42.25	42.30	42.36	42.42	42.48	42.53	42.59	42.65
46	42.71	42.76	42.82	42.88	42.94	42.99	43.05	43.11	43.17	43.22
47	43.28	43.34	43.39	43.45	43.51	43.57	43.62	43.68	43.74	43.80
48	43.85	43.91	43.97	44.03	44.08	44.14	44.20	44.25	44.31	44.37
49	44.43	44.48	44.54	44.60	44.66	44.71	44.77	44.83	44.89	44.94
50	45.00	45.06	45.11	45.17	45.23	45.29	45.34	45.40	45.46	45.52
51	45.57	45.63	45.69	45.75	45.80	45.86	45.92	45.97	46.03	46.09
52	46.15	46.20	46.26	46.32	46.38	46.43	46.49	46.55	46.61	46.66
53	46.72	46.78	46.83	46.89	46.95	47.01	47.06	47.12	47.18	47.24
54	47.29	47.35	47.41	47.47	47.52	47.58	47.64	47.70	47.75	47.81
55	47.87	47.93	47.98	48.04	48.10	48.16	48.22	48.27	48.33	48.39
56	48.45	48.50	48.56	48.62	48.68	48.73	48.79	48.85	48.91	48.97
57	49.02	49.08	49.14	49.20	49.26	49.31	49.37	49.43	49.49	49.54
58	49.60	49.66	49.72	49.78	49.84	49.89	49.95	50.01	50.07	50.13
59	50.18	50.24	50.30	50.36	50.42	50.48	50.53	50.59	50.65	50.71
60	50.77	50.83	50.89	50.94	51.00	51.06	51.12	51.18	51.24	51.30
61	51.35	51.41	51.47	51.53	51.59	51.65	51.71	51.77	51.83	51.88
62	51.94	52.00	52.06	52.12	52.18	52.24	52.30	52.36	52.42	52.48
63	52.53	52.59	52.65	52.71	52.77	52.83	52.89	52.95	53.01	53.07
64	53.13	53.19	53.25	53.31	53.37	53.43	53.49	53.55	53.61	53.67
65	53.73	53.79	53.85	53.91	53.97	54.03	54.09	54.15	54.21	54.27
66	54.33	54.39	54.45	54.51	54.57	54.63	54.70	54.76	54.82	54.88
67	54.94	55.00	55.06	55.12	55.18	55.24	55.30	55.37	55.43	55.49
68	55.55	55.61	55.67	55.73	55.80	55.86	55.92	55.98	56.04	56.11
69	56.17	56.23	56.29	56.35	56.42	56.48	56.54	56.60	56.66	56.73
70	56.79	56.85	56.91	56.98	57.04	57.10	57.17	57.23	57.29	57.35
71	57.42	57.48	57.54	57.61	57.67	57.73	57.80	57.86	57.92	57.99
72	58.05	58.12	58.18	58.24	58.31	58.37	58.44	58.50	58.56	58.63
73	58.69	58.76	58.82	58.89	58.95	59.02	59.08	59.15	59.21	59.28
74	59.34	59.41	59.47	59.54	59.60	59.67	59.74	59.80	59.87	59.93
75	60.00	60.07	60.13	60.20	60.27	60.33	60.40	60.47	60.53	60.60

(continued)

Table VIII *(continued)*

%	0	1	2	3	4	5	6	7	8	9
76	60.67	60.73	60.80	60.87	60.94	61.00	61.07	61.14	61.21	61.27
77	61.34	61.41	61.48	61.55	61.62	61.68	61.75	61.82	61.89	61.96
78	62.03	62.10	62.17	62.24	62.31	62.37	62.44	62.51	62.58	62.65
79	62.72	62.80	62.87	62.94	63.01	63.08	63.15	63.22	63.29	63.36
80	63.44	63.51	63.58	63.65	63.72	63.79	63.87	63.94	64.01	64.08
81	64.16	64.23	64.30	64.38	64.45	64.52	64.60	64.67	64.75	64.82
82	64.90	64.97	65.05	65.12	65.20	65.27	65.35	65.42	65.50	65.57
83	65.65	65.73	65.80	65.88	65.96	66.03	66.11	66.19	66.27	66.34
84	66.42	66.50	66.58	66.66	66.74	66.81	66.89	66.97	67.05	67.13
85	67.21	67.29	67.37	67.45	67.54	67.62	67.70	67.78	67.86	67.94
86	68.03	68.11	68.19	68.28	68.36	68.44	68.53	68.61	68.70	68.78
87	68.87	68.95	69.04	69.12	69.21	69.30	69.38	69.47	69.56	69.64
88	69.73	69.82	69.91	70.00	70.09	70.18	70.27	70.36	70.45	70.54
89	70.63	70.72	70.81	70.91	71.00	71.09	71.19	71.28	71.37	71.47
90	71.56	71.66	71.76	71.85	71.95	72.05	72.15	72.24	72.34	72.44
91	72.54	72.64	72.74	72.84	72.95	73.05	73.15	73.26	73.36	73.46
92	73.57	73.68	73.78	73.89	74.00	74.11	74.21	74.32	74.44	74.55
93	74.66	74.77	74.88	75.00	75.11	75.23	75.35	75.46	75.58	75.70
94	75.82	75.94	76.06	76.19	76.31	76.44	76.56	76.69	76.82	76.95
95	77.08	77.21	77.34	77.48	77.61	77.75	77.89	78.03	78.17	78.32
96	78.46	78.61	78.76	78.91	79.06	79.22	79.37	79.53	79.69	79.86
97	80.02	80.19	80.37	80.54	80.72	80.90	81.09	81.28	81.47	81.67
98	81.87	82.08	82.29	82.51	82.73	82.96	83.20	83.45	83.71	83.98
99.0	84.26	84.29	84.32	84.35	84.38	84.41	84.44	84.47	84.50	84.53
99.1	84.56	84.59	84.62	84.65	84.68	84.71	84.74	84.77	84.80	84.84
99.2	84.87	84.90	84.93	84.97	85.00	85.03	85.07	85.10	85.13	85.17
99.3	85.20	85.24	85.27	85.31	85.34	85.38	85.41	85.45	85.48	85.52
99.4	85.56	85.60	85.63	85.67	85.71	85.75	85.79	85.83	85.87	85.91
99.5	85.95	85.99	86.03	86.07	86.11	86.15	86.20	86.24	86.28	86.33
99.6	86.37	86.42	86.47	86.51	86.56	86.61	86.66	86.71	86.76	86.81
99.7	86.86	86.91	86.97	87.02	87.08	87.13	87.19	87.25	87.31	87.37
99.8	87.44	87.50	87.57	87.64	87.71	87.78	87.86	87.93	88.01	88.10
99.9	88.19	88.28	88.38	88.48	88.60	88.72	88.85	89.01	89.19	89.43
100.0	90.00	—	—	—	—	—	—	—	—	—

Table VIII appeared in *Plant Protection* (Leningrad), Vol. 12 (1937), p. 67, and is reproduced by permission of the author, C. I. Bliss.

Table IX   WILCOXON DISTRIBUTION—UNPAIRED DATA

The numbers given in this table are the number of cases for which the sum of the ranks of the sample of size n_1 is less than or equal to T_1.

Values of U, where $U = T_1 - \frac{1}{2} n_1(n_1 + 1)$.

n_1	n_2	$C_{n_1 n_2}$	0	1	2	3	4	5	6	7	8	9	10	11	12	13	14	15	16	17	18	19	20
3	3	20	1	2	4	7	10	13	16	18	19	20											
3	4	35	1	2	4	7	11	15	20	24	28	31	33	34	35								
4	4	70	1	2	4	7	12	17	24	31	39	46	53	58	63	66	68	69	70				
3	5	56	1	2	4	7	11	16	22	28	34	40	45	49	52	54	55	56					
4	5	126	1	2	4	7	12	18	26	35	46	57	69	80	91	100	108	114	119	122	124	125	126
5	5	252	1	2	4	7	12	19	28	39	53	69	87	106	126	146	165	183	199	213	224	233	240
3	6	84	1	2	4	7	11	16	23	30	38	46	54	61	68	73	77	80	82	83	84		
4	6	210	1	2	4	7	12	18	27	37	50	64	80	96	114	130	146	160	173	183	192	198	203
5	6	462	1	2	4	7	12	19	29	41	57	76	99	124	153	183	215	247	279	309	338	363	386
6	6	924	1	2	4	7	12	19	30	43	61	83	111	143	182	224	272	323	378	433	491	546	601
3	7	120	1	2	4	7	11	16	23	31	40	50	60	70	80	89	97	104	109	113	116	118	119
4	7	330	1	2	4	7	12	18	27	38	52	68	87	107	130	153	177	200	223	243	262	278	292
5	7	792	1	2	4	7	12	19	29	42	59	80	106	136	171	210	253	299	347	396	445	493	539
6	7	1716	1	2	4	7	12	19	30	44	63	87	118	155	201	253	314	382	458	539	627	717	811
7	7	3432	1	2	4	7	12	19	30	45	65	91	125	167	220	283	358	445	545	657	782	918	1064
3	8	165	1	2	4	7	11	16	23	31	41	52	64	76	89	101	113	124	134	142	149	154	158
4	8	495	1	2	4	7	12	18	27	38	53	70	91	114	141	169	200	231	264	295	326	354	381
5	8	1287	1	2	4	7	12	19	29	42	60	82	110	143	183	228	280	337	400	466	536	607	680
6	8	3003	1	2	4	7	12	19	30	44	64	89	122	162	213	272	343	424	518	621	737	860	994
7	8	6435	1	2	4	7	12	19	30	45	66	93	129	174	232	302	388	489	609	746	904	1080	1277
8	8	12870	1	2	4	7	12	19	30	45	67	95	133	181	244	321	418	534	675	839	1033	1254	1509

225

From J. L. Hodges and E. L. Lehmann, *Basic Concepts of Probability and Statistics*. San Francisco: Holden-Day, 1962. Reprinted by permission of Holden-Day, Inc.

Table X TOTAL RUNS

All values are at the .05 significance level. The larger of n_1 and n_2 is to be read at the top and the smaller is to be read in the left margin.

	5	6	7	8	9	10	11	12	13	14	15	16	17	18	19	20
2								2 6	2 6	2 6	2 6	2 6	2 6	2 6	2 6	2 6
3		2 8	2 8	2 8	2 8	2 8	2 8	2 8	2 8	2 8	3 8	3 8	3 8	3 8	3 8	3 8
4	2 9	2 9	2 10	3 10	3 10	3 10	3 10	3 10	3 10	3 10	3 10	4 10	4 10	4 10	4 10	4 10
5	2 10	3 10	3 11	3 11	3 12	3 12	4 12	4 12	4 12	4 12	4 12	4 12	4 12	5 12	5 12	5 12
6		3 11	3 12	3 12	4 13	4 13	4 13	4 13	5 14	5 14	5 14	5 14	5 14	5 14	6 14	6 14
7			3 13	4 13	4 14	5 14	5 14	5 14	5 15	5 15	5 15	6 16	6 16	6 16	6 16	6 16
8				4 14	5 14	5 15	5 15	6 16	6 16	6 16	6 16	6 17	7 17	7 17	7 17	7 17
9					5 15	5 16	6 16	6 16	6 17	7 17	7 18	7 18	7 18	8 18	8 18	8 18
10						6 16	6 17	7 17	7 18	7 18	7 18	8 19	8 19	8 19	8 20	9 20
11							7 17	7 18	7 19	8 19	8 19	8 20	9 20	9 20	9 21	9 21
12								7 19	8 19	8 20	8 20	9 21	9 21	9 21	10 22	10 22
13									8 20	9 20	9 21	9 21	10 22	10 22	10 23	10 23
14										9 21	9 22	10 22	10 23	10 23	11 23	11 24
15											10 22	10 23	11 23	11 24	11 24	12 25
16												11 23	11 24	11 25	12 25	12 25
17													11 25	12 25	12 26	13 26
18														12 26	13 26	13 27
19															13 27	13 27
20																14 28

From C. Eisenhart and F. Swed, "Tables for Testing Randomness of Grouping in a Sequence of Alternatives," *Annals of Mathematical Statistics*, Vol. 14 (1943), p. 66. Reprinted by permission of the authors and the publisher.

Table XI VALUES FOR THE *r* TO *Z* TRANSFORMATION

r	Z	r	Z	r	Z	r	Z
.00	.000	.25	.255	.50	.549	.75	.973
.01	.010	.26	.266	.51	.563	.76	.996
.02	.020	.27	.277	.52	.576	.77	1.020
.03	.030	.28	.288	.53	.590	.78	1.045
.04	.040	.29	.299	.54	.604	.79	1.071
.05	.050	.30	.310	.55	.618	.80	1.099
.06	.060	.31	.321	.56	.633	.81	1.127
.07	.070	.32	.332	.57	.648	.82	1.157
.08	.080	.33	.343	.58	.662	.83	1.188
.09	.090	.34	.354	.59	.678	.84	1.221
.10	.100	.35	.365	.60	.693	.85	1.256
.11	.110	.36	.377	.61	.709	.86	1.293
.12	.121	.37	.388	.62	.725	.87	1.333
.13	.131	.38	.400	.63	.741	.88	1.376
.14	.141	.39	.412	.64	.758	.89	1.422
.15	.151	.40	.424	.65	.775	.90	1.472
.16	.161	.41	.436	.66	.793	.91	1.528
.17	.172	.42	.448	.67	.811	.92	1.589
.18	.182	.43	.460	.68	.829	.93	1.658
.19	.192	.44	.472	.69	.848	.94	1.738
.20	.203	.45	.485	.70	.867	.95	1.832
.21	.213	.46	.497	.71	.887	.96	1.946
.22	.224	.47	.510	.72	.908	.97	2.092
.23	.234	.48	.523	.73	.929	.98	2.298
.24	.245	.49	.536	.74	.950	.99	2.647

From R. A. Fisher and F. Yates, *Statistical Tables for Biological, Agricultural and Medical Research*. Edinburgh: Oliver and Boyd, Ltd., 1948. Reprinted by permission of the authors and publisher.

Table XII   VALUES OF TRIGONOMETRIC FUNCTIONS

deg	rad	sin	cos	tan	deg	rad	sin	cos	tan
0	.000	.000	1.000	.000					
1	.017	.017	1.000	.017	46	.803	.719	.695	1.036
2	.035	.035	.999	.035	47	.820	.731	.682	1.072
3	.052	.052	.999	.052	48	.838	.743	.669	1.111
4	.070	.070	.998	.070	49	.855	.755	.656	1.150
5	.087	.087	.996	.087	50	.873	.766	.643	1.192
6	.105	.105	.995	.105	51	.890	.777	.629	1.235
7	.122	.122	.993	.123	52	.908	.788	.616	1.280
8	.140	.139	.990	.141	53	.925	.799	.602	1.327
9	.157	.156	.988	.158	54	.942	.809	.588	1.376
10	.175	.174	.985	.176	55	.960	.819	.574	1.428
11	.192	.191	.982	.194	56	.977	.829	.559	1.483
12	.209	.208	.978	.213	57	.995	.839	.545	1.540
13	.227	.225	.974	.231	58	1.012	.848	.530	1.600
14	.244	.242	.970	.249	59	1.030	.857	.515	1.664
15	.262	.259	.966	.268	60	1.047	.866	.500	1.732
16	.279	.276	.961	.287	61	1.065	.875	.485	1.804
17	.297	.292	.956	.306	62	1.082	.883	.470	1.881
18	.314	.309	.951	.325	63	1.100	.891	.454	1.963
19	.332	.326	.946	.344	64	1.117	.899	.438	2.050
20	.349	.342	.940	.364	65	1.134	.906	.423	2.145
21	.367	.358	.934	.384	66	1.152	.914	.407	2.246
22	.384	.375	.927	.404	67	1.169	.921	.391	2.356
23	.401	.391	.921	.424	68	1.187	.927	.375	2.475
24	.419	.407	.914	.445	69	1.204	.934	.358	2.605
25	.436	.423	.906	.466	70	1.222	.940	.342	2.747
26	.454	.438	.899	.488	71	1.239	.946	.326	2.904
27	.471	.454	.891	.510	72	1.257	.951	.309	3.078
28	.489	.470	.883	.532	73	1.274	.956	.292	3.271
29	.506	.485	.875	.554	74	1.292	.961	.276	3.487
30	.524	.500	.866	.577	75	1.309	.966	.259	3.732
31	.541	.515	.857	.601	76	1.326	.970	.242	4.011
32	.559	.530	.848	.625	77	1.344	.974	.225	4.331
33	.576	.545	.839	.649	78	1.361	.978	.208	4.705
34	.593	.559	.829	.675	79	1.379	.982	.191	5.145
35	.611	.574	.819	.700	80	1.396	.985	.174	5.671
36	.628	.588	.809	.727	81	1.414	.988	.156	6.314
37	.646	.602	.799	.754	82	1.431	.990	.139	7.115
38	.663	.616	.788	.781	83	1.449	.993	.122	8.144
39	.681	.629	.777	.810	84	1.466	.995	.105	9.514
40	.698	.643	.766	.839	85	1.484	.996	.087	11.430
41	.716	.656	.755	.869	86	1.501	.998	.070	14.301
42	.733	.669	.743	.900	87	1.518	.999	.052	19.081
43	.751	.682	.731	.933	88	1.536	.999	.035	28.636
44	.768	.695	.719	.966	89	1.553	1.000	.017	57.290
45	.785	.707	.707	1.000	90	1.571	1.000	.000	—

INDEX

This book was set in 10/13 Times Roman, a
typeface originally designed by Stanley Morison of
Cambridge University Press in 1931.